EDUCATION IN ENGLAND

IN THE

MIDDLE AGES

AMS PRESS

NEW YORK

EDUCATION IN ENGLAND

IN THE

MIDDLE AGES

THESIS APPROVED FOR THE DEGREE OF DOCTOR OF
SCIENCE IN THE UNIVERSITY OF LONDON

BY

A. W. PARRY, M.A., D.Sc.

PRINCIPAL OF THE TRAINING COLLEGE, CARMARTHEN

LONDON: W. B. CLIVE

University Tutorial Press Ld.

HIGH ST., NEW OXFORD ST., W.C.

1920

Library of Congress Cataloging in Publication Data

Parry, Albert William, 1874-1950.
    Education in England in the Middle Ages.

    Thesis—University of London.
    Reprint of the 1920 ed. published by W. B. Clive,
London.
Bibliography: p.
    Includes index.
    1. Education—England—History. 2. Education,
Medieval. I. Title.
LA631.3.P37   1975   370'.942   77-178584
ISBN 0-404-56659-6

Reprinted from an original copy in the collection of
the Memorial Library of the University of Wisconsin

From the edition of 1920, London
First AMS edition published in 1975
Manufactured in the United States of America

AMS PRESS INC.
NEW YORK, N. Y. 10003

PREFACE.

THE purpose of this book is to give an account of the provision which was made in this country for Education during the period from the Introduction of Christianity to the Eve of the Reformation. Preparatory to writing it, I tried to examine all the relevant, available evidence with the object of discovering the factors which contributed to the educational development of the nation during the period under consideration.

Whilst this work was in progress, the late A. F. Leach published his *Schools of Mediaeval England.*" His book, however, differs essentially from mine, his aim is different, the conclusions he arrives at are different; further, as he does not quote the authorities for the statements he makes, I did not find his work of direct assistance. This criticism does not apply to his *Educational Charters*, a collection of documents of inestimable value to all students of English Educational History.

I have tried to acknowledge in every case my obligations to other writers. In addition, I give in an appendix a list of the authorities I have consulted, and of the other books I have studied for the purpose of this investigation. Still, as a great part of this book was written whilst I was on military service (1914-9) and I was consequently dependent on notes which I had compiled at various times and places, it is probable there may be some omissions and inaccuracies. My defence must be the special circumstances of recent years.

May I take this opportunity of expressing my indebtedness to Professor Foster Watson, D.Litt.   As one of his former students I owe to the stimulus and encouragement I received from him, my interest in matters relating to the History of Education.   I wish also to refer in appreciative terms to Mr. J. E. G. de Montmorency's *State Intervention in English Education*.   Mr. de Montmorency was the first writer to give a connected account of the development of English Education, and it is only fitting that those who essay a similar task should realise their obligations to the one who first " blazed the trail."

I must also thank Mr. G. St. Quintin and Mr. S. E. Goggin for relieving me of the distasteful task of correcting the proofs, and the Rev. Dr. Hughes for kindly preparing the Index.

                                                        A. W. P.

CARMARTHEN,
    January 1920.

CONTENTS.

BOOK III.—EDUCATION PASSING OUT OF CHURCH CONTROL.

INTRODUCTION.

The history of education during the Middle Ages is closely interwoven with the history of the Church. Professor Foster Watson quotes with approval Cardinal Newman's dictum, "Not a man in Europe who talks bravely against the Church but owes it to the Church that he can talk at all." [1]

It is possible to trace three stages in the development of the English educational system during the period with which we are concerned.

The first stage covers a period from the Introduction of Christianity to the Norman Conquest. The Introduction of Christianity was the means by which education became possible for this country, and so it naturally came about that the provision of facilities for education was generally conceived of as a part of the function of the Church. In this connection it is important to realise the relationship of the State to the Church in Anglo-Saxon times As Professor Medley points out,[2] the Church and the State during this period were largely identical. The bishops were *ex-officio* the advisers of the kings, and they sat in the local courts not only exercising jurisdiction in those cases in which the clergy were affected, but also concerning themselves with questions involving the morals of the laity. In a more real sense than at any subsequent time, the Church of England, during the Anglo-Saxon period, was the Church of the English nation. During this time the activities of the Church were essentially the activities of the State, and the work which was done for education might be conceived of, indifferently, as either the work of the Church or of the State.

---

[1] *English Grammar Schools*, p. 10.   [2] *Constit. Hist.*, p. 563.

The second stage dates from the Norman Conquest, which brought to a close this identity of Church and State. William I., impelled by a desire to effect certain reforms in the Church on the model of those he had witnessed abroad, separated the ecclesiastical from the civil courts, and, by the ordinance he issued, authorised the ecclesiastical authorities to utilise the secular power for the enforcement of their sentences. From this time and right up to the Reformation, Church and State were distinct in this country.

This separation of Church and State resulted in a number of duties, other than those which were strictly spiritual, being tacitly regarded as a part of the function of the Church. The provision of Educational facilities is included among these duties, and it was left to the Church to make such arrangements for the organisation, maintenance, and control of education as she deemed fit.

A third stage evolved when the social consciousness of the community (or rather of a part of the community) first realised that education was not a matter for the ecclesiastical authorities alone. The first manifestation of this in England occurred when teachers began to recognise that they exercised a function distinct from the special functions of the priesthood and consequently proceeded to associate themselves in an organisation for the protection of their common interests and thus initiated a movement which ultimately resulted in the establishment of universities. At a later date, various economic developments produced certain social changes which not only made education an object of greater desire but also brought it about that wealthy merchants, gilds, and civic communities, as well as churchmen, took part in the work of providing additional facilities for the education of the people.

For the sake of convenience we may distinguish these three stages as :—

    I.   The Anglo-Saxon Period.

   II.   Education under Church Control.

  III.   Education passing out of Church Control.

BOOK I.

THE ANGLO-SAXON PERIOD.

CHAPTER I.

THE WORK OF THE MONASTERIES.

The introduction of Christianity to this country subsequent to the Saxon invasion was effected by means of two independent agencies—the Roman mission under the leadership of Augustine which arrived in Thanet in 597, and the Scottish missionaries who, in response to the invitation of Oswald, king of Northumbria, took up their residence in the island of Lindisfarne in 635.

The primary task of these missionaries was obviously that of converting a people who professed a heathen religion to an adherence to the Christian faith. The accomplishment of this main task, however, involved two additional tasks, the one moral, the other social. A dismal picture of the moral condition of the settlers in this country in the fifth century has been painted by Montalembert. Basing his account on Ozanam's "Germains avant la Christianisme" he asks, "What could be expected in point of morality from persons accustomed to invoke and to worship Woden, the god of massacres, Freya, the Venus of the North, the goddess of sensuality, and all those bloody and obscene gods of whom the one had for his

emblem a naked sword and another the hammer with
which he broke the heads of his enemies?" He continues,
"The immortality which was promised to them in their
Valhalla but reserved for them new days of slaughter and
nights of debauch spent in drinking deep from the skulls
of their victims. And in this world, their life was but too
often a prolonged orgy of carnage, rapine and lechery."[1]
Herein lay the moral task which awaited the Christian
missionaries. They had to replace the existing national
ideals with the ideals of Christianity—ideals of the highest
standard of personal morality. The social task undertaken by the missionaries was that of elevating this
country from a condition of barbarism into a state of
civilisation. Referring to the results of the introduction
of Christianity, Green writes, "The new England was
admitted into the older commonwealth of nations. The
civilisation, art, letters, which had fled before the sword of
the English conquest returned with the Christian faith." [2]

What means could be adopted by the missionaries to
accomplish the ends they had in view? It is obvious that
continual teaching and instruction would be imperative to
meet the needs of the converts to the new faith, and it is
equally clear that it would be necessary to provide for the
creation of a native ministry in order that the labours of
the early missionaries might be continued. Teaching,
consequently, occupies a position of the greatest importance,
and it is to the educational aspect of the labours of these
missionaries rather than to the religious or the ecclesiastical
aspect that our attention is now directed. It may be advisable for us to remind ourselves that these missionaries
came to this country speaking the Latin tongue, that the
services of the Church were carried on in that language,
and that such books as existed were also written in Latin.
It is necessary to make this point clear in order to show
that schools for instruction in this language would be imperative from the very first.

It is also important to remember, as Montalembert

---

[1] Montalembert : *Monks of the West*, I., 178.
[2] Green : *Short History*, Ch. I., sec. 3.

points out, that the conversion of England was effected by means of monks, first of the Benedictine monks sent from Rome, and afterwards of Celtic monks.[1] We may here lay down a general hypothesis, which the course of this thesis will tend to demonstrate : the educational institutions established in this country were due to an imitation of those which had been in operation elsewhere. The Christian missionaries to England, for example, did not originate a system of education. They adopted what they had seen in operation in the parent monasteries from which they came, and, in so doing, they would naturally adapt the system to the special needs of the country. Some exceptions to this general principle may be found ; they will be noted in their proper place.

Accepting this hypothesis, before we can proceed to consider the special work for education of the monasteries in this country, it is necessary briefly to review the meaning of monachism and to consider the extent to which monasteries had previously associated themselves with educational work.

The origin of Christian monasticism is due partly to the moral conditions prevalent in the early centuries of the Christian era and partly to the mystical and ascetic tendencies which manifest themselves in some individuals. Though the generally accepted view of the moral condition of Roman society in the days of the Early Church[2] may be exaggerated and the description given by Dill[3] represent more fairly the condition of things that actually prevailed, yet even this modified account portrays a social condition in which moral ideals—except in rare cases—barely existed. To yield to the lusts of the body seemed to be almost inseparable from life in the world. Repeatedly did the Apostles and the Church Fathers find it necessary to warn the members of the Church against the grosser sins. The multiplicity of temptations, the low moral standard, the absence of any social condemnation of

[1] Montalembert, *op. cit.* I., 23.
[2] Cf. Draper : *Intellectual Development of Europe.*
[3] Cf. *Roman Society in the Last Century of the Western Empire.*

infractions of the moral code tended to the growth of a belief that bodily mortification and a vigorous asceticism should be practised by those who desired to be real and not merely nominal Christians. Effectively to achieve such an ideal tended to a withdrawal from a participation in social life, from a life of fellowship with others, to a life of isolation, in order that by a severe discipline of the body and a life given up completely to prayer, contemplation, and meditation, the soul might enter into a closer communion with God.

This ideal of isolation was not altogether new. In the deserts of Egypt, during the early centuries, devout Jews had given themselves up to a solitary and austere life of chastity and prayer, combining a system of religious contemplation with a stern régime of physical discipline. Here then was an example ready to be imitated by the enthusiastic Christian. Abandoning life in the world, which in so many cases meant profligacy and vice, the convert, to whom the Christian religion had become a reality, endeavoured to find in the isolated life of a hermit the opportunity for contemplation which he considered imperative for the salvation of his soul.

The reputation for sanctity and austerity gained by certain hermits caused others desirous of a similar life to build their cells in close proximity. Gradually the custom arose of building an enclosure round a small group of cells and of recognising one man as the spiritual head of the group. Certain rules were agreed to, and a common oratory was shared. The first rules for a community of this type were drawn up by Pachomius who founded a coenobitic community at Tabenna in 320 A.D.

For our purpose, it is important to note that Pachomius considered that attention should be paid to the education of the inmates of the community. Classes were to be held for those whose early instruction had been neglected, whilst no one was to be allowed to remain who did not learn to read and was not familiar, at the very least, with the Book of Psalms and the New Testament.[1]

---

[1] *Regula S. Pachomii*, cap. 139, 140.

A third stage in the evolution of monasticism is associated with the name of St. Basil of Caesarea. Instead of
founding his monastery in some remote district, he built it
near a town and received into it not only solitaries who
had become convinced of the dangers of living alone, but
also the poor, the oppressed, the homeless, and those who,
for various reasons, had become weary of life in the outer
world and sought an asylum for their remaining days.
Not only men but also women and children were received
by Basil: so great was his success that he ultimately established in different centres several industrial coenobitic
communities.

The reception of children by Basil naturally brought
forward the question of their education. These children
fell into one or other of two classes; in the one class were
those who, like the infant Samuel, were offered by their
parents for the cloistral life from a tender age; in the
other class were those who were subsequently to return to
the world. St. Basil organised schools for the former of
these classes; children were to be admitted to them when
they were five or six years of age; details with regard to
the mode of their instruction were prescribed; general
rules of discipline were laid down.[1] Under certain circumstances, children who were not destined for the
monastic life could also be received in these schools.[2] In
addition to teaching the elements of grammar and rhetoric
and the facts of scripture history, Basil provided for a
number of trades to be learned and practised as soon as
the children were able to profit by the course. Among the
trades recommended were weaving, tailoring, architecture,
woodwork, brass work, and agriculture.[3]

Cassian was the first to transplant the rules of the
Eastern monks into Europe. He founded two monasteries
in the neighbourhood of Marseilles for men and women
respectively. In 420 he wrote *De Institutis Renuntiatium*,
in which he records the rules to be observed in the institu-

[1] *Regulae Fusius Tractatae*, XV. Interrog. (Pat. Lat., v. 31,
col. 952).
[2] *Regulae Brevius Tractatae*, Interrog. CCXCII.
[3] *Regulae Brevius Tractatae*, XXXVIII.

tions he had founded. The code of rules here enunciated constituted the law of monasticism in Gaul till it gave place to the regulations of Benedict. Cassian in his youth had studied the works of Greek learning, but in his later years he showed a great distrust of pagan literature and strongly opposed its study. He considered that the fascination of such literature distracted the soul, and desired that even the memory of the classical writings should be eradicated from his mind. The underlying conception of the rule of Cassian was that the monastery was a school in which a future stage of existence was the dominating and controlling thought.

Reference must next be made to Cassiodorus (479?-575) —the great Italian statesman turned monk—who did much to develop study among ecclesiastics and to make the cloister the centre of literary activity. He founded a monastery at Vivarium in Bruttium, which he endowed with his Roman library containing a magnificent collection of manuscripts, and to which he himself retired at the age of sixty. During the remaining years of his life he devoted himself to literary work; of his numerous writings the most important is his *Institutiones Divinarum et Saecularium Lectionum.* A more important work accomplished by Cassiodorus than the writings he produced was his organisation of the monastery scriptorium. This served as a model for the series of Benedictine monasteries which subsequently came into existence. Hence to Cassiodorus must be assigned the honour of realising that the multiplication of manuscripts was a recognised employment of monastic life. Consequently, he conferred a boon of the greatest value upon the human race. As Hodgkin expresses it, there was in existence an accumulated store of two thousand years of literature, sacred and profane, the writings of Hebrew prophets, of Greek philosophers, of Latin rhetoricians, perishing for want of men with leisure and ability to transcribe them. Were it not for the labours of the monks it is highly conceivable that these treasures would have been irretrievably lost to the world.[1]

---

[1] *Italy and Her Invaders*, IV., 391.

The number of the monastic institutions rapidly increased. Gradually the evils arising from a lack of definite control and from the want of a code of rules to check individualising tendencies, began to manifest themselves. To St. Benedict of Nursia is due the more adequate organisation of monastic life. In addition to the laws of chastity, poverty, and obedience required from the professed monk, he recognised the importance of labour not only for self-support but also as a duty towards God. The code of rules, drawn up by him for the use of the monasteries under his care, was found to meet a great need of the religious communities of the time, with the result that the Benedictine rules became almost universally accepted by all monastic establishments.

Of these rules, the one that exercised a profound influence upon educational development is headed *Concerning Daily Manual Labour*.[1] It runs:—

"Idleness is the enemy of the soul: hence brethren ought at certain seasons to occupy themselves with manual labour and again at certain hours with holy reading. Between Easter and the calends of October let them apply themselves to reading from the fourth hour until the sixth hour . . . From the calends of October to the beginning of Lent let them apply themselves to reading until the second hour. During Lent let them apply themselves to reading from morning until the end of the third hour, and in these days of Lent let them receive a book apiece from the library and read it straight through. These books are to be given out at the beginning of Lent."

The great importance of this rule arises from the fact that whilst monks were becoming very numerous, books were very few. Hence in order that the requisite number of copies might be available, writing had to be taught; in order that the monks might be able to read the books, it is conceivable that in some cases reading also would have to be taught. Moreover, the copying of manuscripts was considered to comply with the regulation as to manual labour prescribed by the Benedictine rules. Consequently wherever a Benedictine monastery came into existence, there books were multiplied, and a library gradually developed. As the years went on, the Benedictine labours

[1] Chapter XLVIII.

in the intellectual world increased. Mabillon remarks, "Almost alone, the order of St. Benedict for several years, maintained and preserved letters in Europe. There were frequently no other masters in our monasteries, and frequently the cathedral schools drew theirs from the same source."[1]

The purpose of this digression has been to show that by the time that the monks entered upon their mission in this country, the idea of monasticism was firmly established on the continent. The monastic houses consisted of communities of men or of women who, leaving the outer world behind them, dedicated their lives to the worship and the praise of God. They concentrated their attention upon the world to come, and, as far as possible, they endeavoured to anticipate it in the present stage of existence. Labour, either physical or mental, was one of their special obligations. Limiting ourselves to intellectual labour, we note that to some was entrusted the instruction of the children who were brought to them and of those members of the community who still needed education; to others was assigned work in the scriptorium; to others was allotted the task of giving instruction in singing and of making due preparation for the musical part' of the monastic services; others, according to their capacity, continued their studies, and, by the chronicles which they wrote, enable posterity to reconstruct the history of their days.

Our problem is now a narrower one: does any evidence exist to show that the educational organisation of the monasteries in this country corresponded with the educational work of the continental monasteries? Fortunately, for our purpose, a complete answer in the affirmative can be obtained from the works of the Venerable Bede.

That it was customary for schools to be established in monasteries is a fact that can be readily demonstrated. Bede writes that he "was given at seven years of age to be educated by the most reverend Abbot Benedict and afterwards by Ceolfrid; and spending all the remaining time of my life in that monastery, I applied myself wholly

[1] *Etudes Monastiques*, p. 18.

to the study of scripture, and amidst the observance of regular discipline and the daily care of singing in the Church, I always took delight in learning, teaching, and writing." [1] This passage, alone, practically establishes the fact that the educational activities described as existing in continental monasteries were also to be found as a normal part of the monasteries which were established in this country. Lest it might be maintained that the monastery at Wearmouth was exceptional the decree of the Council of Cloveshoo may be quoted. At that council it was decreed that " abbots and abbesses should take care that scripture reading was everywhere studied." Again it must be borne in mind that copies of the scriptures existed only in the Latin language and that for the reading of scripture it was an essential condition that ability to read Latin had been previously acquired. Further, at the same council, it was enacted that boys " everywhere in the schools were to be compelled to address themselves to the love of sacred learning." [2]

The work of the monasteries in connection with higher education is also attested by Bede. The Irish monasteries, in particular, acquired a reputation in this respect. Many English youths of every social grade crossed over to Ireland, attracted thither by the greater fame of the monasteries, for the purpose of extending their studies. [3] Bede records that scholars went about from cell to cell, gathering learning from monastic teachers. [4] It is noteworthy that at these monasteries food, books, and teaching were supplied freely and willingly. Aidan instructed, among others, twelve boys of the English nation at his monastery at Lindisfarne : some of these acquired fame in later years, *e.g.* Basil, who became Bishop of Lindisfarne, and Eata, who became Prior of Melrose. Briefly, we may say that nearly all the learned men of this period were either monks or were closely connected with monasteries. Among them we may mention

---

[1] *H.E.*, V., 24.
[2] Haddon and Stubbs : *Councils and Documents relating to Britain and Ireland*, Vol. III, pp. 364-5.
[3] *H.E.*, III., 27.   [4] *H.E.*, III., 27.

Aidan, Bede, Wilfrid, Theodore, Hadrian, Benedict Biscop, Aldhelm, and Augustine.

The formation of libraries and the work of the scriptorium occupied as high a place in the newly-established English monasteries as they did in those monasteries which served as models for them. Benedict Biscop—the father of English culture [1]—who was the founder of the twin monasteries of Wearmouth and Jarrow, is particularly famous for his labours in connection with the establishment of libraries. He visited Rome six times in all, and each time he returned he brought back books with him to this country. Of his fourth journey Bede remarks that he "brought back with him a very large number of books of all kinds." [2] Biscop's sixth journey to Rome was almost entirely devoted to the purpose of acquiring additions to his collection of books, a collection which included classical as well as ecclesiastical literature. [3] In some cases monasteries arranged for the mutual exchange of books. [4] As an instance of the activity of the scriptorium may be quoted the famous library of York, which was composed of transcripts of the parchments collected by Biscop. Ceolfrid, who became Abbot of Jarrow, and who subsequently was also placed in charge of the monastery of Wearmouth, took considerable interest in the scriptorium. Montalembert quotes the statement that Ceolfrid had had made two complete copies of the Bible according to the version of St. Jerome, as a refutation of the "stupid calumny" which represents the Church as having interdicted the reading and study of the scriptures. [5] The preservation of such Anglo-Saxon literature as remains, is undoubtedly due to the action of some of the monastic scribes. The poems of Caedmon were written first of all in the monastery of Whitby; so, too, the Northumbrian poet, Cynewulf, owes the preservation of his works to the scriptorium of the monastery he ultimately entered.

The teaching of singing naturally occupied an important

[1] Sandys : *History of Classical Scholarship*, I., 52.
[2] " Eum innumerabilem librorum omnis generis copiam apportasse."
[3] Alcuin. *Ep.*, 13.   [4] *H.E.*, V., 15.   [5] *Monks of the West*, IV., 464.

place among the educational activities of the monasteries.
Bede describes himself as being in charge of "the daily
care of singing in the Church." [1] John, Abbot of the
monastery of St. Martin's and precentor of St. Peter's,
Rome, one of the most famous of the teachers of music of
the day, came to this country for a time on the invitation
of Biscop and at the request of Pope Agatha. Abbot John
taught the monks not only how to sing but also how to
read aloud. His efforts were not limited to Wearmouth
alone; those who were experts in music, from "almost all"
the religious houses, came to him for further instruction,
and in this way the influence of his teaching was widely
spread. [2]

When we pass to the question of what was taught in
the monasteries, we find that the scholars were trained to
read the scriptures in Latin and to be familiar with the
services of the monastery, and that writing and singing
were also subjects of instruction. Two of Bede's works
are probably school-books: his "Librum de orthographia,
alfabeti ordine distinctum" and his "Librum de metrica
arte, et huic adjectum alium de schematibus sine tropis
libellum, hoc est de figuris modisque locutionum, quibus
scriptura sancta contexta est."

Though it may not be just to regard Bede as the typical
product of the English monasteries of the time, yet it may
fairly be pointed out that the whole of Bede's education
was received in these monasteries. Even if we regard him
as the best-educated of the English monks, his example
will still serve to show the extent of learning which could
be acquired in the monasteries of this period. Sandys
writes, "His skill in Latin verse is shown in his elegiacs on
Queen Ethelfrida and in his hexameters on the shrine of
St. Cuthbert. . . . His Greek learning is indicated in his
treatises and in the references to a Greek MS. of the Acts
which are to be found in his *Liber Retractionum*. The
Latin authors most frequently quoted by him are Cicero,
Virgil and Horace and (doubtless at second hand) Lucilius
and Varro." [3]

[1] *H.E.*, V., 24.   [2] *H.E.*, IV., 18.
[3] Sandys: *History of Classical Scholarship*, I., p. 53.

Apart from the education, in the technical sense of the word, given by the monks, they were also responsible for reforms which, in the wider sense of the term, were also educational. Thus, the higher ideals of life prevalent in the monastery were introduced into the country as a whole. The age was a turbulent and disordered one, in which neither moral nor ethical obligations prevailed and in which might alone was right.[1] The monks established, in the country of their adoption, a number of communities, in which the ruling principles were those of Charity, Chastity, and Obedience. The ideals prevailing in these monasteries reacted upon the social customs of their neighbourhood. The strong individualism of the Teutons was modified by the attitude of obedience to recognised authority characteristic of the monk; the qualities of savagery tended to yield to the examples of self-denial, self-control, and care for others.

The monasteries also played an important part in the economic development of the country. At times, and in certain localities, the economic condition of the people seems to have sunk to a low ebb. Bede tells us that "very often forty or fifty men being spent with want, would go together to some precipice or to the seashore and there, hand in hand, perish by the fall or be swallowed up by the waves."[2] From the earliest times industrial activity had been a feature of monastic life. Speaking of St. Basil, his biographer tells us that "by the labour of his monks over wide desert places, hopeless sterility gave place to golden harvests and abundant vintages."[3] Manual labour was a common employment in the English monasteries.[4] The builders of the monasteries also necessarily introduced new arts into the country. Thus Benedict Biscop brought over masons and glaziers from France.[5] Lamps and vessels for the use of the Church were made, and the craft taught to the Northumbrians.[6] All the furniture and vestments

---

[1] Cf. Traill: *Social England*, I., p. 177.   Bede: *H.E.*, II., 20: III., 11.   [2] *H.E.*, IV., 13.
[3] Smith and Wace: *Dictionary of Christian Biography*.
[4] *H.E.*, IV., 13.
[5] Bede: *Hist. Abb.* V., cf. *H.E.*, III., 4.   [6] *Hist. Abb.*, V.

"which Benedict could not procure at home he took care
to purchase abroad." [1]   The knowledge of the art of fishing
by means of nets, which apparently was not known in
some parts, was introduced by the monks.[2]   Though
slavery was not condemned by the Church at this time,[3]
yet the Church fostered the feeling that slavery was not
consonant with the dignity of the human soul, and the monasteries used their influence in opposing this custom.
Aidan employed some of the gifts of money he received
for the monasteries, for the redemption of slaves.[4]   Wilfrid
granted liberty to the slaves on the land that had been
bestowed to the monastery founded by him.[5]

It must be borne in mind that in this country the monasteries originally were not merely communities of men or
women who were dedicated to a life of contemplation, but
were essentially centres of missionary enterprise.   Bede
tells us of monks who went into the surrounding country
and villages to preach, baptize, and visit the sick.[6]   Of
Aidan and his company of "shorn monks" and laymen,
we learn that they traversed the country trying to convert
those who were not yet converts to Christianity, and stirring
up those who had previously accepted the faith to alms
and good works.[7]   Similarly Chad, one of the disciples of
Aidan, proceeded to preach the gospel "in towns, in the
open country, cottages, villages, and castles." [8]   In brief,
at the period with which we are now concerned, these
monasteries served the purpose of spiritual outposts, from
whence messengers went out to extend the message of the
Christian faith.

It is interesting to note that the monasteries were
thoroughly democratic in their selection of members.   The
monks preached that " Christian men are brothers, whether
high or low, noble or ignoble, lord or slave.   The wealthy
is not better on that account than the needy.   As boldly
may the slave call God his Father as the king.   We are

---

[1] *Hist. Abb.*, V.   [2] *H.E.*, IV., 13.
[3] Cf. "homo XIII. annorum sese potest servum facere " Theod.
Penit. XIX., sec. 29.
[4] *H.E.*, V., 5.   [5] *H.E.*, IV., 13.   [6] *H.E.*, III., 27.
[7] *H.E.*, III., 5.   [8] *H.E.*, III., 28.

all alike before God, unless anyone exceeds another in good works." [1] So, whilst on the one hand kings like Ceolwulf and Ini became monks, on the other hand redeemed slaves were admitted as inmates of the monasteries, and, if they proved themselves capable of profiting by instruction, were advanced to the priesthood.[2] Certain undesigned effects followed. With the progress of civilisation, the warlike qualities which originally had gained territory for the Teutonic invaders needed to be supplemented by the intellectual gifts necessary for legislation and administration. These abilities could only be found in the ranks of the clergy. As a result, priests became in practice the ministers of the Crown; the names of Dunstan and Lanfranc readily occur as illustrative instances. A general study of Bede, apart from specific instances, tends to support the suggestion that Cuthbert, Theodore, Wilfrid, and Aidan, among others, also exercised a considerable influence over kings. As a second undesigned effect may be mentioned the fact that, as the monasteries admitted boys who showed vocation and promise, regardless of their social position, and gave them the best education of which the monasteries were capable, so it happened that the monastery was practically the only avenue through which promotion became possible to the able and competent who were handicapped by circumstances of their birth. Passing outside our period, we may refer to the case of Nicholas Breakspear, who from being a servant lad at St. Albans rose to the position of Pope.

[1] Aelfric, *Homilies*, vol. I., p. 261.
[2] *H.E.*, V., 3.

CHAPTER II.

EDUCATION UNDER THE SECULAR CLERGY.

In the preceding chapter we stated that the evangeli-
sation of England was mainly the work of monks. Though
this statement is true, yet we must not lose sight of the
fact that the work of the secular clergy was slowly developing side by side with that of the regular clergy, and
ultimately superseded it. It is consequently necessary
that we should next investigate into the work for education
which was effected by them.

By way of introduction, we may point out that the
method of work of the secular clergy and their mode of
organisation closely resembled that of the regular clergy,
and at times was scarcely distinguishable. Just as Augustine and his band of monks settled in the capital of the
kingdom of Kent and built there a monastery, in which
the bishop shared a community life with his monks, and
which served as the centre from which their labours were
directed, so a secular bishop with his companions settled
in the chief town of another kingdom, where a church was
ultimately built and a community life established. Thus
in 604, Mellitus was consecrated bishop and sent to preach
to the East Saxons. The new faith was accepted both by
the king of the East Saxons and his people. A church
dedicated to St. Paul was subsequently built at London—
the capital of the kingdom. This church, instead of being
a monastic church, as was Christ Church, Canterbury,
belongs to that category of churches known as collegiate
churches.

For the sake of convenience, we may here point out the main differences between monasteries and collegiate churches. A monastery consisted of a community of men or women under the rule of an abbot or abbess. The members of a monastery had taken certain vows and were bound to live in accordance with the rules of that Order to which the monastery belonged. A collegiate church consisted of a number of clergy forming a corporate body and living under the supervision of a Dean or Provost and responsible to the bishop. The origin of such churches has been traced to St. Augustine of Hippo, who arranged for his clergy to live together under his direction in a kind of community, though without the imposition of monastic vows. A further development took place about 750 when Chrodegang, bishop of Metz, drew up certain rules for the use of the clergy who were living with him. The clergy who lived according to these rules were called "canons." The rule of Chrodegang was introduced into England, but it was not generally accepted;[1] and consequently the term "canon," in this country, originally meant little more than a man who was a member of a college of clergy, who served a church in common and had a common claim on its revenue.

We may also note here that when a bishop's official seat or throne (cathedra) was placed in a church, it thereby became a cathedral church. Sometimes the cathedral church was a monastic church, sometimes a collegiate church; in each case the church was known as a cathedral. From the standpoint of the development of education, as will be subsequently shown, the distinction between a collegiate cathedral church and a monastic cathedral church is an important one, but this distinction cannot always be clearly made, because during the early centuries of Christianity in England, a cathedral church was at times in the possession of the regular clergy, and at other times in the hands of the secular clergy. Thus Christ Church, Canterbury, was originally monastic but is said to have fallen into the hands of the seculars during

[1] Hunt : *Hist. of the Eng. Ch.*, p. 239.

Monastic vs. Secular

the archiepiscopate of Ceolnoth (837-870), after which it again returned to the monks and remained monastic till the Reformation. So too, Gloucester Cathedral was originally monastic, then Offa transferred it to the secular clergy, later it again became monastic.

Whether or not the cathedral church of a diocese was monastic, the bishop of a diocese was the head of the secular clergy and obedience was due to him from them; on the other hand, the monks owed their obedience directly to their abbot, from him to the head of their order, and ultimately to the pope.[1]

bishop / Secular

Abbot / monks

In this chapter we propose to limit ourselves to the labours for education of the bishop and the secular clergy, though, as we have previously indicated, the line of demarcation between the work that was definitely monastic and that which may definitely be assigned to the secular clergy cannot always be clearly drawn.

The educational problems which had to be faced by a bishop and his band of secular priests were similar to those which had to be dealt with by the missionary monks. Latin, the language of the Church, had to be taught to those who were ignorant of it and who wished to be attached to the Church in an official capacity. A knowledge of music was necessary for those who desired to take a personal part in the worship offered by the Church. In addition, the principles of Christianity had to be taught more fully to converts; the children of the faith required instruction; arrangements had to be made for more advanced instruction for those who were desirous of receiving it. Schools had to be founded for these purposes, and these schools were the original schools of England.

Latin

We have already adopted as our hypothesis that the schools of this country were not a new discovery but were modelled on those which existed elsewhere. Our first problem consequently, is to discover where these models were found.

Mr. Leach, in his *Schools of Medieval England*, maintains that " the true models and source of the schools of

---

[1] Cf. Medley, *Constitutional History*, p. 557.

England are not the schools of the Church but the schools
of heathendom, the schools of Athens and Alexandria, of
Rome, of Lyons, of Vienne. They were in fact the very
same "heathen" or "pagan" or, in other words, Graeco-
Roman institutions, in which Horace and Juvenal, Jerome
and St. Augustine had learned the scansion of hexameters
and the accredited methods of speech-making and arguments." [1]

This statement calls for examination. The schools to
which Mr. Leach refers came into existence about 50 B.C.
and owed their distinctive characteristics to the influence
of Greek thought upon Roman activities. Three grades
of these schools are usually recognised :—

(1) The Schools of the Litteratores. In these schools
only reading, writing, and calculation were taught ; they
were never very highly esteemed, and their teachers, who
were generally slaves, were frequently ill-remunerated.

(2) The Schools of the Grammatici. Originally these
schools dealt simply with grammar, *i.e.* with words and
their relations ; but the conception of grammar developed
so that it came to include both a study of Latin and Greek
Literature and also a range of subjects embracing mathematics, music, and elementary dialectic. Ultimately these
schools were to be found in almost every city of the empire
and, generally speaking, were supported either by public
funds or by endowments.

(3) The Schools of the Rhetores. These were the most
important schools ; admission to them was not possible
until the "toga virilis" had been assumed. Here the
pupils studied carefully and minutely all matters relating
to success in the art of oratory—an art which at that time
had to be mastered by all who purposed to devote themselves to public life. But oratory, as the term was then
understood, denoted much more than the art of declama-
tion. It included a mastery of the existing literature, an
acquaintance with the knowledge of things so far as that
knowledge was then available, and a good vocabulary. To
this must be added the power of playing upon human

---

[1] *Op. cit.*, p. 13.

emotions, combined with grace of manner and effective delivery.

The following reasons may be advanced in support of our contention that Mr. Leach is in error in considering these Graeco-Roman Schools as the models of our English Schools, which, as Mr. Leach himself admits, owed their existence in the first place to the labours of Christian missionaries.

(1) In the pagan schools, there was no thought of the moral aspect of instruction. The literature on which the schoolboy was nourished was created in the atmosphere of paganism and teemed with mythological allusions.[1] The scholar was taught that the ideal age lay in the past rather than, as Christianity taught, in the future. The great deeds held up for his admiration were those associated with the Roman heroes who had read the fate of their campaigns in the flight of birds or the entrails of the victims at the altar.

(2) As Professor Woodward points out, "it is an invariable law that the accepted ideals of the adult generation shape its educational aims."[2] At the period in which the schools referred to by Mr. Leach were flourishing, scepticism in religious matters was prevalent. Terentius Varro had urged that the anthropomorphic gods were mere emblems of the forces of nature. Lucretius had argued against the immortality of the soul. Cicero, the greatest thinker of the time, barely veiled his scepticism. Moreover, it was generally recognised that religion had lost its control over the moral life of man. It is thus evident that the ideals of Christianity and the ideals of the Graeco-Roman schools were fundamentally opposed. In no essential respect could the schools of paganism furnish a model for the schools of Christianity.

(3) The attitude of the Christians of the early centuries towards classical literature serves to illustrate still further the attitude of the Christians towards the pagan schools. Classical literature was obnoxious to the early Christians

---

[1] Dill: *Last Century of the Western Empire*, p. 67.
[2] *Erasmus*, p. 73.

because the general interpretation of life revealed by these books was hostile to the Christian view. The beauty and charm of the mode of expression made little or no appeal to men who were confronted by the hideous reality of current licentiousness, even though the prevailing manner of life might be cloaked by the elegance and grace of its presentation.

As an alternative hypothesis we suggest that the schools founded by the bishops in England were modelled on the schools of Christendom rather than on the schools of paganism. To substantiate this hypothesis, it is necessary that we should briefly consider the origin and character of these early Christian schools.

The germ of the essentially Christian Schools may be traced from the custom of the great apostles of gathering round them their disciples and the aspirants for the priesthood, for purposes of instruction and discipline.[1] Gradually three types of schools were evolved : —

(1) Schools for Catechumens. It is assumed that some form of instruction would be given to Christian catechumens prior to their admission to the Church. These classes were held either in the porch of the church or in some other part of the building, and were controlled by a master appointed for that purpose. The first of these schools of whose existence we have any evidence was established by St. Mark in Alexandria.[2]

(2) Catechetical Schools. This type of school also originated at Alexandria, and arose out of the intellectual activities which made that city so important a centre during the first and second centuries of the Christian era. Pantaenus, a converted Stoic philosopher who took charge of the school at Alexandria in 170 A.D., introduced a wide range of studies into the curriculum and made use of his old learning to illustrate and defend his new faith.[3] Pantaenus was succeeded by two of the most noted of the Fathers of the Early Church, Clement, who was formerly

[1] Hodgson : *Primitive Christian Education*, p. 103.
[2] Jerome : *Lives of Illustrious Men*, Ch. VIII.
[3] Eusebius : *H.E.*, VI., pp. 3, 26.

his assistant, and Origen, who assumed the direction of
the Catechetical School at the age of eighteen years.[1]

(3) Bishop's Schools. The origin of these schools may
be traced to the fact that circumstances compelled Origen
to leave Alexandria in 231. Subsequently, at the invitation
of two bishops, he opened a school at Caesarea. It proved
so successful that similar schools were opened at a number
of centres. Teaching was carried out either by the bishops
in person, or by a deputy appointed by them. To these
schools came candidates for ordination, the younger clergy
whose instruction needed to be continued, as well as those
who, for some reason or other, wished to avail themselves
of the educational facilities thus provided.

One other type of educational institution must also be
referred to. We have already indicated the service rendered
to the Church by St. Augustine of Hippo in connection
with the establishment of collegiate churches, and it is
equally important to note his contribution to the educational organisation of the Church. Prior to his conversion
to Christianity, St. Augustine had been a teacher of
rhetoric, and was the author of certain treatises dealing
with the seven liberal arts. Subsequent to his consecration
to the episcopate, he established a seminary for those who
were in course of preparation for ordination. This seminary, though planned on community lines, was essentially
an educational establishment with the avowed object of
making its members as efficient as possible in the ministry
which awaited them.[2] The institution proved a great
success. Many priests, who were trained there, subsequently became well-known; the seminary itself furnished
a model to be imitated by various bishops.[3] Ultimately,
this idea of St. Augustine's was adopted by Pope Leo I.;[4]
and the example thus set by Rome was followed by several
bishops in Gaul, notably by Sidonius Apollinaris, Bishop
of Clermont, St. Hilary, Bishop of Arles, and Gregory,
Bishop of Tours.

[1] Jerome : *Lives of Illustrious Men*, Ch. XXVIII.
[2] *Sermo* CCCLV., sec. 2, 6, 7.   [3] *Vita S. Augustini*, c. 11.
[4] Theiner : *Histoire des Institutions d'Education Ecclesiastique*,
v. 1, pp. 103-117.

The schools established by the bishops in Gaul are of
special interest to us, because the first available reference
to education in this country is the statement by Bede
that Sigebert "wishing to imitate what he had seen well
ordered among the Gauls " "instituit scolam in qua pueri
litteris erudirentur." [1] It is consequently necessary that
we should next turn to the educational system of Gaul at
this time.

There had existed in Gaul from Roman times (as in
other parts of the Empire) schools of the Graeco-Roman
type to which we have previously referred. The barbarian
invasions, however, brought these schools to an end. When
social conditions reasserted themselves, the old condition
of things had passed away and Christianity had become
a power in the land. In the educational reconstruction
which followed, the bishops played an important part and
two types of schools were ultimately to be found in Gaul,
the monastic schools and the episcopal schools.

The monastic schools taught theology mainly, but instruction was also given in speaking, reading and writing
Latin, in copying manuscripts, in painting and architecture,
and in elementary notions of astronomy and mathematics. [2]
The most famous of these schools were those of Luxeuil,
Soissons, Lérins and Saint-Vandrille. At the last-named
school there were about three hundred scholars.

The Episcopal Schools were closely modelled on the type
originated by St. Augustine. They were mainly intended
for those who proposed to offer themselves for ordination.
The curriculum of these schools was narrower and more
definitely theological than that of the monastic schools.
The best known were those of Paris, Poitiers, Le Mans,
Clermont, Vienne, Chalons-sur-Saône and Gaps. These
schools, however, differed from the seminary of St. Augustine
on which they were modelled because the special circum-

---

[1] Bede, *H.E.*, III., 18.
[2] Cf. Fischer de Chevrier: *Histoire de l'Instruction Populaire en
France*, Ch. IV. ; Mullinger: *University of Cambridge*, p. 11 ;
Ampere: *Histoire Littéraire de la France avant le Douzième Siècle*,
II., 278 ; Joly: *Traité Historique des Ecoles Episcopales et Ecclésias-
tiques*, pp. 144-599.

stances of the time rendered it necessary that classes were also held in connection with them for the boys, who were attached in some capacity or other to the cathedral church. Thus the choir boys and others who were desirous of preparing themselves for subsequent employment in any capacity in which the education available would afterwards be of service to them, found in these classes the opportunities they sought.

Our analysis of the educational institutions existing in Gaul in the sixth century has brought out that there existed, as models for imitation, the monastic schools and the episcopal schools. In addition, schools had also developed in connection with the parish churches, but we propose to deal with that development later. We have already considered the monastic schools of this country; our present problem is then to consider whether there is any evidence that schools, conducted by the bishop himself or by his deputy, similar to those we have shown to have existed in France, were to be found in this country.

Our reply is emphatically in the affirmative. Thus there was a school at Hexham. Bede tells us of Herebald, who was a member of the school kept by St. John of Beverley, whilst Bishop of Hexham. "When in the prime of my youth," Herebald is reported to have said, "I lived among his clergy[1] applying myself to reading and singing."[2]   Another school existed at Canterbury, and during the time it was conducted by Archbishop Theodore and the Abbot Hadrian it ranked as the most famous of the episcopal schools of this country. With regard to these two famous teachers, Bede writes: "They gathered a crowd of disciples, and there daily flowed from them rivers of knowledge to water the hearts of their hearers; and, together with the books of Holy Writ, they also taught them the arts of ecclesiastical poetry, astronomy, and arithmetic. A testimony of which is, that there are living at this day some of their scholars who are as well versed in the Greek and Latin tongues as in their own in which

[1] *I.e.* the clergy of the Bishop of Hexham.
[2] *H.E.*, V., 6.

they were born." [1]   It is owing to the labours of these two
men that England, for a time, occupied the leading place
in the schools of the west.[2]   One of the most celebrated
scholars of the school of Canterbury was Aldhelm, who
can claim the distinction of being the first Englishman
who cultivated classical learning with any success, and the
first of whom any literary remains are preserved.[3]   Bede
describes Aldhelm as "a wonder of erudition in the liberal
as well as ecclesiastical learning." [4]   It is from a letter
written by Aldhelm that we gain an insight into the
curriculum followed at Canterbury, and learn that the
course of study pursued there included grammar, geometry, arithmetic, metre, astronomy, and Roman Law.[5]

A third famous episcopal school was that of York, of
which we possess a full account in Alcuin's poem "De
Pontificibus Sanctae Ecclesiae Eboracensis." Alcuin writes
in most eulogistic terms of the work of this school, and,
more particularly, of the educational labours of Archbishop
Albert, to whom Alcuin was personally indebted for the
instruction he received.

"He gave drink to thirsty minds at the fountain of the sciences.
To some he communicated the art and the rules of grammar; for
others he caused floods of rhetoric to flow; he knew how to exercise
these in the battles of jurisprudence, and those in the songs of
Adonis; some learned from him to pipe Castalian airs and with
lyric foot to strike the summit of Parnassus; to others he made
known the harmony of the heavens, the courses of the sun and the
moon, the five zones of the pole, the seven planets, the laws of the
courses of the stars, the motions of the sea, earthquakes, the nature
of men, and of beasts and of birds, and of all that inhabit the forest.
He unfolded the different qualities and combinations of numbers;
he taught how to calculate with certainty the solemn return of
Eastertide and, above all, he explained the mysteries of the Holy
Scriptures." [6]

The library of the school at York was particularly
famous, and included the works of Jerome, Hilarius,
Ambrose, Augustine, Athanasius, Orosius, Gregory, Leo,

[1] *H.E.*, IV., 2.
[2] Mignet : *Memoire sur la conversion de l'Allemagne par les
Moines*, p. 25.   [3] Sandys : *History of Classical Scholarship*, I., 451.
[4] *H.E.*, V., 18.   [5] *Aldhelmi Opera*, ed. Giles, p. 96.
De Pontiff. Ebor., lines 1431-1447, trans. by Munroe.

Basil, Fulgentius, Cassiodorus, Chrysostom, Aldhelm, Bede, Victorinus, Boethius, Pliny, Aristotle, Cicero, Virgil, etc. Mullinger remarks of this library: "The imposing enumeration at once calls our attention to the fact that the library at York at this period far surpassed any possessed by either England or France in the twelfth century, whether at Christ Church, Canterbury, St. Victor at Paris, or at Bec." [1]

The school at York is also important because it is the first known instance in English educational history of the bishop's school being conducted by a member of the staff of clergy associated with the bishop, instead of by the bishop himself. On the death of Archbishop Albert, his successor, instead of taking personal charge of the school, entrusted that duty to Alcuin. This was a special case of the principle of the division of labour, and the example thus set at York was of considerable importance in the subsequent development of education in this country.

As Alcuin is commonly regarded as the most important educator of the first half of the Middle Ages, and as it was through Alcuin that England influenced continental education, a slight digression from the main purpose of this chapter, for the sake of indicating the importance of Alcuin, may be allowed. The only education which Alcuin received was obtained at the bishop's school at York, and a consideration of this fact should assist us in realising that these schools were in practice the universities of the period. The reputation which Alcuin gained must have spread beyond the borders of this country, because Charles the Great, who had determined upon a scheme of educational reform in the dominions ruled by him, invited Alcuin to come to his court to occupy a position analogous to that of a Minister of Education of modern days. This position Alcuin occupied for fourteen years, and during that period the famous capitularies of 787, 789, and 802 were issued.[2] The effect of the reforms carried out by

[1] *Schs. of Charles the Great*, p. 61.
[2] For capitulary of 787 and 789, see Pertz: *Leges*, I., pp. 52, 65; for that of 802, Pertz, I., 107; for translation see *Schools of Charles the Great*, pp. 97-99.

Alcuin was, that scholars were attracted from all parts of Europe to the court of Charles the Great, the Palace Schools were developed and invigorated, learning was promoted among the clergy, and the activities of the monastic and episcopal schools were stimulated. It has been suggested that the reforms attributed to Alcuin owed little to his individual genius, but were based entirely upon the practice he found in operation in York.[1] If this is so, then the educational facilities provided in this country in the eighth century must have been of much greater importance than is commonly conceived. The available evidence is, however, too scanty for any definite statements to be made on the subject.

Alcuin was a voluminous writer, and his works bear further witness to the intellectual activity of his day. They include epistles, poems, exegetical works, dogmatic writings, liturgical writings, biographical writings, studies, and dialogues.[2] His educational writings include works *On Grammar*, *On Orthography*, *On Rhetoric*, *On Dialectic*, etc. They are written in the characteristic Anglo-Saxon dialogue form. In his *On Grammar*, Alcuin shows that true happiness is to be found in the things peculiar to the soul itself rather than in those things which are alien to it; of these things, "wisdom is the chief adornment." Progress in wisdom was to be obtained, so far as secular knowledge was concerned, by the "seven ascents of theoretical discipline," *i.e.* the trivium and the quadrivium.

We have thus brought forward evidence to show that episcopal schools existed at Canterbury, York, and Hexham, and that advanced instruction was available at these centres. The general hypothesis we submit is that the cathedral city of each diocese became gradually recognised as a place of higher education, and that it was commonly regarded as the duty of the bishop to provide, either personally or by deputy, such higher education as the circumstances of the time rendered possible.

Facilities would also be required at these centres for

[1] Mullinger : *op. cit.*, p. 50.
[2] *Alcuini Opera Omnia* ; Migne, *Pat. Lat.*, Vols. C., CI.

elementary instruction, and also for instruction in the
"specialist" art of writing. As the demand for such instruction arose, so the Church endeavoured to meet it, and
classes were established for this purpose. Thus, in a letter
written c. 796 by Alcuin to Eanbald II. Archbishop of
York, he recommends that separate masters should be appointed to teach those "qui libros legant, qui cantilenae
inserviant, qui scribendi studio deputentur." [1]

With the spread of Christianity in this country, the
parochial system originated. For this purpose, the Saxon
"tun" was taken as the unit of ecclesiastical organisation
and it became known as the "parish," the specific area
placed under the spiritual over-sight of the parish priest.
We must again remind ourselves that Latin was the
language of the Church, and that to participate in the
worship offered by the Church, to join in its psalms, to
understand its doctrines properly, or in fact to become in
any sense of the word a "churchman," a knowledge of
Latin was imperative. A custom naturally arose that the
parish priest should keep a "school of grammar," or, as we
should term it to-day, should hold a Latin class for those
who were desirous of learning that language. In course
of time this custom became obligatory and a part of the
law of the Church. Thus, at the Council of Vaison held
in 529, it was decreed that each priest, who was in charge
of a parish, should also have at his house a class of young
men for the purpose of preparing them for the sacred
ministry. These young men were also to be engaged in
teaching the small children. The bishop in his visitatio
of the parish made enquiries as to whether this law was
carried into effect.[2]

The enactment of Vaison was repeated by subsequent
decrees of the Church, notably by that of Tours, and the
establishment of schools of grammar to be taught by the
parish priest was a definite part of the system of the
Church.[3] This requirement was reiterated from time to

[1] *Alcuini Epistolae*, Migne, *Pat. Lat.*, 1851, Vol. C., p. 222.

[2] Heinemann: *Statutes of* 852, XI.   *Acts of the Province of Rheims*,
I., p. 211.   Azarias : *Essays Educational*, p. 180.

[3] Mansi : *Concilia*, vol. IX., p. 790.

time. Thus Theodulf of Orleans, the coadjutor of Alcuin
in carrying out the educational reforms of the kingdom of
Charles the Great, issued a letter to his clergy in 797 in
which he reminded them that " Presbyteri per villas et
vicos scolas habeant, et si quilibet fidelium suos parvulos
ad discendas litteras eis commendare vult, eos suscipere et
docere non renuant." [1]

Were these parochial grammar schools to be found in
England ?   The direct evidence is very slight.   In a letter
which Alcuin wrote to Offa, King of Mercia, about 792, he
recommends to him a schoolmaster ; [2] this schoolmaster,
however, does not appear to possess a strong moral character,
as Alcuin warns Offa not " to let him wander about with
nothing to do nor to become a slave to drink, but to provide
him with scholars and require him to teach these diligently."
Then in another letter written by Alcuin and attributed to
797, the Bishop of Hexham is advised to pay attention to
the education of boys and youths.   It is stated in this letter
that " it is a great work of charity to feed the poor with
food for the body but a greater to fill the soul with
spiritual learning."

Apart from this evidence, there are a few references in
Domesday Book which tend to support the idea of parochial
schools and which we will subsequently consider.   All that
we can do here is to assume that, just as the Church in
this country followed the general practice of the Church in
the establishment of schools in connection with monasteries
and cathedral churches, so she also followed the custom
and precept of the Church in establishing schools in connection with the parish churches.

[1] Migne : *Pat. Lat.*, vol. CV., p. 196.
[2] *Alcuini Epistolae*, ed. Migne, *Pat. Lat.*, vol. C., p. 214.

CHAPTER III.

THE EDUCATIONAL REVIVAL.

The Danish invasions checked temporarily the remarkable educational progress this country was making. Beginning early in the ninth century, the era of Danish reconnoitring excursions closes with the year 855; the era of methodical plundering with the year 876. As a consequence of their various immigrations, the greater part of the English coasts were ruined and devastated. Towns and ecclesiastical buildings were plundered and burnt. "The Church with its civilising and cosmopolitan influences was for a time swept out of great districts which fell momentarily into heathen hands." [1]

After a long and fierce struggle with the invaders, Alfred, the West Saxon king, held them in check, and compelled them to make peace with him. Subsequently, in the tenth century, through the successive efforts of Alfred's son, daughter, and grandson, the territory formerly yielded was regained.

From the ruin and desolation that the Danes had occasioned, it was the aim of King Alfred to raise his country. No sovereign could recognise more fully the value of Education than Alfred did. His general attitude is evidenced by the preface he wrote to his translation of Gregory the Great's *Pastoral Care*. In it he refers to the reputation that this country at one time enjoyed on account of the wisdom and learning of its clergy. Then he proceeds to

[1] *Social England*, I., p. 141.

show that the decay that had set in had been so great that
learning had practically disappeared from the country.
He aimed at making his people familiar with the contents
of some of the chief religious books, and, as the knowledge
of Latin had by this time practically died out in the
country, he sought to get them translated "into their own
land-speech." Not content with simply expressing a wish
that this might be done, he endeavoured to stimulate the
efforts of others by the example he set. In order that
education might make greater progress in the future, he
suggested that every English child born of free condition
and who had the means or faculty, should during his youth
"be given over to teachers . . . till such time as they may
know well to read English writing." Those who evinced
an interest in letters should then proceed to a study of
Latin.

It is an interesting question to consider how and where
these educational advantages were to be secured. Alfred
himself had written: "So clean was learning fallen off
from among English folk that few there were on this side
Humber that could understand the service in English or
even turn an errand writing from Latin into English.
And not many were there, I ween, beyond Humber. So
few they were that I cannot bethink me of so much as one
south of the Thames when first I took the kingdom."
The suggestion of Alfred is that "now we must get these
from without if we would have them." Unfortunately no
reliable evidence is available to assist us in suggesting an
answer to the problem.

The educational activities of Alfred are described at
length in Asser's *Life of Alfred*.[1] The authenticity of this
life, however, has been called in question, and though
Stevenson argues strongly in its favour yet the evidence
against is so strong that it is difficult to admit its claim to
be considered what it professes to be. Still, even if the
work is not a ninth century production, there is indisputable evidence of its existence in the tenth century. We
can, therefore, regard the work as setting out the educa-

---

[1] Asserius, *de Rebus Gestis Alfredi*, ed. W. H. Stevenson, 1904.

tional ideas which tradition, at any rate, considered to be in harmony with the character of King Alfred. From this pseudo-Asser, we learn that Alfred first acquired the power of reading Anglo-Saxon by the aid of a master, who was most probably one of the priests associated with the court. Alfred's ambition to learn Latin was difficult of accomplishment because of the scarcity of teachers of that subject. For the education of his children, Alfred arranged that they, together with the young nobles and some promising youths of lower origin, should be instructed by masters who should teach their pupils to read both Latin and Saxon. Thus the king established at his court a Palace School similar to that founded by Charles the Great.

Though all the details given in Asser cannot be accepted as true, yet the general statement that Alfred played an important part in stimulating the educational activity of his country is unquestioned. His efforts must be regarded as the beginning of a national concern for education, as Alfred, though a pious and religious king, was actuated not by a desire to recruit the ranks of the priesthood but by a wish to make his subjects capable of discharging more effectively the duty they owed to the state. This, he considered, could be secured through education. If this contention is sound, then Alfred was the first Englishman to recognise the sociological significance of education.

There is, unfortunately, no evidence that the efforts of Alfred, in the direction of improving the education of his country, met with any success. There would be practical difficulties in securing a sufficient number of keen and capable priests from abroad ; the secular clergy of this country had scarcely proved equal to the trust reposed in them. To the thoughtful observer of the day the end in view could be obtained only through the restoration of monasticism. We learn that Edgar, as a youth, had made a vow to restore as many monasteries as possible,[1] but "until Dunstan and Athelwold revived learning in the monastic life, no English priest could either write a letter

[1] Stubbs : *Memorials of St. Dunstan*, p. 290 ; *Chronicon Abbatiae Rameseiensis*, p. 25.

in Latin or understand one." [1] We must therefore turn
to those "three torches" of the Church—Dunstan, Oswald,
and Athelwold—in order to learn how a revival of interest
in education was effected.

We are fortunate in possessing two biographies of
Dunstan which were practically contemporary writings, as
one was written within sixteen, and the other within twenty-
three years of his death. "Both of these are dedicated to
his successors, who knew him well, as being his fellow
scholars and his own disciples." Dunstan was born at
Glastonbury in 925, and the old monastic buildings in a
semi-ruinous condition still existed there at that time.
They were then tenanted by some Irish scholars who had
come to Glastonbury to visit the tomb of Patrick the
Younger.[2] To these clerks Dunstan was sent at an early
age for instruction. He made rapid progress and not only
acquired a mastery of grammar, but also showed excellence
in other branches of study.[3] Consequently, he exposed
himself to the charge of "studying the vain poems and
trifling histories of ancient paganism, to be a worker of
magic." [4]

Dunstan, whilst still a young man, was introduced to
the court of King Athelstan by Aldhelm, Archbishop of
Canterbury, stated by Adelard, one of the biographers of
Dunstan, to have been his uncle. A serious illness and
the jealousy of some of the nobles led to Dunstan's retire-
ment from court. On the advice of Alfeah the Bald,
bishop of Winchester, he took the monastic vows,[5] and in
946 was made Abbot of Glastonbury. He did all in his
power to develop the growth and importance of the monastery, and it is interesting to find that under his rule, the
establishment of Glastonbury was more of a school than
a monastery ; "the words ' scholasticus ' and ' discipulus '
come more naturally than ' monachus ' " [6] After holding
various bishoprics, Dunstan became Archbishop of Canterbury in 959, and was then in a position to undertake

---

[1] *Aelfrici Grammatica Latino-Saxonica*, p. 2.

[2] Stubbs, *op. cit.*, pp. 10, 74, 256.   [3] *Op. cit.*, p. 257.

[4] *Op. cit.*, p. 4.   [5] *Op. cit.*, p. 14.   [6] *Op. cit.*, p. LXXXV.

the task of restoring the monastic conditions of the country and consequently of stimulating its educational activities.

Turning to the coadjutors of Dunstan in his work of reform, we note that Athelwold (who became Abbot of Abingdon in 953, and Bishop of Winchester in 965) was one of his pupils. He attained "a most generous skill in the art of grammar and the honeyed sweetness of verse; he was not only familiar with the Bible, but also with the catholic and most famous authors."[1] Oswald, the other colleague of Dunstan, had been for some time an inmate of the monastery at Fleury.

The point which we wish here to emphasise is that the men of the time who were in a position to judge were of the opinion that the only effective method of producing a reform in the educational condition of the country was primarily through the erection of monasteries, destined to be centres of intellectual activity. With this object in view, they used every possible means to build or restore monasteries in different parts and to place over them men who were not only spiritually minded but who were also men of learning and ability. We learn that in pursuance of this policy, forty monasteries for men and eight for women were erected during the reigns of Edgar and his sons.[2] The men at the head of these institutions taught personally in the schools. Thus we learn of Dunstan being in charge of the school at Glastonbury,[3] and of Aethelwold who " did not scorn ever to explain the difficulties of Donatus and Priscian to little boys."[4]

Efforts were also made to keep in touch with foreign monasteries, especially those of Ghent, Corbeil, and Fleury. These monasteries were appealed to, to send men of learning to the English monasteries, and also for advice in the conduct of the monasteries.[5] In 968 the Abbot of Ramsey sent to Fleury for a master to rule the schools, because " the study of letters and the use of schools had almost

[1] Wulfstan: *Vita St. Aethelwoldi*, Migne: *Patrologia Cursus Complexus*, CXXXVII., p. 87.
[2] Stubbs, *Memorials*, p. 214.   [3] *Op. cit.*, p. 28, 46.
[4] Aelfric, *op. cit.*, p. 1.
[5] Stubbs, *op. cit.*, p. 101; *Chron. Mon. de Abingdon*, I., p. 129.

died out in England."[1] The master sent in response to
this appeal was Abbo, who is described as being well versed
in the trivium and the quadrivium.[2] Abbo spent two years
at Ramsey and wrote a book *Quaestiones Grammaticales* for
the purpose of testing the knowledge acquired by the
monks of his monastery.[3] Among the pupils of Abbo was
the anonymous author of the *Vita S. Oswaldi* (a work
which shows that the writer was a man of culture and
learning), and Byrhtferth, who wrote commentaries on
Bede's mathematical treatises and shows a knowledge of
Latin authors.[4]

In 817, by the council of Aachen, it had been decreed
that no one was to be admitted to the monastery schools
unless he was destined for the monastic life. It does not
appear that this distinction was observed in England
during the Saxon period, and it seems probable that the
English monasteries continued to receive pupils irrespective of whether or not they intended ultimately to enter
the monastery. Thus we learn that the scholars of Dunstan at Glastonbury were of all ages, from the little boy[5]
to the man who had already taken priest's orders.[6] Then,
of the pupils of Wulfstan, we learn that they included
both young and old, and that many of them subsequently
became secular priests.[7] Again, in the picture drawn by
Aelfric of a monastery school of the period,[8] it will be
noted that the pupils included not only a professed monk
but also others who were engaged in secular pursuits. We
also read that the boys who attended the school at
Ramsey Abbey were allowed to go outside the cloisters
for play and recreation.[9]

We may summarise the educational work of Dunstan
and his comrades by pointing out that a new race of
scholars sprang up in the restored cloisters, some of whom
were not unworthy to be ranked with the disciples of

[1] *Chron. Abbat. Ram.*, p. 42.

[2] *Vita Sancti Abbonis*, Migne, *Pat. Cur. Com.*, CXXXIX., p. 390.

[3] *Chron. Abb. Ram.*, p. XXVII.

[4] Stubbs, *op. cit.*, XVIII., XIX.   [5] Stubbs, *op. cit.*, pp. 28, 46.

[6] *Op. cit.*, p. 261.   [7] Wulfstan, pp. 91, 95.

[8] See below, p. 38.   [9] *Chron. Abb. Ram.*, pp. 112, 113.

Alcuin and Bede. One of these pupils was Aelfric,[1] at one time Abbot of Eynsham, who is of special interest as the writer of certain educational and other works: an Anglo-Latin Grammar, a Glossary, and a translation of various extracts from Latin writers into Anglo-Saxon under the title of *Homilies*. Aelfric's *Grammar* is of special interest from the point of view of the study of the principles of teaching, as it indicates the writer was desirous of presenting his subject to his pupils in such a manner as to facilitate their progress. "I am well aware," he writes, "that many will blame me for being willing to devote my time to such a pursuit as to turn the *Art of Grammar* into English. But I destine this lesson book for little boys who know nothing, not for their elders. I know that words can be construed in many different ways, but to avoid raising difficulties I follow the simplest meaning."[2]

From Aelfric's *Colloquy* we are able to learn something of a monastic school at work. The *Colloquy* consists of a dialogue between the master and various boys, and was intended as a First Latin Exercise book. Aelfric accompanies the Latin prose with an Anglo-Saxon interlinear translation. The dialogue opens with the request from the boys that the master would teach them to speak correctly. This, of course, relates to the ability to converse freely in the Latin tongue. Incidentally, the next question throws some light on the mode by which it was then customary to stimulate the boys to apply themselves to their school tasks.

Master : "Will you be flogged while learning?"
Boy : "We would rather be flogged while learning than remain ignorant; but we know that you will be kind to us and not flog us unless you are obliged."

Then, towards the end of the *Colloquy*, there is a conversation between the Master and a professed monk.

M.—"Were you flogged to-day?"
B.—"I was not because I was very careful."

[1] C. 940-1006.   [2] *Ed. Ch.*, p. 39.

M.—"And how about the others?"

B.—"Why do you ask me that? I daren't tell you our secrets. Each one knows whether he was flogged or not."

Of the boys in the supposed school, one was a professed monk, others were ploughmen, shepherds, hunters, fishermen, hawkers, merchants, shoemakers, salters, and bakers. The daily routine of each of them is gone through, and in this way an extensive vocabulary is introduced. One of the passages implies that the school was not restricted to the "free" classes. Thus, after the ploughman has given an account of his day's work, the dialogue continues :—

M.—"O magnus labor est."

A.—"Etiam, magnus labor est, quia non sum liber."

Then the boys in turn argue which occupation is the most useful, and a counsellor is called in to decide the question. The *Colloquy* closes with some good advice: "All you good children and clever scholars, your teacher exhorts you to keep the commandments of God and behave properly everywhere. Walk quietly when you hear the Church bells and go into Church and bow to the Holy Altar, and stand quietly and sing in unison, and ask pardon for your sins, and go out again without playing to the cloister or to school." [1]

So far we have described the monastic revival that took place under Dunstan. Dunstan, however, quite clearly realised that the monasteries alone would not provide sufficient opportunities for the revival of education in England. Though nearly fifty monasteries had been erected, yet that number would meet the need of only a comparatively small section of the community. Further, no monastic institution north of the Humber (with the doubtful exception of Ripon) had escaped the destruction wrought by the Danes. Under these circumstances, Dunstan determined to stimulate the parish priests to a sense of their duty in the matter of education. In the preceding chapter[2] we noted that about 797, Theodulf of Orleans had promulgated certain canons at a diocesan synod;

[1] *Ed. Ch.*, p. 43.   [2] P. 30.

these canons Dunstan adopted, and secured their enact-ment for this country. They run:—[1]

10. And we enjoin that no priest receive another's scholar with-out the leave of him whom he formerly employed.

11. And we enjoin that every priest in addition to lore d, dili-gently learn a handicraft.

12. And we enjoin that no learned priest put to shame the half-learned, but amend him if he know better.

13. And that every Christian man zealously accustom his children to Christianity and teach them the Pater Noster and Creed.

22. And we enjoin that every man learn so that he know the Pater Noster and Creed, if he wish to lie in a hallowed grave, or to be worthy of housel ; because he is not truly a Christian who will not learn them, nor may he who knows them not receive another man at baptism, not at the bishop's hands ere he learn them.

21. And we enjoin that priests diligently teach youth, and edu-cate them in crafts that they may have ecclesiastical support.''

It is impossible to estimate the extent to which these canons were complied with. It is, however, noteworthy that evidence exists that in the first half of the tenth century it was customary for boys of good family to receive education from a priest. Thus Odo, who was Archbishop of Canterbury from 942-959, was taught "by a certain religious man while a boy in the household of the thane Athelhelm." [2] Again, Odo's nephew, Oswald, was taught by a priest named Frithegode, who is said "to have been skilled in all the learning of that age in England, both secular and divine." [3]

In dealing with education in Anglo-Saxon times, it is necessary to use even the slightest evidence of the ex-istence of educational activity. Domesday Book is, of course, the great authority for the social condition of England at this period, and it is essential we should turn to that work for the purpose of investigating whether or not it contains any references which in any way relate to education.

As Professor Vinogradoff tells us, we get a good deal of information in the "Survey" about the tenure of

[1] *Ancient Laws*, p. 396.   [2] *Hist. Ch. York*, I., p. 404.
[3] *Chron. Abb. Ram.*, p. 21.

churches.[1] "They are a necessary element of every township organisation. The parish church is the "tun kirke" of Old English times, and a tenement of a hide or two virgates is of right reserved to it." The parish priest was remunerated in various ways, partly by tithes, partly by glebe, partly by "church scot." It is in connection with this latter payment that we can trace a connection between the churches and education. In 376 A.D., Gratian issued an edict, which was applied in Britain, that teachers were to be paid in "annones," that is, a measure of corn. Now "church scot" was a species of tax imposed on houses or buildings for the payment of the priest.[2] There are two passages quoted by Vinogradoff which seem to connect this payment of "church scot" with the "annones," which were perhaps originally intended as payments for the work of the priests as teachers of schools. On page 441 he writes :—

"Every socman possessed of a hide has to pay one carriage load of corn, called annona, to his parish church, and there is a provision for the case of non-performance of this duty as in Worcestershire." And on page 418 we read that "the shire gave evidence that the church of Pershore ought to have church rent from 300 hides, that is, one load of corn from every hide in which a franklin is settled."

It is not suggested that any stress should be laid on these extracts. They are interesting as indicating the possibility that a part of the remuneration of the parish priest was a payment for his services as a teacher.

In Domesday Book itself, three references to education have been traced :—

1. Wilton Church in Wiltshire was endowed for teaching.[3]

2. Lands in Oxfordshire were given by King Edward the Confessor to the Abbey of Westminster for the education and support of a novice.[4]

---

[1] *English Society in the Eleventh Century*, p. 373.
[2] *Op. cit.*, p. 143.   [3] D.d.I., f. 68, Ellis, I., 332.
[4] I., f. 1546, Ellis, I., 304.

3. Aluuid, a young woman, held half a hide of the demesne lands at Oakley (Bucks) for teaching the daughter of Earl Godric.[1]

Taken alone, these instances do not amount to much, but when they are considered in relation to the decrees and custom of the Church and the canons promulgated in the reign of King Edgar, they tend to support the contention that provision for education was actually made in the various parishes of this country.

Turning next to the Collegiate Churches, whether of a cathedral dignity or not, we note that no evidence of their scholastic activities is available until after the Danish conquest. Then we learn that when Canute visited a famous monastery or borough, he sent there " at his own expense boys to be taught for the clerical or monastic order." [2] This statement is made by a contemporary of the king and is consequently worthy of credence. It was repeated by Abbot Samson who wrote about a century later. Samson, however, exaggerates matters and states that Canute was " so great a lover of religion " that he established public schools [3] in the cities and boroughs " charging the expense on the public purse." [4]

It is difficult to say what these statements mean. They may mean that Canute gave further endowments to particular churches on the understanding that an additional priest, who would be responsible for the teaching of the boys, would be maintained, or that endowments were given to monasteries with the implied understanding that they were given to meet the expenses incurred in the support of the boys intended for a monastic profession. Again, it is probable that by now the custom had grown up of requiring payments from the boys who attended the classes of the priests ; in that case the statements would simply mean that Canute made certain grants to the particular church to free those whom he nominated from any further charges.

[1] I., f. 149, Ellis, I., 267. See also *Times' Educational Supplement*, 10th Oct., 1918.

[2] Hermanus : *De Miraculis Sancti Eadmundi*, sec. 16 in Mem. of St. Edmund's Abbey (R.S.) p. 46. [3] "Publicas instituens scholas."

[4] *Memorials of St. Edmund's Abbey*, p. 126.

The account available of the foundation of Holy Cross
Collegiate Church, Waltham, and its re-foundation by
Earl Harold,[1] enables us to understand the organisation
of the Collegiate Churches of the period and the nature
of the provision made for education. Originally, there
were only two clerks on this foundation; Earl Harold by
additional endowments made it possible for eleven further
clerks to be added. Just as the monasteries sent to Fleury
and other monasteries of note for guidance in the conduct
of their monasteries, so it appears that some of the
Collegiate Churches sent abroad for guidance in the direction of their institutions. Thus we learn that, at Waltham
a certain " Master Athelard " came from Utrecht that he
might " establish at Waltham Church the laws, statutes,
and customs both in ecclesiastical and in secular matters
of the churches in which he had been educated." [2] The
church seems to have been organised on the model of a
monastic community; a number of clerks lived together
under specified rules; discipline was strictly enforced. A
dean, described as " a religious man, illustrious for his
character, well known for his literary learning," was placed
over the clerks. The schoolmaster was apparently a most
important official; his authority seems to have equalled
that of the dean; he taught reading, the composition of
prose and verse, and singing.[3] A stringent discipline prevailed. We learn that the boys of the choir " walked,
stood, read and chanted, like brethren in religion, and
whatever had to be sung at the steps of the choir or in
the choir itself they sang and chanted by heart, one or two
or more together, without the help of a book. One boy
never looked at another when they were in their places in
choir, except sideways and that very seldom, and they
never spoke a word to one another; they never walked

[1] 1060. See *Tractatus de inventione Sante Crucis*, ed. W. Stubbs,
1861.
[2] *Ibid.*, p. 15. These customs were probably due to the influence
of the reforms instituted by Chrodegang of Metz. We may assume
that the Godwin family supported the secular clergy in opposition
to the regular clergy who followed Edward the Confessor from
Normandy.   [3] *Ibid.*, p. 35.

about the choir ... And in walking in procession from school they go to choir, and on leaving the choir go to school." [1]

Between thirty and forty churches of secular canons are registered in Domesday Book, the majority of which were founded during the reign of Edward the Confessor. Among these pre-Conquest Collegiate Churches were All Saints' Church, Warwick, Beverley Minster, and St. Martins-le-Grand, London. At each of these churches one of the priests acted as schoolmaster, and so we assume that wherever a Collegiate Church was founded, there it was customary to delegate the task of giving instruction in Latin and Music respectively to definite persons. We know that at Warwick and Beverley there was a separate master for Song, and hence we may infer that, wherever possible, separate instructors were provided for these subjects.

It must, however, be admitted that the direct evidence of general education during the Anglo-Saxon period is slight and that we are consequently largely driven to conjecture. We are justified in definitely asserting that some of the monasteries were centres of intellectual activity, and that systematic education was given in connection with some of the collegiate churches. It is also extremely probable that it was a general custom for the parish priest to give instruction in Latin to those who wished for such instruction, but it is impossible, so far as our knowledge goes now, to assert anything more than probability in this connection.

[1] *Ibid.*, p. 35.

BOOK II.

THE CHURCH IN CONTROL OF EDUCATION.

INTRODUCTORY.

The second stage which we propose to trace in connection with the evolution of education, is that in which the responsibility for the provision of educational facilities, the organisation of education, the control and the recognition of teachers, were tacitly regarded by the State as among the functions which ought to be undertaken by the Church.

A consideration of this question will involve, as a necessary preliminary, some reference to the political ideas of the Church in the Middle Ages. It would be difficult to discover any ideas which could be considered as political in their character in connection with the labours of those mission priests who were responsible for the introduction of Christianity into England. Separation from the body politic, rather than a desire to participate in its activities, was a distinguishing characteristic of those monks who formed the nucleus of the Catholic Church of this country. With the progress of time, however, a change in this respect became evident. The Church tended to develop into a great social and quasi-political institution, and the question of the relation of the ecclesiastical to the secular power became of increasing importance. Various factors

contributed to produce this result. Not the least significant of them was the development of the Feudal System,
to which is due, to a great extent, the development of the
temporal power and rank of the Church, because the great
ecclesiastics were not only the leading men of the Church
but also great feudal lords.

By the Feudal System is meant the system of government prevailing in Western Europe in medieval times.
Though the problems connected with its origin and development cannot yet be regarded as definitely settled, yet
opinion is practically united upon the main points ; such
differences as continue to exist relating mainly to minor
points of detail. We may summarise the essential features
of Feudalism in its more complete forms by saying that
" the State no longer depends upon its citizens, as citizens,
for the fulfilment of public duties, but it depends upon
a certain few to perform specified duties, which they owe
as vassals of the king, and these in turn depend upon their
vassals for services which will enable them to meet their
own obligations towards the king." [1] In other words, the
individual citizen had little or no consciousness of any
duty he might owe to the State; his horizon was limited
by his responsibilities to his over-lord.

It is possible to trace the origin of the Feudal System
to two practices known to Roman Law. One of these was
the " precarium." Under this form the small landowner,
induced by a fear of the effects of the disordered condition of the times, gave up his land to some powerful
landowner whose position was strong enough to command
respect. This land he received back again no longer as
owner but as tenant. The other practice—the " patro-
cinium "—was of a similar character. The poor freeman,
desirous of the protection he could not otherwise secure,
attached himself to the household of a great lord, and
in return for the protection thus gained he gave to the
rich man such services as a freeman might perform.

At the time of the Frankish invasion of Gaul, these
practices were found in operation, and as they corres-

[1] Adams : *Civilisation in the Middle Ages*, p. 197.

ponded in their main features to customs current among the Franks, the German customs and the Roman customs merged the one in the other and in their new form were adopted by the invaders. The coupling of the special obligation of military service as a condition of land tenure was strengthened by the efforts of Charles the Great. The growth in size of the Frankish empire, resulting in campaigns being necessary at great distances, produced a modification of the existing practice. Of special significance was his ordinance that the vassals should come into the field under the command of their lords; as a result, each lord endeavoured to secure as fine a body of vassals as possible. Gradually it thus came about that the inherent duty of the citizen to defend his country " was transferred from a public obligation into a private contract." The Feudal System developed further when other functions of the State passed into the hands of individuals. Of great importance in this connection was the acquisition of the power of " jurisdiction," by which the administration of justice passed out of the power of the State so far as persons residing within the limits of the fief were concerned. Thus it gradually came to pass that all real power passed from the State and centred in individual lords with the result that patriotism and a common national feeling were almost entirely wanting.

Yet, from the very time of its origin, the Feudal System contained within itself factors which influenced its decline and fall. The only force that held together a fief was the personal ability of the successive generations of lords, coupled with the nature of their success in maintaining order and security and in compelling outlying landlords to recognise their supremacy. But vassals were ever ready to throw off their allegiance and to assert sovereign rights, if the opportunity occurred, and neighbouring great barons would not scruple to entice the vassals of a rival to change their over-lord. When the Feudal System became fixed, such things might become less frequent, but, generally speaking, the law of the survival of the strongest prevailed.

Sooner or later, the Feudal System was certain to result in a period of anarchy. In this country, that period occurred on the death of Henry I , when the feudal party refused to abide by the oaths which the late king had made them swear to his daughter Mathilda. The Peterborough continuation of the English Chronicle describes this period of anarchy " in words with which in their pregnant simplicity no modern description can possibly vie." [1] " They filled the land full of castles, and filled the castles with devils. They took all those that they deemed had any goods, men and women, and tortured them with tortures unspeakable : many thousand they slew with hunger . . . and they robbed and burned all the villages so that thou mightest for a day's journey nor ever find a man dwelling in a village nor land tilled. Corn, flesh, and cheese, there was none in the land. The bishops were for ever cursing them but they cared nought therefor. . . . Men said openly that Christ and His saints slept. Such and more than we can safely say we suffered nineteen years for our sins."

Apart from the practical and tangible effects of the Feudal System, medieval theorising on politics brought forward arguments to support the contention that the Church was not only distinct from, but was in certain essential respects superior to, the State. The starting point in such theorising was the dogma of the two powers, the Spiritual and the Temporal, the power of the priesthood derived from the King of Kings, the power of the State derived from the ability to exercise force.

Ecclesiastics maintained that of these two powers the greater dignity pertained to the spiritual. This arose directly from the views of the early Church as to the relative importance of the earthly life and of the life to come. To save souls was more important than to regulate physical life ; hence, those whose function it was to save souls were not only more worthy of honour than those who simply sought to control temporal activities, but they possessed an authority of a higher and more responsible character. The claim of the Church to a power of inspection and correction in reference to the behaviour and motives of secular

[1] Traill : *Social England*, I., p. 257.

rulers enhanced its authority still further. To the sacer-
dotal mind not only were princes laymen, but of all laymen
they were the class most prone to sin and consequently
were most in need of clerical censure. Among the duties
of the kings which were imperatively insisted upon were
" respect for and protection of the Church and her ministers." Hincmar, Gregory VII., and Innocent III. are
prominent among those who may be quoted as the pro-
tagonists of the claim to ecclesiastical pre-eminence.

A weapon of great value in the enforcement of ecclesiastical demands was that of excommunication and anathema.
This was considered to correspond to the death penalty of
the Mosaic law, the employment of the sword of the Spirit.
If, however, the fear of excommunication was insufficient
to gain from a reluctant monarch respect for the wishes of
the Church, then the power of deposition was resorted to.
The authority to do this was based on the power claimed
by the Church of absolving their members from the oaths
of allegiance they had taken. This power was of special
significance in a feudal state of society, at a time when the
tendency to renounce allegiance was continually present
and opportunity and pretext alone lacking.

The Norman Conquest not only intensified the development of the Feudal System in this country, but it also
contributed largely to the recognition of the separate
power of the Church. The Conquest had resulted in the
administration of the country passing under the control of
men who were "better managers, keener, more unscrupulous, less drunken and quarrelsome, better trained,
hardier, thriftier, more in sympathy with the general
European movements, more adventurous, more temperate
. . . The result was inevitably better organisation, quicker
progress, great exactions and oppressions in Church and
State."[1] Moreover, the invasion had claimed to possess a
religious character and to have for its object the regaining
of an heritage which had been "filched by a perjured
usurper." The existing archbishops, bishops, and abbots
fled or were deprived of their positions, and their places

[1] Traill, *op. cit.*, I., p. 243.

were filled, generally but not always, by men of foreign race. These men were not merely ecclesiastics, but were feudal lords in addition, and the temporal possessions they held in virtue of their dignities were not only considerable in themselves but, owing to various causes, were continually increasing. The clergy were thus in possession of increasing powers and additional interests, separate from and independent of the rest of their countrymen. The tendency was more and more marked for the Church to become conscious of her temporal powers, to feel jealous of her privileges, and insistent upon her rights.

This analysis of the relationship of Church and State, as it developed subsequent to the Norman Conquest, is necessary to enable us to realise the part taken by the Church in regard to education. The Church was not conceived of as a spiritual organisation existing simply for the purpose of promoting a closer fellowship between God and man, but rather as the partner of the State, and as having under her control all those national activities which might be described as "spiritual" in the special sense in which the term was employed at that time. Hence the central authority of the State was merely the organisation which controlled the activities which were definitely temporal. Regarded from the point of view which was common from the eleventh to the thirteenth centuries, education was essentially "spiritual," and consequently was classed under the activities for which the Church alone was responsible.

We pass next to consider the social and economic condition of the country during that period in which the Feudal System was the prevailing system of government. This is necessary because experience has shown that a close connection exists between the social and economic condition of a country and its system of education, in fact, it is impossible properly to understand the educational organisation of a country apart from its social development.

The Manorial System may be regarded as the social counterpart of the feudal mode of government. When the Manorial System first emerges upon the stage of history it is recognised that two elements enter into its constitution, the seignorial and the communal; a lord and a group of dependents having rights in common. The origin of the manor is a problem which is still obscure. The question at issue is whether a servile population, working for a superior who was absolute owner of the land, existed "from time immemorial," or whether, at a particular stage of the development of a free community, an overlord succeeded in gaining the ascendancy and in imposing his will upon it. Two theories have been advanced. The Mark theory[1] maintains that a certain district, marked off from districts of a similar character, was held in common ownership, and that the Manorial System arose when through some particular cause the authority of a lord became recognised. The other theory is that set out by Seebohm in his *English Village Community*, where a connection is traced between the early English village and the Roman vill, and the conclusion arrived at that the English villages were servile and manorial from the earliest days of the Anglo-Saxon period.

Without attempting to express an opinion as to these two hypotheses, we may take "Domesday Book" as our starting point. From that book, we learn that over the greater part of England, villeins, cottars or bordars, and slaves made up the whole of the population of the country apart from the governing classes. Subsequent to the Norman Conquest, we can trace a rapid increase in the number of free tenants, due to a variety of circumstances, of which the chief were (1) the commutation by villeins of their services for money payments, (2) the enclosure and letting out of portions of the waste land, (3) the renting of portions of the lord's own demesne. The term "free tenants," as Professor Ashley has shown, is elastic enough to cover men in very different positions, " from the military tenant who had obtained a considerable holding in return for service in the field, down to the tenant who had received at a money rent one or two acres of the

---

[1] Advocated by Kemble in his *Saxons in England*.

demesne, or of new cleared ground." [1] The larger number of those who were known as free tenants were clearly virgate-holding villeins or their descendants, who had commuted their more onerous labour services of two or three days a week for a fixed sum of money, and who had been freed from what were regarded as the more servile " incidents " of their position.

In practice the manorial system implied that freedom of movement and choice of occupation scarcely existed. Even before serfs could send their children to school, it was necessary that the consent of the lord should be obtained, and in many cases fines were exacted before this permission was granted. Thus, in the single manor of Woolrichston, in Warwickshire, we learn that in 1361, Walter Martin paid 5s. for the privilege of putting his son " ad scholas "; in 1371, William Potter paid 13s. 4d. that his eldest son might go " ad scholas," and Stephen Prout paid 3s. 4d.; in 1335, William at Water paid for a licence for his younger son William " ad sacrum ordinem promovendum." [2]

The point which we wish to emphasise here, is that the only real social distinction on a manor was that between a lord and his tenants. Between these two grades there was a great gulf fixed. Socially, they were as far asunder as the poles. Between the tenants themselves the social separation was slight. " The yardling and the cotter worked in the same way; their manner of life was the same." [3] Even the priest in charge of the majority of the village churches belonged to the same social grade as his parishioners, and, in many cases, he was as poor as any of them, and glad enough to get a few acres and to add to his income by joining in the common agriculture. [4]

Passing from the villages to the towns, we may note that at the time of the Norman Conquest there were only about eighty towns in England, and that most of these towns were distinguishable from the villages only by the

[1] *Econ. Hist.*, I., p. 20.
[2] Thorold Rogers : *Agriculture and Prices in England*, vol. II., pp. 613, 615, 616.
[3] Ashley, I., p. 42.　　　　[4] *Ibid.*, p. 34.

earthen mounds which surrounded them. Even a town of the first rank cannot have had more that 7,000 or 8,000 inhabitants. Until the second half of the twelfth century, the majority of the burgesses still occupied themselves principally in the cultivation of the common fields, and only a minority specialised in trade or handicraft.[1]

Meredith distinguishes four stages in the evolution of a town, but he also makes the important proviso that though the majority of the towns passed through these various stages, yet it cannot be said that any one type of organisation prevailed in any given half-century. Certain factors might combine to make a particular town of great importance and to facilitate its rapid progress; hence the stage of development reached by one town early in the twelfth century might not be attained by another town until a century or more later. The stages are:—

(1) The embryo municipality is but slightly differentiated from a manorial village.

(2) The inhabitants increase in number and in wealth and are able to purchase self-government. At this stage a gild merchant is formed.

(3) The gild merchant loses its importance; its legislative and judicial work is undertaken by the municipality, whilst the separate craft gilds look after the interests of the various trades.

(4) The clear demarcation between town and country breaks down. The capitalist and wage-earning classes emerge and the central government makes inroads into the legislative powers of the municipality and gradually dispenses with the executive work of the crafts.

Is it possible to trace a connection between a social and economic condition such as we have described as existing in the manors and towns, and education? It is obvious that there could be little or no demand for education, because, before education is demanded, its value must be perceived. During this period there could not exist any idea of the culture value of education, the value of education for its own sake. Those who held official positions

---

[1] Meredith: *Econ. Hist.*, p. 49.

as bailiffs or stewards in connection with manorial estates might find a certain amount of education of value, but neither the demands of commerce nor the amenities of social life were sufficiently insistent to create a wish for education.

The main demand for education at this time came from those who desired some position or other in connection with the Church. As will be shown in a subsequent chapter, the Church provided facilities for education for three reasons: as a partner of the State she was responsible for providing it; as holding the view that intellectual training was necessary for moral perfection it was, of necessity, her mission to supply it; and in order that a sufficient number of adequately equipped clerks should be forthcoming, it would be imperative that she should take the necessary action.

An important question now arises. To whom did the Church offer facilities for education? To the gentry and nobility? To the middle classes? Or to the labouring classes? This question must be considered, partly because it arises out of our analysis of the social structure, and partly because of the views expressed by various writers on English education.[1]

The nature of the education received by the children of the "nobility and gentry" will be considered in Chapter VI.; here it will be sufficient to state that the intellectual part of their education was given by a priest, but it was provided at the expense of the relatives of those who received it; hence, in the ordinary acceptation of the term, the Church did not "provide" facilities for the education of the children who were of "gentle" lineage.

Two social classes remain: the middle classes and the "gutter poor," as Mr. Leach elegantly terms them.[2] Which of these two classes did the Church endeavour to educate?

The answer is obvious when we consider the social structure of the period. For practical purposes,[3] the middle

[1] Cf. Leach: *English Schools at the Reformation.* Holman: *English National Education.*
[2] *Winchester College*, p. 92.　　　[3] See Book III., Ch. I.

class in England did not exist until about the close of the fourteenth century. The social distinctions between the various classes of tenants on a manor were so slight as to be negligible; one class tended to merge into the other, so that it was impossible to draw a clear line of demarcation between them. Consequently when the question is asked as to the social grade for whom the Church provided educational facilities, the answer is that such facilities were offered regardless of social standing, and were available for the poorest, even the "gutter poor" if the term is desired.

Indisputable evidence of the social grade of those who attended the schools of the Church in the tenth century is available. Not only were the various classes of persons who were employed on agricultural labour, such as shepherds, cowherds, swineherds, represented, but even members of the "unfree" class are described as being present in the school of which Abbot Aelfric gives us a picture.[1]

As we shall be obliged to return to this subject again, on account of the common misconception, we may now defer further consideration.

[1] See p. 37.

CHAPTER I.

EDUCATIONAL LABOURS OF THE MONASTERIES.

The place of the monasteries in connection with the educational life of the country will become evident from a consideration of the special circumstances of the time. Monasticism, as we have shown, originated mainly from a sense of inability to lead a Christian life in an atmosphere largely tinged with paganism, and in which the prevailing ideal of life had sunk to a very low standard. The remarkable success of monasticism led to a great increase in the number of those who desired to enrol themselves as members of an organised religious community. In course of time, not only had Christianity become the generally accepted religion of the western world, but the monks had come to be regarded as the élite among the clergy. As a class, the secular clergy of this country of the ninth and tenth centuries had not shown themselves inspired with the same zeal, self-sacrifice, and fervour, which had marked the early missionaries; apparently they had been attracted to the clerical profession by a variety of motives, and not invariably from a sense of vocation. Learning does not appear to have been highly esteemed among them, and it would be a difficult matter to name, in this country at this period, many secular priests of outstanding ability. Generally speaking, the term "secular clergy" had come to denote men of lower ideals, of less learning, of less spirituality, and of less efficiency, than the regular clergy.

The monastic mission of the eleventh and twelfth centuries consequently differed appreciably from that undertaken by the Benedictine and Celtic monks in the seventh century. Originally the aim of the monks was the introduction of Christianity; now the task of the monks is to make the Church more efficient and powerful. Efficiency and power can be acquired by the Church in various ways —by its temporal wealth, by its political power, by its spiritual zeal, by its intellectual activities. It is only with the last named aspect of the work of the Church that we are here concerned. Education and religion were generally regarded as identical at the period with which we are dealing; the progress of religion was held to involve the spread of education. "Zeal for letters and religion," remarks William of Malmesbury, "had grown cold many years before the coming of the Normans."[1]

Here, then, is indicated the task which awaited the leaders of the Church, the revival of zeal for religion and letters. How were they to approach and solve the problem? We may legitimately assume that those who lived at the time, and who were in a position to know the special circumstances of the period, would also be in a position to consider the best policy to adopt. The method actually adopted by them for promoting the cause of "religion and letters" was, in the first place, by the establishment of monasteries. We learn that between 1066 and 1135, three monastic cathedrals, thirteen important monasteries for women, eleven important monasteries for men, seventeen Cluniac priories and sixty cells for foreign houses were founded in this country.[2]

One of the main effects of the Norman Conquest upon England, from an ecclesiastical point of view, was the substitution of Norman for the existing English bishops and abbots. Of the twenty-one abbots who attended the Council of London in 1075, thirteen were English; of these, only three held office at the accession of William Rufus.[3] From among the Normans of learning who came to occupy positions of importance in England may be

---

[1] *De Gestis Regum Anglorum*, II., 304.
[2] Böhmer: *Kirche und Staat in England und in der Normandie*, p. 113, n. 1.   [3] *Ibid.*, p. 107.

mentioned Lanfranc and Anselm, successively Archbishops of Canterbury, Gundulf, Bishop of Rochester, Paul, Abbot of St. Albans, Water, Abbot of Evesham, Gilbert Crispin, Abbot of Westminster, Ernulf, Prior of Christchurch, Canterbury, and Thurstan, Abbot of Glastonbury, all of whom had been connected with the school attached to the monastery of Bec. Instances might also be given of ecclesiastics who came to this country from the schools of Rouen, of Cluny, of Mont St. Michel, of Bayeux, and of Laôn.[1]

These appointments are all the more significant because the Church in Normandy at this time was in a very flourishing condition, and was conspicuous for its learning;[2] hence the Norman Conquest, among other things, meant that men of learning and ability were appointed to the chief ecclesiastical positions in England.

Reference should be made here to the reforms effected at Cluny—a Benedictine monastery—in the second half of the eleventh century. Confining ourselves to the reforms that were connected with the intellectual activities of the monastery, we note that manual labour, in its literal sense, became practically non-existent. In its stead additional time was given to study and to the copying of manuscripts.[3]

The importance of Cluny for the educational progress of England arises from the fact that Lanfranc, who was appointed by the Conqueror to the position of Archbishop of Canterbury, had apparently studied the customs prevailing in that monastery,[4] and had based upon them the reforms which he sought to effect in his own Cathedral monastery at Canterbury,[5] and also endeavoured to introduce into other monasteries in this country.[6]

---

[1] See Bateson: *Medieval England*, Ch. IV.
[2] Böhmer: *Op. cit.*, pp. 3-24.
[3] Cf. Pignet: *Histoire de l'Ordre de Cluny*, III., p. 41. Maitland: *The Dark Ages*, pp. 375, 389, 390.
[4] Cf. D'Achery, *Spicilegium*, IV., 4-226.
[5] Cf. *Constitutiones Lanfranci*.
[6] Cf. *Gesta Abbatum Monasterii Sancti Albani*, I., p. 52.

The two men who successively occupied the position of Archbishop of Canterbury after the Conquest are of special importance both from an ecclesiastical and from an educational point of view. Lanfranc had acquired a reputation as a schoolmaster before he took up residence in this country. His first school was conducted at Avranches, where he attracted many scholars; subsequently he entered the monastery of Bec, where he opened a school in connection with the monastery, the fame of which spread widely. Scholars educated at this school subsequently occupied most important ecclesiastical positions both here and on the continent. Among them were Pope Alexander II., and Ivo who afterwards became famous in connection with the school at Chartres.

After Lanfranc became Archbishop of Canterbury he issued his "Constitutiones," a series of regulations for the control of the monastery of Christ Church, Canterbury. For the most part, these regulations relate to the stringent discipline which Lanfranc wished to enforce; educationally, they show that he followed the course of study in the monastery which had been customary since the council of Aix-la-Chapelle in 817. The curriculum of the school included the psalms, writing, and reading and speaking Latin.

After the death of Lanfranc, the see of Canterbury was vacant till a dangerous illness frightened William Rufus into the necessity for taking action in the matter. He compelled Anselm, who had succeeded Lanfranc as Prior of Bec, to accept the position. Under Anselm the reputation of the school at Bec had been enhanced, so that it had become generally regarded as the principal centre of learning in Western Europe. Little direct evidence of the connection of Anselm with education in England is available, but it may fairly be assumed that a man, whose learning was so generally recognised and whose influence on European thought was so great, would of necessity react upon the condition of learning in this country and tend to bring education into greater repute.

The work of the monasteries for education during the eleventh and twelfth centuries may be considered under three heads : (1) the part they played in connection with a revival of learning, (2) their connection with schools, and (3) their contribution to the production of books.

I.—THE REVIVAL OF LEARNING.

To bring about an increased interest in learning was generally regarded as the first of monastic reforms.[1] This opinion was so common that it almost became proverbial : Claustrum sine armario castrum sine armamentario.[2] How was this interest in letters to be secured ? Obviously by requiring the monks to spend a greater amount of time in study, and by causing them to copy a greater number of books, which would afterwards be available for the use of the monastery. The first of these was, as we have seen, an essential reform at Cluny, the model for the English monastic reformers. A considerable amount of evidence is available to show that the new abbots of the monasteries regarded it as important that their libraries should be well stocked with books. At St. Albans the Abbot Paul built a scriptorium in which hired writers copied the MSS. lent him by Lanfranc, and he provided an endowment to secure the continuance of the work.[3] A subsequent abbot, Simon de Gorham, initiated the custom that the abbot should always maintain one writer in the scriptorium at his own expense.[4] At Malmesbury the Abbot Godfrey paid special attention to the formation of a library and to the education of the monks. Under his rule the monks, who had previously been considered as ignorant, equalled, even if they did not surpass, those of any other monastery in the country.[5] Other instances which may be quoted are those of Bath,[6] Thorney,[7] and Abingdon.[8]

---

[1] Wm. of Malmesbury, *De Gestis Pontificum*, p. 249.
[2] Martini et Durand: *Thesaurus Anecdotorum*, I., 511 ; quoted Graham, *Trans. Hist. Soc.*, XVII.
[3] *Gesta S. Albani*, I., p. 57.   [4] *Ibid.*, pp. 76, 184, 192.
[5] *De Gestis Pontificum*, p. 431.   [6] *Ibid.*, p. 194.   [7] *Ibid.*, p. 32.
[8] *Chron. Mon de Abingdon*, II., 44, 289. See also *Hist. Intro. Rolls Series*, ed. Stubbs, p. 43 ; Rashdall, *Universities*, II., p. 476 ; J. Willis Clark, *The Care of Books*, p. 74 ; *De Gestis Regum*, I., pp. xx-xxii.

II.—THE PROVISION OF SCHOOLS.

The question of the provision of schools by monasteries is a matter of considerable controversy. Turning first to the continental custom, we note, on the one hand, that the decree of the Council of Aix-la-Chapelle of 817 provided that "schola in monasterio non habeatur nisi eorum qui oblati sunt"[1]; and, on the other hand, that there is the incontrovertible case of the school in connection with the monastery of Bec, conducted first by Lanfranc and later by Anselm.[2] In addition, reference might also be made to the hostel maintained at Cluny, at the expense of the monastery, for clerks of noble birth who attended the schools in the town.[3] It is not suggested that any general conclusion as to the existence of external monastic schools can be drawn from these instances, but it does establish the point that the decree of the Council of Aix-la-Chapelle alone cannot be considered as sufficient evidence that, after the ninth century, the monasteries ceased to interest themselves in the provision and maintenance of schools.

Turning next to this country, we find that schools for the inmates of the monasteries and for their prospective members were instituted as a matter of course. This point is so generally admitted as not to call for specific evidence in its support.[4] The question at issue is: did the monasteries in England make any provision for the education of external pupils? We are not concerned here with the further question why they should interest themselves in the subject; our only task is to enquire whether or not they actually did so. To summarise the main evidence to support the statement that some of the monasteries took an interest in the provision of schools, we may note that there existed a secular school in con-

---

[1] The case for the non-existence of schools in connection with monasteries is effectively set out by Mr. G. G. Coulton in his *Monastic Schools of the Middle Ages.*

[2] See Lanfranc, *Opera*, ed. Giles, I., 296. Cf. *L'Abbaye du Bec et ses Ecoles* par M. L'Abbé Porrée.

[3] Migne, *Patrologia Cursus Completus*, CLXXXIX., 1051.

[4] Coulton, *op. cit.*, p. 3.

nection with the Abbey at St. Albans, and that among
the famous headmasters of this school were Geoffrey of
Maine[1] and Neckham[2]; a cell in connection with the
monastery of St. Albans was in charge of a monk who
kept school[3]; the Abbot Samson of Bury St. Edmunds
gave an endowment towards the payment of a master of a
secular school at Bury,[4] and provided a hostel in connection with the school[5]; schools existed on two of the
manors belonging to St. Edmund's Abbey to which the
Abbots appointed the masters.[6] Schools were also supported by monasteries at Evesham, Bruton, and other
places.[7] In those cases in which monastic orders took the
place of secular canons, they continued the work of their
predecessors, e.g. at Waltham,[8] at Huntingdon,[9] at Canterbury,[10] and at Christ Church, Twinham.[11]

The conclusion seems to be that monasteries directly
provided schools for their own members only within the
walls of the monasteries, and that, when opportunity
occurred and necessity demanded, they also undertook the
responsibility of providing schools in their neighbourhood
for all who might care to attend. As is shown by the
appointments at Bury St. Edmunds, in those cases in
which the monasteries were in charge of schools, the
masters appointed to these schools were men of high intellectual attainments. This is what would naturally be
expected when the mental calibre of some of these Norman
abbots is considered; thus, Warin[12] was a master of the
University of Salerno,[13] John de Cella, his successor,[14] was
a master of Paris, and is described as " in Greek, esteemed
a Priscian, in verse an Ovid, in Physic, a Galen "[15]; and
the Abbot Samson, the hero of Carlyle's *Past and Present*,

---

[1] *Gesta S. Albani*, I., 73.   [2] *Ibid.*, I., 196.
[3] *Mem. St. Edmund's Abbey*, I., 77, 78, 145.
[4] *Ibid.*, p. 296.   [5] *Ibid.*, p. 249.
[6] Cf. *Mem. St. Edmund's*, III., 182.
[7] See pp. 85, 86, 105, infra.
[8] *Foundation of Waltham Abbey*, pp. 15, 35.
[9] *Monasticon*, VI., pt. I., p. 79.
[10] *Ibid.*, VI., pt. II., p. 615.   [11] *Ibid.*, VI., pt. I., pp. 304, 305.
[12] Abbot of S. Albans, 1183-1195.
[13] *Gesta S. Albani*, I., p. 194.   [14] 1195-1214.   [15] *Ibid.*, p. 217.

was at one time the "magister scolarum" at Bury St. Edmunds.[1]

III.—THE WRITING OF BOOKS.

Though a full consideration of this topic would serve to illustrate the intellectual activities of the monasteries, yet such a discussion lies outside the scope of our investigation. For our purpose a brief reference only is necessary, merely to illustrate the point that interest in educational matters was continued in the monasteries, and to mention that we owe to the monkish scribes most of the material that is available at the present time for the reconstruction of the historical development of this country. As representative writers of the eleventh and twelfth centuries may be mentioned William of Malmesbury, Orderic Vitalis, Henry of Huntingdon, Geoffrey of Monmouth, Florence of Worcester, Simeon of Durham, Roger Wendover, Matthew of Westminster, and Eadmer of Canterbury.

[1] *Mem. S. Edmund's Abbey*, XLIII.

CHAPTER II.

SOME TERMS IN DISPUTE.

It is inevitable that confusion of thought occurs in dealing with any department of knowledge, unless there is a general agreement as to the meaning to be assigned to the terms which are employed. With the possible exception of Economics, Education suffers more than any other science from the ambiguous use of terms. Consequently it is advisable, at this juncture, to indicate the sense in which some of the terms frequently used in this thesis are understood. This is particularly necessary because the terms we propose to consider are often used in a sense different from that in which, in our opinion, they were employed in medieval times. We have selected the following for consideration—School, Free, Grammar, Song, Writing, and Reading.

SCHOOL.

When the term " school " is employed to-day, it is usually taken to mean the " school-house," *i.e.* the building in which the work of the school is carried on. It must, however, be emphasised that in medieval times a school-house was an " accident." Specific buildings for teaching purposes were a comparatively late development in the history of schools. The term " school " considered etymologically means " leisure," and probably the modern idea of school developed from the fact that the leisure time to which σχολή specially related was that which was given up to discussion. A second stage of development is reached when the term is

restricted to organised school. The essential idea of a
school at this stage is that of a master and his scholars.
The master might be a man of over seventy years of age
and his pupils men of middle age (as was probably the
case in the school conducted by Archbishop Theodore), or
the master might simply be a youth, and his pupils a few
village children learning their letters, as would be the case
in the schools taught by the youths preparing for the
priesthood in the house of the parish priest; in each case
the term "school" was equally applied and considered
equally appropriate. The place where the school was held
was a matter of indifference. It might be held in the open
air, in the cloisters of a monastery, in some part of a
collegiate church, or possibly in some more suitable place.
Then, too, the school might be held at regular intervals or
it might simply meet occasionally. Briefly we may say
that the conception of "school" was in a state of flux, and
merely implied that a master and pupils met together for
purposes of instruction.

We may point out here that it would assist in clear
thought if the use of the term "school" could be restricted
to those cases in which the erection of a school-house constituted a definite and objective sign of the existence of a
school, and to employ the term "class" for such gatherings
of teacher and pupils as were held otherwise. If this
suggestion could be adopted investigations into the origin
of schools would become much more definite and valuable.
To illustrate this statement, we may consider the statement
in Bede, that Sigebert in 631 "instituit scolam, in qua
pueri litteris erudirentur." [1] What does this phrase
precisely mean? If the statement had been that Sigebert
founded a monastery or a church, then we should not be
in any doubt on the matter. We have not been able to
trace in any edition of the writings of Bede any interpretation of "scola," as the various editors take it for granted
that its meaning is not in dispute. Thus Bright in dealing
with the passage in Bede we have quoted, assumes that a
school existed at Canterbury in connection with the monas-

[1] *H.E.*, III., 18.

tery of SS. Peter and Paul, and that the school which
Bishop Felix established at the wish of King Sigebert was
probably attached to the primitive East Anglian Cathedral
which had been erected at Dunwich, then a town on the
Suffolk coast, but now annihilated by the sea.[1]   But neither
at Canterbury nor at Dunwich would a specific building for
the school be provided.   Consequently the phrase from
Bede, which is an important passage in the history of
English educational history, simply means that certain
priests, who had obtained some experience in the art of
teaching, were specifically assigned the duty of teaching
the Latin language in classes held in the church buildings,
to those who might care to attend.

We have not found it possible in this thesis to distinguish
carefully between a " class " and a " school."   We are
obliged to content ourselves with indicating the danger
that exists of reading into the medieval use of the term
school the meaning commonly applied to the term at the
present time.

Grammar.

The term " grammar " gradually superseded that of
" letters " as the specified purpose for which schools were
founded.   So far as England is concerned, the first occasion
on which the actual words " scola grammatice " occur, is in
a document of the latter half of the eleventh century.[2]
The term became more common in the thirteenth century
owing to the necessity of distinguishing grammar schools
from the " schools " of the higher faculties in the universities.
" The first actual use of the term ' grammar school ' in
English appears to be in 1387 A.D. when John of Trevisa,
translating from the Latin of Ralph Higden's ' Polychronicon,' mentions a ' gramer scole ' held at Alexandria." [3]   By
the fourteenth century therefore the phrase " grammar
school " had entered into ordinary colloquial speech.

But what does this term " grammar " exactly denote?
On the plinths of the right bay of the great west doors of

[1] *Early English Church History*, p. 125.
[2] Foster Watson: *Old Grammar Schools*, p. 2.   [3] *Op. cit.*, p. 2.

Chartres Cathedral are to be found statues of the Seven
Liberal Arts. With reference to these statues, Dr.
Clerval in his work on "Chartres, sa Cathédrale et ses
Monuments," writes :—

"Les autres cordons représentent les sept Arts libéraux qui
ornaient l'esprit de la Vierge symbolisés chacun par une femme
portant les attributs de chaque science, et par un homme, le cory-
pliée de cette science, assis devant un pupître, avec plume, canif,
encre, éponges, règles. Ainsi au bas du premier cordon de droite,
c'est la Musique frappant trois cloches avec un marteau, et dessous
Pythagore. Au second cordon à gauche en bas, c'est la Dialectique,
portant un lizard subtil et un sceptre, et dessous Aristotle ; puis la
Rhétorique, discourant, et dessous Ciceron ; la Géométrie avec un
compas, et dessous Euclide ; l'Arithmetique (en redescendant) avec
un livre, et dessous Boèce ou Pythagore ; l'Astronomie regardant le
Ciel et portant un boisseau, et dessous Plotonée, portant une
lunette ; enfin la Grammaire, assise, menaçant de verges deux jeunes
écoliers lisant à ses pieds, et au-dessous Priscien ou Donat. Ces
représentations des Arts très curieuses sont les plus anciennes avec
celles de Laôn. Elles s'expliquent à Chartres par les écolâtres de
cette Eglise, spécialement Thiery, auteur de l'Heptabuclion, vers
1140." [1]

This passage may assist us in determining the meaning
assigned to Grammar as one of the Seven Liberal Arts.
It suggests that everything which was not music, eloquence,
logic, mathematics, astronomy, geometry, was grammar,
i.e. nearly the whole of the humanities ; or, in other words,
the study of grammar was synonymous with the study of
"letters" so far as the term was then understood.

In actual practice, however, grammar did not possess
this connotation. This was due to the fact that a study of
letters was not possible until a mastery of Latin had been
acquired, and consequently it resulted that the term
"grammar school" was applied to denote a place in which
instruction was given in "Donat" or "Priscian." Donat
was a Roman rhetorician who wrote *Ars Grammatica*
about the middle of the fourth century. His grammar
was the most generally used elementary text-book on the
subject. In its abbreviated form, which was the one in
common use, it only consisted of eight or nine pages.
Priscian was a grammarian who flourished in the early

[1] *Op. cit.*, pp. 58, 59.

part of the sixth century, and who published, about 526, his *Institutiones Grammaticae*, a most elaborate and systematic treatise on Latin grammar. For over a thousand years Priscian's work was regarded as the leading and authoritative text-book on the subject.

We may also note here that classical Latin literature was rarely used for school purposes. This was the result of the attitude of the early Christian Fathers towards these writings. We have previously pointed out that this classical literature was closely associated with pagan beliefs and practices, and consequently was not regarded as suitable for introduction into classes taught by Christian priests. Even as late as 1518, the statutes of Dean Colet prescribed that the books to be studied in his school were to be the works of such " auctours Christian as lactantius prudentius and proba and sedulius and Juvencus and Baptisa Mantuanus."

This analysis will help us to realise that when the term " grammar school " is used with reference to the schools of Medieval England, what is generally meant is a class in which elementary instruction was given in " Donat," and in the power of speaking Latin. If advanced work was attempted, then Priscian would be studied and the works of " Christian authors " read.

FREE.

We next pass to consider the term " free "—an epithet which usually accompanies the expression " grammar school " and which has given rise to a certain amount of controversy. A special meaning was given to this term in 1862 by Dr. Kennedy, headmaster of Shrewsbury School, in a paper which he submitted to the Public Schools' Commission and which was published by them. This special meaning was that the term " free " denoted a " school free from the control of a superior body, *e.g.* a chapter, a college, a monastery." He advances the following arguments in support of his contention.

(1) " Most of the schools being then gratuitous, such a fact would hardly have been chosen to give the distinctive title of these schools."

(2) " That free school is in Latin ' schola libera ' and that ' liber ' appears never at any period to be used by itself to mean gratuitous." [1]

(3) " That whatever franchise or immunity was denoted by the word, it would, according to ordinary usage, be an immunity for the school or its governors, not for the scholars."

(4) " That the nearest analogies are ' free town,' ' free chapel,' and that these mean free from the jurisdiction of the sheriff and of the bishop respectively."

(5) " That the imposition of some charge (*e.g.* admission and quarterages) was not at all compatible with the title of free school." [2]

On the other hand, Mr. Leach maintains that the average school of the period did charge fees and that the schools which were described as "free" grammar schools were those in which no tuition charges were made.[3] He quotes the case of the Newland Grammar School which was founded under licence in mortmain of 1445-6 for " an honeste and discrete preste beinge sufficiently lerned in the arte of gramer to kepe and teche a grammer scole ther half-free for ever; that is to saie to take of scolers lernynge grammer 8d. the quarter and of other lernynge lettres and to rede, 4d. the quarter, within a house there called the chauntrie house or scoole house."

In replying to the suggestions of Dr. Kennedy we would point out that the nature of the control exercised by bishops, monasteries or colleges over schools is so slight as to be practically non-existent. Consequently, to make the fact of such freedom the distinctive epithet of such schools seems scarcely to be warranted. Moreover, these " free " schools were founded as a general rule either by bishops personally or by ecclesiastical persons or by persons in the closest sympathy with the existing ecclesiastical system. It is highly improbable that they would deliberately found

---

[1] In the *Cyclopaedia of Education* Mr. Leach points out that there are three passages in Livy alone (XXX., 17; XXXV., 23; XLI., 6) in which "libera" is used in the sense of free from payment.

[2] *Report of Schools' Inquiry Commission*, pp. 122, 123.

[3] Art. "Free Schools," *Cyclopaedia of Education*.

an institution which was to be " free " from association with the Church.

A similar criticism applies to the contention advanced by Mr. Leach. As Dr. Kennedy points out, the official schools of the Church were gratuitous from the time of their origin. Then, as we shall show in a subsequent chapter, the schools in which fees were charged were as a general rule those which may be classed as " private adventure " schools. Payment of fees in Church schools is probably due to the custom which would naturally arise that boys would make offerings to their teachers at certain times,[1] and that in course of time this custom would become an unwritten law. The point we wish to emphasise here is that the official schools of the Church were always " free schools " in the sense of being free from payment. This was such a generally well-known and recognised fact that no need existed to apply the term " free " as the distinctive epithet for the purpose of distinguishing between one grammar school and another. In other words, our contention is that all the Church schools were " gratuitous " whether or not they were described as free schools.

It is therefore necessary for us to advance another hypothesis to account for the use of the term, and we suggest that the term " free " means " open to all comers," *i.e.* that admission to the school was not restricted to any particular social grade or to those who were preparing for any particular profession or to those who were living in any particular locality. A free school, in fact, denotes a public school. The following reasons in support of this suggestion may be advanced.

(1) Certain schools of the period were necessarily restricted. Thus, only those who were destined for the monastic life were allowed to attend the monastery schools ; the almonry schools were confined to those who gained admission to them, and were not open to all who wished to attend ; some of the cathedral schools also were open only to specified classes of persons.[2]

---

[1] Cf. "cockpennies." See p. 113, infra.
[2] *Linc. Chapter Act*, Bk. A.2.30 : *Ed. Ch.* p. 386.

(2) As the general idea of the period was that each parish was self-sufficing and concerned with its own parishioners only a *free* school would mean one available for the public generally. Each town regarded every non-burgess of that town as a "foreigner," and freedom of trade was only allowed to townsmen. Each parish had a responsibility for its own poor; the claim to burial in the churchyard was limited to actual parishioners. This same idea passed on to educational matters. Thus, an entry in the York Episcopal Registers of June 1289 states that the schools of Kinoulton were to be open to parishioners only, "all other clerks and strangers whatsoever being kept out and by no means admitted to the school." [1]

(3) The term "public" school gradually becomes a substitute for "free" school. Thus, in the "Acte for the due Execution of the Statutes against Jesuits, Seminaries, Preists, Recusants, etc.," there is a specific reference to "publike or free Grammer Schools." [2]

(4) The warrant granted in 1446 to Eton College not only provided that it should have a monopoly of teaching grammar within a radius of ten miles, but specifically stated that the school should be open "to all others whatsoever, whencesoever and from whatever parts coming to the said college to learn the same science, in the rudiments of grammar, freely." [3] This extract clearly shows a different attitude from that specified in (2) above. We may consequently regard the institution of "free" grammar schools as marking a stage in the policy of breaking down the barriers which separated parish from parish and township from township.

We now proceed to consider a special case to test these various suggestions. A school founded by the citizens at Exeter in the sixteenth century was expressly described in the statutes of the school as a "Free Grammar School." But the same statutes proceed to decree that

[1] *V. C. H.* Notts, II., 216, *Ed. Ch.* 235, *Epis. Reg. York, Romanus,* X., 75.
[2] *Stat. of the Realm,* ed. 1819, IV., pt. II., sec. 8.
[3] *Chancery Warrants,* Series I., file 1439, *Ed. Ch.,* 412.

"one month after Michaelmas yerely . . . everyone that is admitted . . . shall pay unto the schoolemaister of the said schoole for the tyme beinge as followeth, viz every childe of any ffreeman of the said city sixe pence, every childe of any inhabitant of the said city that is not ffree of the said City Twelve pence, and every Childe of any strangers Two shillinges respectively."[1]

We consequently plainly see that a school might be a "free" school and yet charge fees. On the other hand, our contention that "free" denotes "public," *i.e.* open to all comers is supported by this extract which also shows incidentally that the idea that the school was one for citizens only was but slowly disappearing.

Song.

A discussion of the term "song" has become necessary, because of a tendency to regard a song school as the elementary school of the Middle Ages. This position has been strongly taken up by Mr. Leach and has been adopted by all writers who rely upon him. Apparently the only evidence for this opinion is an incident arising out of a misunderstanding between the master of grammar and the master of song with which Mr. Leach has dealt fully in his *History of Warwick School*.[2] As a result of this dispute, the dean and chapter of the Collegiate Church decided upon a specific enumeration of the duties of the two masters. The master of grammar was to have the "Donatists" and "scholars in grammar or the art of dialectic, if he shall be expert in that art," whilst the master of song was to be allowed to "keep and teach those learning their first letters and the psalter."[3]

The "Donatists," as we have shown, were those who were receiving the most elementary lessons in Latin. To "learn a Donat" had passed into colloquial speech as the equivalent of acquiring the elements of knowledge of any subject. If the decision at Warwick had been that the master of grammar was to have taught the scholars "Priscian," and the master of song to have taught them

---

[1] Izacke's MS. : *Memorials of the City of Exeter*, fo. 178 *seq.* ; reprinted Parry : *Founding of Exeter School*, pp. 104-112.
[2] *Op. cit.*, p. 66.   [3] *Ed. Ch.*, p. 273.

" Donat," then the inference might legitimately have been drawn that the master of song was the elementary schoolmaster. Since, however, Latin was the only subject of instruction at a Grammar School, and as the elements of Latin Grammar were to be taught by the master of grammar, it would seem as if Mr. Leach was in error in regarding the song school as the elementary school of the period.

The two subjects, which were taught in the various schools held at this time, were Latin and Music, and, wherever possible, separate masters for these subjects were appointed. To attempt to estimate the relative importance of these subjects from a social point of view, is to expose one's self to the charge of snobbishness. Latin and Music alike were taught because of the fact that they were of outstanding importance in connection with the worship of the Church. Thus one of the events recorded by Bede, as obviously an event of great importance, was the visit paid by the Abbot of St. Martin's, Rome, for the purpose of teaching song to the monks at the Northumbrian monasteries [1] and to all others who cared to resort there for instruction. Bede also tells us that when Bishop Putta was temporarily without an episcopal charge he devoted his time to the teaching of music.[2]

We wish, therefore, to emphasise that the song schoolmaster was not the elementary schoolmaster of the middle ages. The duty of the master of song, as set out in the Statutes of Rotherham College, was to teach the art of music and " presertim in plano et fractu cantu secundum omnes modos et formas ejusdem artis." [3] Song occupied a prominent place in the curriculum of the schools of the middle ages and it probably exercised a greater refining influence upon the nation than is commonly realised. The abolition of the schools of song was not the least disastrous of the effects of the Reformation in this country, and it is of considerable significance that the recent Royal Commission into University Education in Wales recommends

[1] *H.E.*, IV., 18.   [2] *H.E.*, IV., 12.
[3] *Yorkshire Schools*, vol. II., p. 116.

that steps should be taken for the greater encouragement of the study of music, not only within the university itself but also in the schools of the Principality.

One other point may also be mentioned here. It was a very frequent occurrence for the same master to be responsible for the instruction both in grammar and in song. Thus, in 1385, the same master was appointed "ad informandos pueros tam in cantu quam in gramatica,"[1] in 1440, a master was appointed "ad informandos pueros in lectura, cantu et gramatica,"[2] and in 1426, there is a record of an appointment of a master for "scola lectuali et cantuli."[3]

READING.

It is not easy to arrive at a decision as to the meaning of the term "reading school." The books which were read were probably the service books of the Church, and these, of course, were written in Latin. Is it possible that a reading school would be a class in which boys were taught to read Latin only, whilst in a grammar school they would not only be taught to read Latin but also to speak it? Sometimes the references to be found to schools seem to lead to the conclusion that "reading schools" and "grammar schools" were but different terms for one and the same school. Thus, the entries in various Chapter Act Books contain references to appointments to schools of grammar, side by side with references to schools of reading as if the meaning in each case was the same, e.g. at Howden in 1394, a master was appointed "ad informandum pueros in lectu et cantu," and again in 1401, "in lectura et cantu."[4] Sometimes the nature of the reference leads to the conclusion that the term "reading" denoted a lower grade of instruction in Latin than did the term "grammar," e.g. at Northallerton a master was appointed, in 1456, for the purpose "ad informandos pueros in lectura et gramatica."[5] The record

---

[1] *Yorkshire Schools*, II., 61.   [2] *Ibid.*, p. 62.   [3] *Ibid.*, 87.
[4] *Ibid.*, p. 85. Cf. with the appointments recorded in pp. 62 and 87.   [5] *Ibid.*, p. 87.

of a previous appointment in 1440 was, that the master
was responsible " ad informandos pueros in lectura, cantu
et gramatica." As the evidence is so scanty, it scarcely
seems possible to arrive at a definite conclusion, though
the probability appears to be that the use of the term
"reading" implies that the work of the school was not
carried on to so advanced an extent as it was when
" grammar " was used as the descriptive term.

Since the topic of elementary education has been mentioned and as it is obvious that elementary instruction
must of necessity have been arranged for, we may here
consider briefly how this would be effected. We suggest
that, as a general rule, there would be found some clerk
or other in minor orders attached to every church who
would be prepared to give this instruction. In course of
time express provision for elementary instruction seems to
have been made. Thus at Brecon, the A B C was taught
to young children by the chaplain of the college[1]; at the
collegiate church of Glasney the founder, Bishop Goode
of Exeter, provided that the bellringer was to receive
" 40s. yerely as well for teachynge of pore mens children
there A B C as for ryngynge the belles "[2]; at Launceston,
a benefaction existed for the purpose of paying "an aged
man chosen by the mayor to teche chylderne the A B C."[3]

WRITING.

Three distinct stages in the meaning to be attached to
this term can be traced. Originally it was a specialist
craft, as only the skilled man would be able to write out
the charters which were required and to copy the manuscripts which were so highly esteemed. In Saxon days
there were two distinct styles of writing in this country,
the Canterbury style and the Lindisfarne style. The
Roman mission introduced the Canterbury style of writing. The characteristics of this style were that the
Roman uncials were adopted but with the addition of
some local peculiarities. The Canterbury psalter,[4] which
is now in the British Museum, is an example of the work

---

[1] *E. S. R.*, II., p. 31.   [2] *Ibid.*, p. 31.   [3] *Ibid.*, p. 34.   [4] C. 700.

of this mode. The Lindisfarne style had a greater influence upon our national handwriting, as, with certain modifications of its half-uncial characteristics, it was the recognised English style until a new fashion of writing was introduced from Gaul about the end of the tenth century.[1] The next stage in the evolution of writing is connected with its practical value as a means of communication and for business purposes. Now it is known as the " scrivener's art." We can trace the appointment of masters to teach writing for this purpose in this country from the fifteenth century. Thus, of the three masters appointed to the college of Acaster in 1483, one was to teach grammar, the second, song, " and the third to teche to Write and all suche thing as belonged to Scrivener craft." [2] The third stage in the evolution of writing is reached when ability to write is considered to be one of the earliest of the school tasks to be undertaken, and when writing is considered indispensable for all intellectual progress. This stage was reached about the time of the Renaissance. We stop at this point because a further consideration would carry us outside the limit of our task.[3] Our only purpose has been to show that the establishment of a writing school in any place in the Middle Ages did not mean the establishment of an elementary school as the term is understood to-day. As a matter of fact, the first elementary schools, in the modern sense, cannot be traced further back in England than to the establishment of the charity schools of the seventeenth century. Preparatory schools, of course, are much older, but not elementary schools.

[1] Hunt: *English Church*, p. 202.   [2] *Yorkshire Schools*, II., 89.
[3] For additional particulars, see article on " Writing" in the *Cyclopaedia of Education*.

CHAPTER III.

ORGANISATION OF EDUCATION BY THE SECULAR CLERGY.

In a previous chapter we have pointed out the nature of the work of the monasteries in connection with the educational development of this country. Important as this work was, yet it did not influence the country as a whole to any appreciable extent, as each monastery concerned itself only with those matters which affected its own interests or the interests of the order to which it belonged. The secular clergy were more in touch with the ordinary life of the people, and it is through their work that we trace the beginnings of an organised system of education.

Though the Norman Conquest effected a distinction between Church and State, yet it did not involve any change in the existing ecclesiastical system, and as education at this period was inseparable from religion, neither was any radical change effected in educational development. The Norman contribution to religion was threefold: it brought the Church in this country into closer connection with the Church in the continental countries; it stimulated the activities of the Church; and it appointed to the chief administrative posts men who were foreigners but who were also, in many cases, men of ability and energy. The effect of this upon the educational development was, that there gradually emerged a definite and systematic educational organisation, and it is in this fact that we find the distinctive Norman contribution to educational progress.

This organisation consisted of :—

(a) The establishment of Schools of Theology in connection with Cathedral Churches.

(b) The recognition of the Chancellor of the Cathedral as the head of the " Education Department " of the diocese.

(c) The establishment of Grammar Schools and Song Schools in connection with Collegiate and Parochial Churches.

Except for the recognition of the Chancellor as the responsible head of the educational aspect of the work of the Church, the post-Conquest educational arrangements did not essentially differ from the pre-Conquest arrangements. There was a real continuity of educational effort from the days of the introduction of Christianity. The main difference is that, after the Conquest, the educational arrangements seem to be more definite and more effectively organised.

We now proceed to consider, in turn, the various parts of the educational organisation which we have enumerated.

(a) Schools of Theology.

As we have already shown, it had been the custom of the Church from the earliest date to establish schools of theology in connection with 'the more important centres in which the work of the Church was carried on. With the progress of time this custom crystallised into law. We must emphasise that these schools of theology existed before canon law definitely refers to them. Canon law enactments on education simply mark the transition from a voluntary to a compulsory condition. The first definite ecclesiastical enactment relating to schools of theology dates from 1179.[1] This was repeated in 1216 when Innocent III., in general council, decreed that in every metropolitical church a theologian should be appointed " to teach the priests and others in the sacred page and to inform them especially which are recognised as pertaining to the cure of souls." [2]

[1] Rashdall, *Univ.*, I., p. 283. Mansi, *Concilia*, XXII., ch. 228.
[2] Dec. V. it. 5 : *Ed. Ch.*, pp. 142-145.

The custom of establishing schools of theology in connection with cathedral churches was common to all those
countries in which the Church had made progress. The
Church of France had gained special fame in this respect,
and the reputation of its schools had extended throughout
the civilised world. Among the celebrated continental
schools of this period may be mentioned Tourney, under
Odo, Chartres, under Fulbert and Bernard Sylvester, Paris,
under William of Champeaux, and Bec, which became
famous under the mastership of Lanfranc and enhanced
its reputation under Anselm. The fame of these schools
became so great that they attracted scholars to them both
from this country and from other parts of the continent of
Europe. John of Salisbury, who was one of the scholars
who went from England to France for the purpose of
obtaining the best education available at the time, has left
us in his writings a valuable account of the mode by which
such an education was gained. He tells us that he went
over to France whilst he was still a youth,[1] and studied
first at Paris, under Adelard and Alberic, then at Chartres,
under Richard the Bishop and William of Conches. Subsequently he returned to Paris to continue his studies
under Robert Pullus and Simon of Poissy successively.
Among other Englishmen, of whom records remain that
they went to France for their education, may be mentioned
Adam du Petit Pont, who afterwards became Bishop of
St. Asaph, Alexander Neckham, the famous Latinist, and
Samson, the celebrated Abbot of St. Albans.

It may also be interesting to note here, as indicative of
the social grade from which the majority of the students
of the time came, that they found it necessary whilst they
were in France to find some means of self-support. Thus,
both John of Salisbury and Adam du Petit Pont maintained themselves by teaching private pupils, whilst Samson was supported by the sale of holy water, a method
which seems to have been at the time a favourite one for
providing an exhibition fund for poor scholars.[2]

[1] "Quum primum adolescens admodum studiorum causa migrassem
in Gallias." *Metal.*, Bk. II., ch. 10.
[2] Cf. *Reg. Pontissera*, f. 55 ; *Ed. Ch.*, p. 232.

So far we have shown that the immemorial custom of the Church as well as the express decree of Canon Law required that the various metropolitical churches at least should provide schools of theology. We have also seen that this custom was widely prevalent in France. We still have to consider whether the practice prevailed in this country. It is necessary for us to point out here, that the evidence must necessarily be indirect and that the fact that evidence is lacking must not be regarded as establishing that schools of theology did not exist in cathedral cities. It is only when some dispute arises or some special incident occurs that we find references, e.g. that a well-known churchman was educated at a particular school, or that a particular official was in charge of the school at a specified time, which assist us in drawing the conclusion that theological schools existed. If these incidents had not occurred then we should not possess any knowledge of the existence of the school. Again, we know that large numbers of clergy were ordained at the appointed seasons, by the bishops of the Church. Thus in the first year of the episcopate of Bishop Stapledon of Exeter,[1] 539 were ordained to the first tonsure, 438 acolytes, 104 sub-deacons, 177 deacons, 169 priests; in the diocese of York in 1344/5, there were ordained 1,222 persons, of whom 421 were acolytes, 204 sub-deacons, 326 deacons, and 271 priests.[2] Now these clergy must have received systematic education, and it is a legitimate inference that most of them received their education in this country.

We may next proceed to consider the evidence which is available of the existence of the schools of theology. We know there was a school of theology at York because Thomas, who became Archbishop of York in 1108, and who had previously held the position of Provost of the Collegiate Church, in Beverley, was educated there.[3] We also know, incidentally, that there existed a school of theology

---

[1] 1308-9.   [2] Cutts : *Parish Priests*, p. 46.
[3] " Erat enim apud nos sub patruo suo amabili et amicabili educatus, et decenter eruditus." *Hist. Ch. of York*, II., 124.

in connection with St. Paul's Cathedral because it is referred to in a deed which is dated about 1125.[1] Similarly, we know that a school of theology existed in Lincoln because the vicar of a Lincolnshire parish was directed to attend the school there to learn theology for a period of two years.[2]

This evidence, which is all incidental and merely the outcome of special circumstances considered in conjunction with the general custom of the Church and the requirement of Canon Law leads us to maintain that schools of theology existed at most, even if not all, of the Cathedral Churches of the period.

(b) THE EDUCATIONAL FUNCTION OF THE CHANCELLOR.

We have previously shown that the bishop of a diocese was originally personally responsible for the preparation of those candidates whom he subsequently ordained. With the progress of time and the increase in the duties of the episcopate, it was impossible for the bishop to undertake the personal responsibility for this work, and consequently a tendency arose for it to be entrusted to a member of the collegiate body associated with him. In the case of a secular bishop, a member of the Cathedral body was appointed. This officer was definitely known as the " Scholasticus," and it was his recognised duty to read theology with approved students.

We are able to trace the existence of a " scholasticus " in connection with the English cathedrals from an early date. Thus we learn that when Thurstan, Archbishop of York, visited the Pope at Blois in 1120, he was accompanied by "duo archidiaconi ecclesiae nostrae et scholasticus." [3] We also know that a " scholasticus " existed in

[1] For additional references to the Chancellor's School of Theology at St. Paul's, see reprint in Archaeol., vol. 62, pt. 1, p. 219 of deeds in St. Paul's Mun. Box. 21, No. 621 and 865 ; Gregory's *Chronicle* (Camden Soc. N.S. XVII., 1876, ed. J. Gairdner) p. 230 : and Register of Bishop Fitz-James, f. 127 b., printed in Sparrow Simpson's *Registrum Statutorum*, p. 413.

[2] *Ep. Reg. Linc.*, *Rot. Hug. de Wells*, III., 101.

[3] *Hist. Ch. of York*, II., p. 162.

connection with St. Paul's, London, because the expression
"magister scolarum" occurs in a deed whose date is
assigned to c. 1110.[1]

In course of time the term "chancellor" was substituted for that of "scholasticus," probably because the
schoolmaster was the most highly educated member of the
cathedral staff and was therefore the most suitable person
to entrust with the care of the cathedral seal and with the
dispatch of the official letters of the cathedral body. This
statement is definitely established by the statutes of the
Church of York, which date from 1307 but which are
regarded by their editor as existing from 1090 at least
On page 6 of these statutes it is stated that "Cancellarius,
qui antiquitus magister scolarum dicebatur, magister in
theologia esse debet, et juxta ecclesiam actualiter legere."
The same change of term can be traced at St. Paul's,
London. One of the witnesses to a deed dated about
1205 who describes himself as Chancellor is the same
person who, when acting in a similar capacity at an earlier
date, described himself as "magister scolarum."[2]

We must remember that this change of designation did
not involve any essential change in his duties or in the
functions he discharged. The qualification required of
the Chancellor as previously of the Schoolmaster was,
that he was to be a "master in theology."[3] His duty
was that he was to teach theology either by himself or by
a suitable substitute[4] to all students who cared to present
themselves. If the Chancellor became lazy (as there is a
general tendency to become when men lose their ideals
and no pecuniary inducement to energy exists) then,
apparently, in some places, a custom arose for other
persons to keep schools of theology for prospective priests
in return for payment, whereas the Chancellor was expected to admit students to his classes without the impo-

[1] Reprinted in *Archaeol.*, vol. 62, pt. I., p. 211.
[2] Deed reprinted in *Archaeol.*, vol. 62, pt. I., p. 211.
[3] *Statutes of the Ch. of York*, p. 6; Sparrow Simpson, *Registrum Statutorum*, p. 413.
[4] *Hist. Ch. of York*, III., 320; *Corpus Juris Canonis*, ed. H. L. Richter, Dec. V. tit. 5; *Ed. Ch.*, p. 143.

sition of any fee. The Church resolutely set itself against this custom of charging fees for instruction, and by a synod held at Westminster in 1138 decreed that "si magistri scholarum aliis scholas pro pretio regendas locaverint, ecclesiasticae vindictae subjaceant." [1]

In order to benefit by the school of theology conducted by the Chancellor, it would be necessary that the pupil should have received a sufficient knowledge of Latin. It is highly probable that many of the clerks who were attracted to a school of theology for the purpose of continuing their studies would not have studied Latin to the extent necessary to profit by the course given. In consequence, a demand would arise for teachers of Latin. Now it is an accepted rule of Economics that whenever a demand for a particular commodity exists, then an attempt to meet the demand is forthcoming. Since scholars were to be found in a cathedral city who wished for instruction in Latin, and since other clerks were to be found there who considered themselves capable of giving such instruction and who were desirous of taking private pupils, it is only natural to conclude that the holding of Latin schools in order to meet the demand became common.

But the danger of such a practice soon became evident. It is highly probable that many who would attempt to earn an income by professing to teach pupils Latin, were incapable of doing so. To meet this contingency, the custom arose that the Chancellor should grant a licence to those whom he considered capable of acting as teachers.

This is an event of the very first importance in the history of Education, because it is the first separate recognition of the teaching profession in England. In addition, the custom led indirectly to the rise of the university system. The custom continues, even to the present day, because the degrees in Arts and Theology in our oldest universities are in reality merely licences issued by the Chancellor of the University to teach those subjects.

We may also note that the necessity for the recognition of qualified teachers was imperative not only in the interests

[1] Mansi: *Concilia,* I., 415.

of the scholars, but also in the interests of the Church itself, as it had become customary to require that priests who were in charge of parishes, and who were discovered at episcopal or archidiaconal visitations not to be sufficiently learned, should return to their cathedral city in order to pursue a further course of study.[1] Such priests would certainly require more individual attention than they would secure at the ordinary school of theology.

In course of time, apparently, some chancellors saw in this granting of licences to teach to approved teachers an opportunity of exacting fees. The Church opposed this practice. In 1160 Canon Law prescribed that " For licence to teach nothing shall be exacted or promised; and anything exacted shall be restored and the promise released."[2] Pope Alexander III.[3] wrote to the Bishop of Winchester requiring him " strictly to prohibit for the future any exaction or promise of anything from anyone in your diocese."[4] This was again repeated in 1170 by the Canon Law of that year.

The duty of the Chancellor in the granting of licences was defined more rigidly by the Fourth Lateran Council of 1179. At that Council it was enacted that the Chancellor should grant, without fee of any kind, a licence to teach to every and any person who was qualified to act as a teacher. The decree laid down that " the seller of a licence to teach or preventer of a fit person from teaching is to be deprived of his benefice."[5]

The Chancellor is consequently the head of the educational work of the diocese. He is required to prepare all clerks who desire to offer themselves for ordination, to supervise the studies of all incumbents whose education has been found to be defective, and he has also the responsibility of passing judgment upon the abilities of these who are desirous of acting as teachers and of granting certificates to teach to those of whom he approves.

[1] *Ep. Reg. Lincoln.*, III., 101.
[2] Dec. V., tit. 5, ch. 2.   *Ed. Ch.*, p. 119.
[3] 1159-1181.   [4] *Ed. Ch.*, p. 119.
[5] *Ed. Ch.*, p. 123; see also Rashdall, II., p. 283; Mansi, XXII., c. 228.

(c) The Grammar Schools.

We have seen in a previous chapter that it had been the custom of the Church from the earliest times to establish schools in connection with the various churches. Just as in course of time schools of theology which had previously been customary, were made the subject of express ecclesiastical enactment, so, too, the holding of Grammar Schools was also definitely prescribed. Thus in 1215, Innocent III. decreed that in connection with "every cathedral or other church of sufficient means" masters were to be appointed who were to be able to teach theology and Latin respectively. [1] These masters were to be remunerated out of the common fund of the cathedral church. If, however, the revenues of the Church did not permit of this, then provision was to be made for the remuneration of the grammarian out of the funds of some other church of the city or diocese. [2] At the risk of exposing ourselves to the charge of repetition, we must reiterate that this enactment did not indicate a new departure on the part of the Church or constitute a decree for the establishment of schools. The provision of facilities for education in any locality practically dates from the foundation of a church in that locality. The value of this enactment is twofold: it indicates the considered mind of the Church towards education, illustrating still further, that the Church realised the importance of education and recognised it as her duty to make provision for it; and in the second place it would act as a stimulant to those dioceses or centres in which the ecclesiastical authorities had not been sufficiently alert to their responsibilities and duties. The Lateran Council of 1179 had not only decreed that "in every cathedral church a competent benefice shall be bestowed upon a master who shall teach the clerks of the same church and poor scholars freely," but it had also enacted that it was the duty of the Church to provide free education "in order that the poor, who cannot be assisted by their parents'

[1] Decretal V., tit. 5, cap. IV,
[2] *Ed. Ch.* p. 145,

means, may not be deprived of the opportunity of reading and proficiency."[1]

Since then the immemorial custom of the Church and Canon Law alike required that schools should be established in connection with the various churches, we have next to consider a narrower problem, to what extent was this requisite complied with in this country.

In this connection we must first of all note the difficulty of finding the necessary evidence. The schools were not a separate foundation but an integral part of the work of the Church. All that can possibly be done is to collect references which will justify us in the inference that schools were carried on in connection with the different churches. Complete evidence for the whole of the educational work of the Church will never be forthcoming. We can only hope to obtain representative evidence and then to submit that this was typical of the general work of the Church, and consequently to maintain that wherever a church, or at any rate a collegiate church, was found, there a master of grammar would also be found.

There is abundant evidence that schools existed in the cathedral cities of England practically from the date of the foundation of these cathedrals.[2] Turning next to collegiate and parochial churches we note that prior to the close of the thirteenth century, schools have also been traced in connection with the church at Bury St. Edmunds,[3] Waltham,[4] Warwick,[5] Pontefract,[6] Hastings,[7] Christ Church, Hants,[8] Beverley,[9] St. Albans,[10] Thetford,[11] Huntingdon,[12] Dunstable,[13] Reading,[14] Bristol,[15] Derby,[16] Bedford,[17] North-

---

[1] *Ed. Ch.*, p. 123, from Decretal V., tit. 5, cap. I.
[2] *H.E.*, III., 18 ; IV., 1 ; *Hist. Ch. of York*, I., p. 390.
[3] *Mem. St. Ed. Abbey*, I., 46-7.
[4] *Tractatus de inventione Crucis*, p. 15.
[5] *History of Warwick Sch.*
[6] *Early Yorkshire Schools*, II., 1.
[7] P.R.O. Anc. Deeds, 1073, *Ed. Ch.*, p. 69.
[8] *V.C.H., Hants*, II., 251.   [9] *Hist. Ch. of York*, I., 281.
[10] *Gesta Abbatum Mon. St. Alb.*, I., 72.
[11] *V.C.H., Suffolk*, II., 303.   [12] *Ed. Ch.*, p. 93.   [13] *Ibid.*
[14] *V.C.H., Berks*, II., 245.   [15] *V.C.H., Gloucester*, II., 355.
[16] *V.C.H., Derby*, II., 209.   [17] *V.C.H., Beds*, II., 152.

ampton,[1] Marlborough,[2] Newark,[3] Southwell,[4] Kinoulton.[5] In addition to these instances, we learn quite by accident, as it were, of six schools in the diocese of Lincoln, viz. Barton, Partney, Grimsby, Horncastle, Boston, and Grantham.[6]

The cumulative effect of all this evidence, we venture to think, is that it establishes the suggestion that the Church of England was not negligent of the custom of the Catholic Church and made the requisite provision for the establishment of schools in connection with her churches.

It is also important to remember that a school of song was also established in connection with the various churches, as well as a school of grammar. There does not appear to be any express decree to this effect, but there is abundant evidence of the common existence of such schools, e.g. at London,[7] York,[8] Lincoln,[9] Beverley,[10] and Warwick.[11] The master of song was not licensed by the Chancellor, but by the Precentor, the official of the Cathedral body who was in charge of the musical part of the services.[12]

Up to this point we have considered mainly the provision for education made by the collegiate churches where it would be possible for a definite person to take charge of the teaching of grammar. But schools were not limited to these churches. On the contrary, the priest in charge of practically every parish church would be expected to keep school. This was a part of the traditional custom of the Church, a custom that was enforced, as we have seen by the Council of Vaison,[13] the canons of Theodulf,[14] and the so-called canons of King Edgar.[15]

Passing to the period with which we are more immediately concerned in this chapter, we find the requirement that parish priests should keep school reiterated by Canon

[1] V.C.H., Northampton, II., 234.   [2] Ed. Ch., p. 152.
[3] Mem. Southwell Minster, XLI.   [4] Ibid., p. 205.
[5] V.C.H., Notts, II., 216.   [6] V.C.H., Lincs., II., 449.
[7] Achaeol., v. 62, pt. I., p. 211. [8] Statutes of the Ch. of York, p. 6.
[9] V.C.H., Lincs., II., 423.   [10] Mem. of Beverley Min., p. 292.
[11] Hist. War. Sch., p. 66.   [12] Statutes of the Ch. of York, p. 5.
[13] A.D. 529.   [14] A.D. 797.   [15] A.D., C. 960.

Law "ut quisque Presbyter, qui plebem regit, clericum habeat, qui secum cantet, et epistolam et lectionem legat, et qui possit scholas tenere, et admonere suos parachianos, ut filios suos ad fidem discendam mittant ad Ecclesiam: quos ipse cum omni castitate erudiat." [1] The Council of Westminster, held in 1200, also decreed that:—

" Priests shall keep schools in their towns and teach little boys freely."

" Priests ought always to have a school of schoolmasters in their houses and if any devout person wishes to entrust little ones to him for instruction, they ought to receive them willingly and teach them kindly." [2]

The teaching of the Church on the matter was consequently clear and explicit. The question next arises, to what extent did the parish priests in this country comply with the regulations of the Church. Rashdall is of the opinion that " it may be stated with some confidence that at least in the later Middle Ages the smallest towns, and even the larger villages possessed schools where a boy might learn to read and acquire the first rudiments of ecclesiastical Latin." [3] The available evidence to support the contention that it was customary for the parish priests of the Middle Ages to keep school is admittedly slight, but it establishes clearly that it was regarded as a common practice for schools to be held in the various parishes. Thus, we learn in *Philobiblon* of " rectores scholarum ruralium puerorumque rudium paedagogos." [4] Roger Bacon [5] tells us that schools existed everywhere " in every city, castle and burg." [6] Abbot Samson in speaking of the days of his boyhood at Diss in Norfolk says that he attended a school which was held there,[7] and John of Salisbury narrates that when he was a boy he went in company with other boys to a priest " ut psalmos addis-

---

[1] *Decret. Greg.* IX., Lib. III., tit. 1 : Rashdall, Univ. II., p. 601.
[2] Wilkins, *Concilia*, I., p. 270, *Ed. Ch.*, p. 139. Cf. this with Theodulf's Capitularies of 797. See p. 30 supra. and Mullinger, Schs. of Charles the Great, p. 130.   [3] *Univ.* II., p. 602.
[4] *Op. cit.*, ed. Thomas, p. 79.   [5] A.D. 1212-1294.
[6] *Opera Inedita*, ed. Brewer, p. 398.
[7] *Mem. St. Edmund's Abbey*, I., p. 248

cerem."[1]   Then, again, an interesting passage, which supports our contention, occurs in the correspondence (usually assigned to a date between 1119 and 1135) which took place between Theobald of Etampes and an anonymous critic. The writer of this passage is supposed to be attacking a statement that there was a scarcity of secular clerks. He urges: " Are there not everywhere on earth masters of the liberal arts, who also are called clerks ?   You yourself, a nobody, are you not said to have taught as a master sixty or one hundred clerks, more or less ?   Have you not been a greedy seller of words to them, and perhaps have wickedly deceived them in their ignorance as you have deceived yourself ?   Where then, I pray, is this want of clerks of yours ?   For not to mention other parts of the empire, are there not nearly as many skilled schoolmasters in . . . . England, not only in boroughs and cities, but even in country towns, as there are tax collectors and magistrates ? "[2]

One other important question still remains to be considered: when were definite school houses first erected ? We have used the term " school " to describe the classes which were held in connection with the churches, but, as we have pointed out, these were for the most part merely classes in which a priest or a youthful clerk taught boys their " Donat."   These schools were usually held in some part of the church building.   Shakespeare refers to this :—

> " Like a pedant that
> Keeps a school i' the Church."
> *Twelfth Night.*

Similarly, in the *Memorials of Southwell Minster* it is recorded on the occasion of one of the visitations, that one of the clerks complained that the boys who were being taught made so much noise as to disturb the services which were in progress.[3]   It is not until a school possesses a definite building of its own that it can be said to possess a real independent existence.   This question is also of interest in connection with the conflicting claims to the title of being the " oldest public school in England " which

---

[1] *Polycraticus*, II., 28, ed. Giles, p. 155.
[2] *Oxford Hist. Soc. Collectanea*, II., 156.   [3] *Op. cit.*, p. 49.

have been set up. If we content ourselves with the definition of a school as "a class held in a church for the purpose of teaching Latin," then the question of the relative antiquity of schools is that of the relative antiquity of churches, a question of comparatively little interest from the point of view of the history of education. We contend that we are on much firmer ground when we ask, when was the first building for specific school purposes erected in England. This is a question which still awaits investigation and can only be solved by one school establishing evidence to maintain the date of its first building and then waiting until its claim is overthrown by a school which can show a still more ancient origin. So far as we have been able to trace, the earliest record of a separate school building dates from about 1150 when Abbot Samson bought a stone house at Bury St. Edmunds and gave it for a schoolhouse.[1] We note also that about the same date, Wakelin of Derby and his wife Goda gave certain buildings in Derby "on this trust that the hall shall be for a school of clerks and the chambers shall be to house the master and clerks."[2] It is highly improbable that these are really the first instances.

CHORISTERS' SCHOOLS.

It is necessary that we should add here some reference to schools for choristers. It is obvious that for the adequate rendering of divine service, the use of boys' voices would be imperative, and consequently the need of providing instruction for them and of maintaining them would arise. The general rule was that the choir boys would be taught Latin by the master of grammar attached to the cathedral, and similarly music would be taught by the master of song.

The duty of the cathedral master of grammar in relation to the choristers is evidenced by various disputes which occurred. Thus at Beverley in 1312, the master of grammar refused to teach, without the payment of fees, more than seven choristers. The dean and chapter enquired into the

---

[1] *Chron. Jocelyn de Brakelonde*, p. 3.
[2] *V.C.H. Derbyshire*, II., 213, from Cott. Mss. Titus, C. IX., f. 58.

"ancient customs" and reported that the grammar master was obliged to teach all the choristers freely.[1]

Again, at St. Paul's, a similar dispute took place in the fourteenth century. Here, also, the dean and chapter investigated the matter, but their decision—though supporting the contention that the choristers were taught by the cathedral master of grammar—was that a certain payment was to be made to him for these services from the cathedral funds. The entry in the almoner's register runs :—

"If the almoner does not keep a clerk to teach the choristers grammar, the schoolmaster of St. Paul's claims 5/- a year for teaching them, though he ought to demand nothing for them, because he keeps the school for them, as the treasurer of St. Paul's once alleged before the dean and chapter is to be found in ancient documents." [2]

In addition to providing instruction, it was also necessary that the choristers should be lodged, clothed, and fed. Various devices to effect this seem to have been tried at various times. In some cathedrals, an arrangement was made with an individual to provide the necessary accommodation at an arranged charge ; [3] in others, the duty of attending to the welfare of the choristers was assigned to the almoner.[4] Gradually it came about in some cathedrals, e.g. Wells, that the choristers were housed together. In 1459-60, Bishop Beckington of Wells drew up an elaborate code of statutes for the control and government of the Choristers' School.[5] These statutes provided, inter alia, that the master of the choristers, who was to be learned in grammar and song, was to be appointed by the Chancellor. Latin was to be spoken in the house. Full details with regard to meals, discipline, and finance were also given.

At the present day, the headmaster of a school is not only responsible for teaching certain specified subjects but

---

[1] *Beverley Chapter Act Bk.* (Surtees Soc.) Vol. I., p. 293.

[2] Reprinted in *Archaeol.* vol. 62., pt. I., p. 198.

[3] *York Chapter Act Bk.* I., f. 25 b.

[4] Sparrow Simpson : *Registrum Statutorum*, pt. V., ch. 8 ; Brit. Mus., *Harl. MSS.*, 1080.

[5] See Reynold's *Wells*, pp. CLXXX-V.

is also in general charge of the organisation, discipline and administration of the school. It is interesting to note that during the Middle Ages, the masters of grammar or of song taught the subjects entrusted to them and had no further duties. The idea of the organisation and disciplinary functions of the master seems to have been evolved from the necessity for exercising control over the choristers, but this duty was at first assigned to an officer distinct from the one who was exercising the teaching function. It was the custom at York, according to the Statutes of the Cathedral, which are dated 1307 but merely codified the customs which had prevailed since the eleventh century, to entrust the government of the choristers to the precentor.[1] The office of taking charge of the choristers developed more completely at other cathedrals. Thus at Lincoln in 1352, Ralph of Ergham was appointed "custos choristatum." The preface to the record of the appointment shows that the function was that of a "canonicum supervisorem et custodem communitatis choristarum."[2]

This custom of appointing a supervisor, as distinct from the schoolmaster, prevailed at the schools, other than schools for choristers, which were founded from time to time. Thus at Winchester, Eton, Acaster, and Rotherham —to name a few instances only—the responsible head of the institution was the provost, while the master of grammar was merely required to give instruction in the subjects assigned to him. The evolution of the schoolmaster as the superintending organiser and controller of an establishment belongs to a later date in English educational history. We must defer, for the present, a further consideration of this topic.

[1] *Statutes of the Ch. of York*, p. 5.
[2] *Registrum Antiquissimum Linc.*, Chap. Mun. A 2, 26, fol. 10. b. *V. C. H. Lincs.* I., 424. Similar appointments are recorded in 1427 and 1432. *Reg. Antig. Lincs.*, fol. 67 b.

CHAPTER IV.

THE MONOPOLY OF SCHOOL KEEPING.

In studying the original sources from which we derive our knowledge of the educational development of this country, we find numerous references to alleged infringements of the monopoly of schoolkeeping claimed by the official schoolmaster. It is, therefore, necessary for us to consider the origin and nature of this monopoly.

The idea of monopoly in connection with trade and industry can be traced back to a very early date in the history of our country. To trace the origin and development of this idea generally, would not only be a valuable, but also an interesting contribution to our knowledge of our economic development. Here, we must content ourselves by limiting our investigation to the educational aspect. The earliest known instance of the claim to this monopoly dates from the eleventh century, and will subsequently be described. It is highly probable that the idea of the monopoly of keeping school in a prescribed area is of much more ancient date, as records, of necessity, only exist when some actual or threatened infringement of the monopoly necessitated recourse to some authority, who possessed the power of enforcing its observance.

A preliminary question naturally arises: if instruction was given gratuitously, why was there any need for the desire to possess this monopoly, why should not all comers teach school, if they so wished? A solution of this problem may be obtained from a consideration of that tendency for social exclusiveness which everywhere manifests itself. Even to-day, in this time of free education, parents, who can barely afford to do so, prefer to send their children to a fee-paying school for social reasons, even though the instruction given in the public free school may be given by better qualified and more efficient teachers than are to be found in the fee-paying schools. By analogy, we can reconstruct the situation in the eleventh and succeeding centuries. A knowledge of Latin was perceived, by this time, to possess value, and the boy who had received an education was recognised as being in a position to make his way in the world. We may, therefore, assume that some parents were prepared to make payments, in order that this education might be obtained. Where was this education to be gained? There were two possibilities. One was that the church schoolmaster might give supplementary attention to fee-paying pupils, or he might teach them separately, and outside the official time which the conditions of his appointment required. The other possibility was, that some other priest might come to the neighbourhood to set up school, and recompense himself by taking fee-paying pupils, leaving to the official schoolmaster only those pupils who were unable or unwilling to make payment for the instruction they received.

An elementary knowledge of human nature readily leads to the conclusion that the second alternative was not one to which the official schoolmaster would quietly consent. He would look upon the new-comer as an intruder, and would take such steps as were possible to prevent interference with what he claimed to be his monopoly of keeping school in his own district.

It is around this question of the monopoly of school keeping that the educational disputes of the Middle Ages mainly centre. The question is a difficult one because (1) this monopoly was not a matter of definite enactment either by Church or State; it simply evolved. (2) The authority by whose aid the monopoly could be enforced was not specified, and the absence of any definite regulating authority, and of any official pronouncements, led to many prospective schoolmasters setting up schools in promising localities. Sometimes this was accomplished without any

interference, *e.g.* we find that at Rotherham a boy, who
subsequently became Bishop of Lincoln, owed his early
education to a schoolmaster who came to that neighbourhood to establish what would to-day be termed a "private
school."[1] This "private" schoolmaster was at times even
welcomed. Thus at Beverley, which was afterwards notorious as the scene of some exciting disputes relative to the
infringement of the monopoly of school keeping, we learn
that "a certain scholar came there, wishing, as the place
was full of clerks, to keep school there; and was received
by the authorities of the church with unanimous approval."[2]
We must therefore conclude that the monopoly was not
always rigorously enforced. It was only when a schoolmaster felt himself aggrieved and possessed energy, that
action was taken in the matter.

The question of the authority by whom the question of
an alleged infringement could be ultimately settled, was
not definitely prescribed. Was the ultimate appeal to be
to the chancellor of the diocese, to the patron of the school,
to the bishop, to the archbishop, or to the pope? Were
such cases to be dealt with, first of all, in an inferior court
and then an appeal to be made to a higher court in the
event of an unsatisfactory verdict being obtained? We
shall be assisted in answering these questions if we consider
the origin of the right of keeping school.

Originally, as we have seen, it was an unwritten custom
of the Church that the parish priest should keep school.
When there was the possibility that pecuniary advantage
could arise through the keeping of a school, then it appears
that this duty became a privilege and was formally
expressed, in some cases, in a deed. In other words, in
founding a church, a patron bestowed upon it not only
certain lands and tithes, but also the right to keep school.
Thus, at a date between 1076 and 1083, Robert Malet,
who founded the conventual church of Eye, gave to the
church "scholas ejusdem villae."[3] Similarly, when Ilbert
of Lacey founded the Church of St. Clement in his castle,

---

[1] *Yorkshire Schools*, II., p. 110.   [2] *Hist. Ch. of York*, I., 281.
[3] *Dugd. Mon.* III., 405.

C. 1080, he "dedicavit ipsam ecclesiam, cum scolis de Kirky et Pontefracti." [1]

It is in this connection that we encounter one of the first disputes relating to the question of monopoly. The question was this, if a new church was established in a particular area, did the erection of this new church diminish the educational rights of the parent church as well as its spiritual rights? We may put the matter in another way by asking whether the patron of a church possessed the power of alienating the monopoly of school-keeping possessed by that church.

Roger, who became Earl of Warwick in 1123, apparently thought that the patron did possess this right. He bestowed the right of holding schools in Warwick upon the Collegiate Church of St. Mary's, thus alienating the right from the Church of All Saints', Warwick, which had previously possessed it. The authorities of All Saints' desired to protest against this alienation and to preserve their rights. To what authority was this appeal to go? No information is available of the whole course of the struggle, but apparently the matter was ultimately referred to the king; for we find that a deed was issued by Henry I. to the bishops of Worcester and Gloucester, to Roger, Earl of Warwick, and to all the barons of Warwickshire, stating the king's command that the Church of All Saints', Warwick, was to retain the schools of Warwick as it had possessed them in the reign of Edward the Confessor. [2]

This decision is a most important one. It is a recognition by the state of the monopoly possessed by a particular church, and, in addition, it establishes the principle that the enforcement of this monopoly was a matter of temporal and not of spiritual jurisdiction.

Whether as the result of this decision or not we have now no means of determining, but the fact remains that many churches seemed to have been in doubt as to whether they possessed, or did not possess, this right of monopoly

[1] *Early Yorkshire Schools*, II., 1.
[2] *Hist. Warwick Sch.*, p. 5, from Chartul, S. Mary's, Warwick, G. R. Eccl. Misc. Bks. 22.

of school keeping. To resolve this doubt, appeal seems to have been made to the king, and a number of documents still exist which show the decision that was arrived at. Thus Henry I. confirmed to St. Oswald's, Gloucester, the monopoly of school-keeping in that city,[1] to the priory of Huntingdon the monopoly of Huntingdonshire,[2] to the priory of Dunstable the monopoly of schools in that town.[3] Even as late as 1446, there was a grant of the monopoly of school-keeping to Eton College.[4]

The principle which seems to be established in these cases is that, when a dispute arose as to the monopoly right of keeping school in a particular area (apart from merely keeping an unlicensed school) the Crown alone possessed the power of deciding the dispute, and that when it was desired to establish an official school in any area, in addition to the existing schools, it was necessary to obtain the consent of the Crown.

This practice continued for several centuries. Thus in 1446, on the petition of the Archbishop of Canterbury and the Bishop of London, Henry VI. ordained that there should be five schools in London, viz. in connection with the Churches of St. Paul, St. Martin, St. Mary-le-Bow, St. Dunstan, and St. Anthony, respectively.[5]

In the following year, another petition was sent to the king asking for four additional grammar schools in London, which were to be established in connection with the churches of St. Andrew's, Holborn, St. Peter's, Cornhill, All Hallows, and with the Hospital of St. Thomas. The reasons why the establishment of these schools is asked for are interesting, " forasmuche as to the Citee of London is the commune

---

[1] *Cal. Pat.*, 12 Rich. II., pt. 2, m. 10 ; *Ed. Ch.*, p 77.

[2] *P. R. O. Cart.*, antiq. H., No. 18 ; *Ed. Ch.*, p. 93.

[3] *Charter Roll*, II., Henry III., pt. 1, m. 27 ; *Ed. Ch.*, p. 93.

[4] *Chancery Warrents*, Series 1, file 1439 ; *Ed Ch.*, p. 413. Dealing with this grant of a monopoly of school keeping to Eton College, Mr. Leach remarks " The remarkable invasion of ecclesiastical jurisdiction, to which alone the grants and still more the enforcement of the monopoly of endowed schools belonged," etc. *Schs. Med. Eng.*, p. 259. Mr. Leach is in error here. The grant of the monopoly of school keeping was a civil matter.

[5] *Pat.*, 24, Hen. VI., pt. II., m. 28.

concours of this lond, wherein is gret multitude of younge
peple, not only borne and brought forthe in the same Citee,
but also of many other parties of this lond, som for lake
of Scole maistres in their oune Contree for to be enfourmed
of gramer there, and som for the grete almesse of Lordes,
Merchaunts and other, the which is in London more plen-
teously doon, than in many other places of this Reaume,
to such pouere Creatures as never shuld have be brought
to so greet vertu and connyng as thei have, ne hadde hit
ben bi the means of the almes aforesaid." [1] They therefore ask that, in connection with the churches we have
enumerated, they should be allowed " to create, establishe
and sette a persone sufficiently lerned in gramer to hold
and exercise a scole in the same science of gramer, and it
there to teche to all that will lerne." [2] The king assented
to this petition " so that it be doone by thadvyse of the
Ordinarie, otherelles of the Archebishope of Canterbury
for the tyme beyng."

The same procedure was even adopted in the seventeenth
century. Owing to a dispute having arisen between the
Master of the Grammar School at Exeter and the City
Authorities, the latter appealed to the bishop, that he
might license an additional master of grammar in the city,
as had previously been done. The bishop did not consider
that the special circumstances warranted him in taking
the step desired by the civic authorities. As they failed to
obtain their request, they appealed to the Crown in Council
for permission to establish and maintain an additional
school in the city, a request which was finally granted in
1631.[3]

A consideration of these cases enables us to understand
why it was not possible, until comparatively recent times,
to establish schools except by the consent of the Crown.
Thus, in the reigns of the Tudor and Stuart sovereigns, a
number of schools were established, but only by royal
authority. When we come to consider the case of the

---

[1] *Rot. Parl.*, V., 137.   [2] *Ibid.*
[3] *Privy Council Register*, vol. VI. ; Parry, *Founding of Exeter
School*, pp. 101-112.

Chantry Schools, we shall find that a number of schools were founded, but even in these cases the consent of the civil and of the ecclesiastical authorities was obtained. A licence to establish the school would be necessary, as well as a licence in mortmain.

The confirmation of the monopoly right of keeping school to a particular church practically meant that the patronage of the mastership of the school was vested in the authorities of that church. This patronage could be transferred, but the proceedings in such a case were of a civil, and not of an ecclesiastical character. This is similar to the procedure involved in the transfer of the right of patronage of an ecclesiastical benefice to-day. The procedure is purely civil and entirely outside the jurisdiction of the ecclesiastical authorities. If there is any dispute as to the rightful power of patronage, the dispute must be settled in the civil courts. One of the earliest recorded cases of the transfer of the patronage of a school is that of Gloucester School. We have seen that Henry I. confirmed to St. Oswald's Church, Gloucester, the right of keeping school in that city [1]; in 1137 Henry II. confirmed the transference of the patronage of the mastership of the school from St. Oswald's Church to the Canons of Llanthony Abbey; and this transference was again confirmed by King John in 1199.[2] The fact that the settlement of disputed right of patronage of schools was a matter for the secular courts, is clearly brought out by a prohibition issued by the Courts in 1343.[3] This document runs: "The King to the Registrar and commissaries of the Court of Canterbury greeting—whereas the pleas relating to the patronage of grammar schools on our kingdom of England belong especially to our Crown and dignity and (whereas) the Abbot and Convent of Beaulieu are bringing before you in the Court Christian, as we have been informed by many, William Pipard, Clerk, relative to the patronage of the grammar schools of Ferendon—we forbid you to entertain

[1] Supra, p. 96.
[2] V.C.H., Gloucester, II., 315, from Rot. Chart., p. 7.
[3] Registrum Brev., 35.

that plea in the ecclesiastical court, such pleas belonging especially to us and to no other in this kingdom." [1]

We have quoted this document in full, because Mr. de Montmorency instances it to support his contention that there existed a collision between Church and State in matters relating to education. He also maintains that this same document shows that the state "controlled the administration of educational foundations." Mr. de Montmorency is in error here. When a vacancy arises in the incumbency of any parish to-day, of which the patronage is not in the hands of the bishop himself, it is possible that a dispute might arise as to the right of presentation. In such a case, the bishop would naturally refer the matter to his legal advisers. It would always be open for any interested party to stay such proceedings and to let the matter in dispute be determined by the High Court. It could hardly be seriously maintained that such action illustrates a collision between church and state in this country.

After a patron had appointed a master to a particular school, that master possessed the monopoly of keeping school in the prescribed area as long as he held the mastership of the school. No other school was allowed to be kept except with the consent of the master of the school. If any individual attempted to establish a school without such consent, then it was open to the schoolmaster to take the necessary steps to end this infringement of his monopoly.

One of the earliest cases of this character, of which records still exist, dates from 1138. Apparently some unlicensed schools had been set up in some parts of London. The schoolmaster of St. Paul's reported the matter to the Bishop of Winchester (who was acting as Bishop of London during a vacancy in the see). The Bishop consequently issued a writ, in which sentence of excommunication was passed against all those who should continue to keep school in the city of London without the permission of Henry, the schoolmaster. [2] Other cases are recorded in the Bever-

---

[1] Quoted by de Montmorency : *State Intervention*, p. 16.
[2] *Ed. Ch.*, p. 91 from St. Paul's Mun. Press A., Box 60, No. 48.

ley Chapter Act Book,[1] one of which may be taken for illustrative purposes. It seems that in 1304 Thomas of Brompton was the recognised master of the school of grammar in connection with the collegiate church at Beverley. An attempt was made by an unauthorised person to set up a school.[2] The schoolmaster reported the offender to the chapter; the chapter determined that if the offence was continued, then the intruding schoolmaster would be, *ipso facto*, excommunicate and that the chapter clerk was to announce, every Sunday, the fact of such excommunication.

There is no real evidence that there was any ground of appeal against such a sentence of excommunication. Only one instance of an appeal having been made is on record. It seems that a dispute as to the right of keeping school arose at Winchester, and that the party dissatisfied with the verdict carried the case to Rome. It has not been found possible, so far, to trace the result of the appeal.[3]

One of the most important of the cases in which an alleged infringement of monopoly took place, is the "Gloucester School Case," which has come to be regarded as the leading case on the subject. Briefly, the facts are: the prior of Llanthony, as patron of the schools at Gloucester, had appointed John Hamlyn to the mastership of the school. A priest named Thomas More, who had previously been "scolemaster atte Herford," set up an unlicensed school at Gloucester. Hamlyn therefore took action against More but, instead of bringing the defendant before a spiritual court, as had previously been customary, he brought the action in the Court of Common Pleas, and the case was tried before the Lord Chief Justice and two other judges.

The considered decision of the court was, that it was not an offence against the Common Law of England to keep a school. If an offence had been committed, it was an

---

[1] Surtees Society, vol. 98. See I., pp. 42, 48, 102, 113, etc.
[2] *Op. cit.*, p. 102.
[3] *Epis. Joh. Saresberiensis*, ed. Giles, No. 19.

offence against ecclesiastical law, and that consequently the remedy was to be found in the ecclesiastical courts.[1]

The significance of this case was that the monopoly of school keeping was partly broken down. Henceforth, anyone who did not fear ecclesiastical censure and excommunication might keep school, if he so desired. The practical effect of the decision was slight since, as we have seen,[2] the monopoly right of keeping school was granted to Eton College thirty years later.

A problem in connection with this question of monopoly arose in Lincoln in 1407-9. There were two recognised schools in Lincoln; the general grammar school attended by the children of the citizens, and to which the choristers formerly went for their instruction in Latin, and the school of the choristers. In course of time, the choristers' school ceased to confine itself to the study of music and added Latin to its curriculum. For some reason or other, this school also attracted outside scholars. The Mayor and Corporation, as representatives of the citizens of Lincoln, objected;[3] ultimately the matter was settled by a compromise; the teachers of the choristers were to be allowed " to teach grammar to the choristers and to the commoners with them, also to the relations of the canons and vicars of the church or those living at their expense and charity or dwelling in their family," provided that a nominal acknowledgement of the rights of the master of the City Grammar School was made each term.[4]

Another problem arose out of the competing claims of the master of song and of the master of grammar. The master of song apparently maintained that he was as much an official master as the master of grammar, and

---

[1] The text of the "Gloucester School Case" is to be found in the Year Book of the eleventh year of Henry IV., p. 47. It is reprinted as an appendix to de Montmorency, *State Intervention*, pp. 241-242. Mr. de Montmorency would seem to be in error in his interpretation of the decision.   [2] Supra, p. 96.

[3] It is interesting to note here that the maintenance of a monopoly was insisted upon by civic authorities no less than by ecclesiastical persons.

[4] *Chapter Act Book*, Lincoln, 1406-7.   *V.C.H.*, *Lincs.*, II., 426.

probably considered himself quite as competent as his colleague to give lessons in Latin. This problem seems to have been particularly acute at Warwick, and so the authorities of the collegiate church made careful enquiries as to the ancient customs on the matter, and ultimately found that the Latin master alone possessed the right of taking classes in Latin. As a concession, they allowed the master of song to take paying pupils in the "first letters" and the psalter.[1]

The grammar master was not alone in his desire to enforce the monopoly of school keeping in his subject; the master of music was equally tenacious of his prerogative. Thus in 1305, the song master of Lincoln Cathedral complained to the Cathedral Chapter that the Parish Clerks of the city were teaching music to the boys in their churches without his permission, and he charged them with holding "adulterine schools to the prejudice of the liberty of the mother church." The chapter compelled the offenders to swear, "holding the most Holy Gospels, that they will not henceforward keep any adulterine schools in the churches, nor teach boys song or music without license from the schoolmaster."[2]

In bringing this chapter to a close, we might quote from the statutes of St. Albans Grammar School, which were confirmed by the Abbot of St. Albans, in 1310, the section which deals with this question of monopoly. It is there stated that "the master for the time being shall annul, suppress, destroy, and eradicate all adulterine schools within our territory or jurisdiction, by inhibiting . . . under pain of excommunication, any persons from resorting to or presuming to keep any schools without the will and assent of the master of our Grammar School within our aforesaid jurisdiction."[3]

Though the privilege of school keeping was highly prized and stoutly defended, yet it has now passed into oblivion. This was effected, not by express decree either

[1] *Hist. Warwick School*, p. 66.
[2] *Linc. Chapter Act Bk.*, A.2f. f. 2 ; *Ed. Ch.*, p. 237.
[3] *Reg. John Whethamstede*, II., 305.

of law court or of state, but simply because the instruction in Latin, which was offered by these schools, ceased to be in demand.   Two forces contributed to produce this result, the Reformation, and the increasing use of the vernacular. The Reformation brought to an end the number of appointments in connection with the Church for which a knowledge of Latin was a necessary qualification; and consequently the demand for grammar schools diminished.   The increasing employment of the vernacular caused Latin to drop out of use as the language of commerce and the medium of written communication.

CHAPTER V.

THE APPOINTMENT AND TENURE OF MASTERS.

We now proceed to consider questions connected with (a) the appointment, (b) the tenure, (c) the remuneration, and (d) the judicial functions of schoolmasters.

(a) THE APPOINTMENT OF MASTERS.

We may distinguish between schools in connection with (1) monasteries, (2) collegiate churches, (3) parishes, (4) chantries and gilds.

I. SCHOOLS IN CONNECTION WITH MONASTERIES.

It is significant that in the monasteries, the position of schoolmaster does not seem to have been definitely recognised. Thus, in the list of the officers and obedientaries of Evesham in the thirteenth century, for example, there is included the prior, sub-prior, third prior, and other "custodes ordinis"; the precentor, sacrist, chamberlain, kitchener, cellarers, infirmarer, almoner, warden of the vineyard and garden, master of the fabric, guest master and pittancer; but there is no mention of a "magister scolarum." We have not been able to discover any instance of a monk, who was pensioned at the time of the dissolution, and who was described as acting in the capacity of a teacher at that time.

Occasionally we come across references to the "master

of the novices." [1] An account of the Novices' School at Durham has been preserved. [2] The school was held in the "weast ally" of the cloisters both in the morning and in the afternoon. The scholars attended for a period of seven years, during which time they received food and clothing. If they were "apte to lernynge ... and had a pregnant wyt withall" they were then sent to the University to study theology; otherwise they were kept at their books in the monastery until they were considered ready for ordination. The Novices' School at Durham was taught by the eldest learned monk in the monastery. At Canterbury the school was under the charge of the "Magister ordinis," and at Abingdon under the "Instructor juvenum." [3] The need for the instruction of the novices was reiterated by the General Benedictine Statutes of 1334, which provided that a secular priest was to be appointed to teach grammar when a monk was not available for the purpose.

The appointment to the scholastic posts within the monastery would naturally be in the hands of the abbot or prior. [4]

There exists evidence that schools for the education of the laity existed in the neighbourhood of most, even if not all, of the greater monasteries. Thus, prior to the thirteenth century, such schools may be traced at Reading, Dunstable, Huntingdon, Bedford, Christchurch (Hants.), Thetford, Derby, Gloucester, Waltham, Bury St. Edmunds, Colchester, Leicester, Cirencester, Lewes, Battle, Arundel, Lancaster, Chesterfield, Bruton, Winchcombe, Malmesbury, and other places in which a monastery is known to have existed. In many of these cases we are able to trace that the appointment of the "magister scolarum" was in the hands of the abbot. Thus the statutes of the Abbey of Bury St. Edmunds state that:—

"The collation of the schools of St. Edmunds belongs to the abbot in the same way as the collation of Churches ... The schools indeed in the manor of Mildenhall and of

[1] *Hist. Mon. Glouc.*, III., 290.
[2] See *Rites of Durham*, (Surtees Society) p. 81.
[3] *Abingdon Obedientaries Accounts*, 1375-6; Camden Soc.
[4] *Roger Prior's Reg.*, V., 261 b.

Beccles are by law to be conferred by those in whose custody the manors are. And it is to be noted that when the ' rector scolarum ' is to be removed he ought to be given notice, by the person who appointed him, before Whitsuntide. If, on the other hand, the master wishes to retire, he is bound to give like notice to the person who appointed him." [1]

A third class of school (which will be described in a subsequent chapter) in connection with the monasteries was the Almonry School. The appointment of the " grammar master " at these schools was usually in the hands of the almoner of the monastery, but the appointment had to be approved of by the Chancellor or Archdeacon who was acting as the head of the educational administration of the diocese. [2]

II. SCHOOLS IN CONNECTION WITH COLLEGIATE CHURCHES.

More definite information is available when we pass to consider the appointments of masters of the schools in connection with collegiate churches. Here, as we have seen, the chancellor (who was previously the schoolmaster) was the responsible head of the education in the diocese. It was his duty to appoint a master of grammar in connection with the cathedral church, and not to allow any other teacher to keep school within the city without his consent. [3] Sometimes the chancellor seems to have taken no steps to make the appointment, possibly because the remuneration of the master came partly out of the benefice of the chancellor. A letter is still extant which was written to the chancellor of York Cathedral in 1344 informing him that unless he took immediate action in making the appointment of a master, he would be liable to punishment. [4]

---

[1] Statutes of the Abbey of Bury St. Edmunds. B.M. Harl. MSS. 1005, fol. 95.6., Trans., *V.C.H. Suffolk.* II., 307. For other instances of appointments of schoolmasters by abbots, see *Gesta Abbatum Mon. S. Albani*, (R.S.) I., p. 72. *V.C.H. Lincs.*, II., 450.

[2] *B M. Landsdowne MS.*, 375 : *Ed. Ch.*, 299. *Westminster Abbey Obedientaries Accounts*, reprinted *Ed. Ch* , pp. 306-315.

[3] Cf. *Statutes of the Church of York*, p. 6.

[4] *Yorkshire Schools*, I., p. 18 from Acta Capituli, G., c. ii. 70.

The general procedure in making an appointment to the master-ship in grammar of a school, in connection with a collegiate church, was that the chancellor should select the man whom he considered suitable and submit his name to the dean and chapter. The appointment was completed by the dean and chapter admitting the nominee of the chancellor to the position.[1]

We have not been able to trace any appointments of a song schoolmaster.[2] The procedure would probably be similar except for the fact that the nomination would be in the hands of the precentor instead of the chancellor.[3]

In the case of those cathedral churches which were served by monks, there would not, of course, be a " chancellor." In such cases, the appointment of the " magister scolarum " was made by the bishop. Thus we read of Archbishop Peckham, during a vacancy of the see of Norwich, appointing a master to Norwich School.[4] The first available record of an appointment to the mastership by a bishop of Norwich dates from 1388 ; after this date the Norwich Chapter Act Book records a continuous stream of such appointments. In Canterbury, which was also a monastic cathedral, the appointment of the schoolmaster was similarly in the hands of the archbishop.[5]

III. SCHOOLS IN CONNECTION WITH PARISHES.

We have used the term " parish " here to denote those districts which were served by a vicar or rector, and not by a college of clergy. The appointments to the parochial church schools, unless arrangements were made to the

---

[1] *Beverley Chapter Act Bk.*, I., pp. 157, 382 ; *Mem. Southwell Minster*, p. 29. The function of the dean and chapter was not simply formal. *Mem. Southwell Minster*, p. 125.

[2] The appointment of a master of song at a monastery was made by the prior. Cf. Roger Prior's *Reg.* V., 261 b.

[3] *Statutes of the Ch. of York*, p. 5.

[4] *Lambeth MSS. Reg. Peckham*, f. 38 a., *Ed. Ch.*, p. 233.

[5] *Lambeth MSS. Reg. Winchelsea*, f. 300. b., *Ed. Ch.*, p. 239. Scholastic patronage in monastic cathedral dioceses was subject to episcopal review. *Worc. Epis. Reg. Silvester*, fol. 202.

contrary, were made by the patrons of the church itself.
In some cases the patrons would be the bishops,[1] in others
the dean and chapter of a collegiate church[2]; in others
again, the patronage would be in private hands, whilst in
other cases a monastery might have the power of nominating.[3] We must remember that when a parish was
subdivided the power of keeping a school did not pass to
the new parish, but continued to be the prerogative of the
parent church, and that consequently the patrons of the
new church did not possess the right of nominating a
master of grammar to keep a school in connection with the
newly-founded church.[4]

Disputes occasionally arose in connection with the
exercise of this right of patronage. It would seem as if
the chancellor of the diocese,[5] in the case of a secular
cathedral, and the "magister scolarum" in the case of a
monastic cathedral, claimed the right of making *all* the
schools appointments in their respective dioceses. Records
are still available of the action which was taken in various
cases to attempt to enforce this claim. We will briefly
describe two of these cases, one of which was due to the
action taken by the chancellor of a secular collegiate
church, the other to the action taken by a "magister
scolarum" in a city served by a monastic cathedral.

Taking first the case of the chancellor of a secular
collegiate church, we note that the prior and convent of
St. Catherine's by Lincoln were the patrons of Newark
Church. In 1238 there occurred a vacancy in the school.
The patrons of the church took the necessary steps to fill
the vacancy. The chancellor of Southwell Minster maintained that the power of nomination was "ex officio"
vested in him. Both parties appealed to the pope. The
result of the action was, that the power of making
the nomination to the school was declared to be the
right of the patrons, but that the admission of the nomi-

---

[1] *Newcourt, Report* II., 86, 87, 88.
[2] *Linc. Chapter Act Bk.*, pp. 2, 24.
[3] See p. 61.   [4] See Chap. IV.
[5] The chancellor of a diocese exercised a considerable amount of
scholastic patronage.

nated master to the position was to be effected by the chancellor.[1]

Turning next to the claim of the "magister scolarum" in connection with a monastic cathedral we note that the Norwich Chapter Act Book records a similar dispute. The prior and convent of Coxford were the patrons of the church of Rudham by Coxford. On a vacancy in the mastership of the schools occurring in 1240, the patrons proceeded to make the necessary appointment. The "magister scolarum" brought an action in the bishop's court to prevent this, as he claimed that he possessed an "ex officio" right to make the nomination. The decision of the court was that the power of appointing the master of the school belonged to the patrons of the church.

We may note here that the authority who possessed the power of determining disputes relating to patronage of schools does not appear to have been definitely prescribed. In the first of the two cases we have referred to here, the authority of the pope was invoked, in the second, the authority of the bishop, whilst records are available of other cases, in which a writ of prohibition was obtained with the view to the case being heard in the king's court.[2]

IV. SCHOOLS ESTABLISHED IN CONNECTION WITH CHANTRIES, GILDS, ETC.

In the latter part of the Middle Ages a number of schools were established in this country by means of endowments. These endowments were usually associated with the foundation of gilds or chantries. The special point we are interested in here is that in such cases arrangements were made for the requisite appointments to be effected when the need arose. Thus the ordinances

---

[1] *Memorials of Southwell Minster*, XII.-XLII., 52.

[2] *Registrum Brevium*, fol 35. The power of patronage to a school could apparently be delegated. Thus the Bishop of Lincoln granted a licence to the rector of Willeford " to chose a lettered and fit man in the parish to teach the boys and others going to him the said science." See *Linc. Epis. Reg. Gynwell*, fol. 135 b. This unusual action was due to the scarcity of schoolmasters after the Black Death.

and statutes in connection with the foundation of the grammar school at Wotton-under-Edge[1] prescribe that "the master of the school was to be presented by Lady Berkeley during her life, and afterwards by Sir Thomas Berkeley and his heirs male, whom failing by Sir John Berkeley her second son, and his heirs male, whom failing by the lord of the manor of Wotton."[2] As a result of this more definite determination of the right of appointment, disputes relating to the exercise of patronage no longer arose.[3]

(b) THE TENURE OF MASTERSHIP.

We find a difficulty in dealing with the question of the tenure of the masterships of the various schools because of the scarcity of evidence and of its conflicting character. Thus, in the Lincoln Chapter Act Book, there is a record that the dean and chapter in 1327 appointed six masters to as many schools in the diocese.[4] In the following year the same men were reappointed and this reappointment continues year after year until 1335, when notices of the appointments of schoolmasters cease. It would therefore appear as if the custom in the diocese of Lincoln was that the masters were appointed for one year only but that if their character and conduct were considered satisfactory they would be reappointed.

In the diocese of York the masters seem to have been appointed for three years. Thus there is a record that at Beverley Collegiate Church, in 1306, the master was appointed to the school for that period[5]; in 1320 there is a record of a similar appointment.[6] It is expressly stated in the note of an appointment made in 1368, that the customary tenure of schools in the diocese of York was three years and that under special circumstances this period might be extended to five years.[7]

In course of time the nature of the tenure changes.

---

[1] 1382.

[2] *Reg. Ep. Worcester, H. Wakfeld,* p. 72. *Ed. Ch.* pp. 331-341.,

[3] See also *Somerset and Dorset Notes and Queries,* III., 241.

[4] *Op. cit.,* A. 2, 24, f. 14.   [5] *Early Yorkshire Schools,* I., 90.

[6] *Ibid.,* p. 97.   [7] *Ibid.,* p. 23.

The first change which we have traced occurred in 1368 when the master appointed was stated to be allowed to retain his appointment until he obtained another benefice. The reason for this change is stated to be the scarcity of priests due to the mortality occasioned by the plague. The triennial tenure was again in vogue in 1426,[1] but in 1486 a departure occurs, as the schoolmaster appointed in that year was to hold his office " durante vitae," if he so wished.[2]

A further change of tenure took place in 1575 when the master was appointed to hold office " durante bene-placito Decani et Capituli." [3]

In the schools which were founded in the sixteenth century and later it began to be common to draw up statutes and ordinances for the administration of the schools. It was usual in these school statutes to refer to the tenure of the mastership. Thus the statutes of Newark School [4] provide that the master at the time of his admission to his post, should be thus instructed :—

" Sjr, ye be chosen to be maister and preceptour of this scoole and to teche chyldern repayring to the same not onely good literature, gramer and other vertuous doctrine but also good maners accordyng to the ordynance of Master Thomas Newark. Wherefore we doe ascertayne you that this ys a perpetual roome of continuance upon your good demeanour and dutie in this scoole." [5]

In making the appointment for life, the founder of Newark School adopted a practice which was different from the common one. Thus William of Wykeham, Waynflete, and Colet, all made the masters of the schools founded by them removeable at will. In fact, Colet arranged that the mastership of St. Paul's was merely to be renewed from year to year.

(c) REMUNERATION OF MASTERS.

We are faced with another difficult question when we proceed to consider the question of the remuneration of

[1] *Ibid.*, p. 27.   [2] *Ibid.*, p. 29.   [3] *Ibid.*, p. 67.   [4] Re-founded 1531-2.
[5] In town muniments of Newark ; reprinted by T. F. A. Burnaby, Town Clerk, 1855.

masters. This problem is one about which contradictory opinions have been held owing to the fact that it is disputed whether or not the education given in the schools of the Middle Ages was free education. It is indisputable that the original schools of the Church were entirely free and that the schoolmaster was remunerated by sharing equally with the other priests in the common fund of the Church. The transition from free education to fee paying education may be said to date from the time when the schoolmaster became the chancellor. The chancellor continued to draw his share of the revenue of the Church, but no express provision was made for the maintenance of the schoolmaster whom the chancellor appointed.[1]

It was probably due to this neglect that the council of 1179[2] decreed that a benefice should be bestowed upon a master so as to enable him to teach the "clericos et scholares pauperes" gratis. This decree was repeated in 1200[3] and 1215.[4] It has not been found possible to trace the appointment to sinecure benefices, subject to the condition that the incumbent of such benefice should hold a school, as the record of the appointment would not also record the condition. We may safely assume that this was done in some cases, as the custom even prevails to-day.[5]

In course of time, the master of a school derived a certain amount of his remuneration from the fees which he received from his pupils. This originated in a natural custom that pupils should make some voluntary offering to those who taught them. Thus, the enactment of 1200, which decreed that "presbyteri per villas scholas habeant, et gratis parvulos doceant" also practically enacted that voluntary contributions on the part of the relations of the pupils would be permitted. It is not difficult to conceive that this custom of voluntary offering would develop into one of compulsory payment.

[1] But cf. *Great Roll of the Pipe* (Rec. Com.) pp. 9-10, which suggests customary arrangements.
[2] Decretal V., tit. 5, cap. I.   [3] Wilkins : *Concilia* I., p. 506.
[4] Decretal V., tit 5, cap. IV.
[5] Cf. appointment of Principal of St. David's College, Lampeter.

The terms used to describe these voluntary offerings are somewhat strange, *e.g.* "cock penny," "potation penny," "nutt money." "Cock pennies" were gratuities given to the schoolmasters in connection with the almost universal custom of cock-fighting which took place in schools on Shrove Tuesday. William Fitzstephen [1] gives an account of the practice, stating that "each boy in the school brings a fighting cock to his master, and the whole of that forenoon is given up to a holiday to watch the cock-fights in the school." Cock-fighting was prohibited in St. Paul's School by Colet's statute of 1518, but the custom seems to have continued at the Manchester Grammar School until 1815.[2] "Potation pennies" were gratuities made when a feast was provided, whilst "nutt money" was the term applied to the gifts made to the schoolmasters at Michaelmas.

In some cases, these offerings were regarded as a natural part of the remuneration of the schoolmaster. Thus the ordinances of Hartlebury Grammar School prescribe that "the schoolmaster shall and may have, use and take the profits of all such cock-fights and potations, as are commonly used in schools and such other gifts as shall freely be given them."[3] In other cases, an effort was made to put an end to the custom. Thus the Coventry Grammar School statutes state that "there shall not be any other or more Potations in any one yeare . . . than one yearely." [4]

In addition to these optional payments, certain other payments gradually became recognised which in course of time were known as "entrance money" (because the payment was made when the pupil was admitted to the school), "quarterages" (payments made at the beginning of each term), "breaking up money" (similar payments made at the end of term). These payments did not become common until the sixteenth century—a period which is outside the time with which we are dealing; consequently, it will not be necessary for us to deal more fully with the question

[1] Who died c. 1191.
[2] See *Notes and Queries*, 8th series, vol. VII., pp. 338, 473-474; *Cyclopaedia of Educ.*, vol. II., p. 42.
[3] Carlisle : *Grammar Schools*, II., p. 759.   [4] *Ibid.*, p. 649.

here. The record of the chantry founded at Newland by
Richard Gryndour, however, may be referred to.[1] At the
school which the chantry priest was required to teach, he
was entitled to charge " scolers lerning gramer, 8d. the
quarter, and of others lerning to rede, 4d. the quarter." [2]
As instances of other types of payments to schoolmasters
we may quote the regulations of Ipswich Grammar School
where it was prescribed in 1476-7 that those attending the
grammar class should pay 10d., the psalter class 8d., and
the primer class 6d. each quarter.[3] A reduction in these
terms appears to have been made for the sons of burgesses
living in Ipswich who were to pay " 8d. a quarter . . . and
not above." [4] Again, the statutes and ordinances of the
Boteler Grammar Schools,[5] described as a *Free* Grammar
School, prescribe that " it shall be lawfull to the schoolmaster to take . . . four pennys by-year that is to say in
the Quarter next after Christmas A cock penny and in
any of the three other Quarters in the year one Potation
Penny." [6] The deed of 1414 which recorded the wishes of
Bishop Langley with regard to his foundation at Durham,
stated that " diligenter instruere et docere pauperes qui
dem gratis pro Deo, si hoc ipsi vel parentes sui pro amore
Dei humiliter petierint, ab illis autem, qui se vel amicos
suos scolares voluerunt recipiendo stipendia moderata in
aliis scolis grammatice vel cantus solvi consueta." [7]

The custom of providing an endowment for the support
of the school and its master, as distinct from the maintenance of scholars, dates from an early period. The
earliest definite instance in this country, which has been
so far traced, occurred C. 1190 when Abbot Samson endowed " the schoolmaster who for the time being taught
in the town of St. Edmunds " with half the revenues of a
rectory.[8] The next available instance is the record at

[1] See *Trans. Bristol and Glas. Archaeol.*, Soc. VI.
[2] *E. S. R.*, II., 82.
[3] *Ipswich Court Bk. Brit. M. Addit.*, MS. 30158, fol. 34.
[4] *Ibid.*   [5] Founded 1520.
[6] *Trans. Hist. Soc. Lancs. and Chester*, VIII., 51.
[7] *V. C. H. Durham*, I., 371.
[8] *Chron. Jocelyn de Brakelonde*, p. 3.

Wells of a house being given to the schoolmaster there, for the time being, together with the prebend of Biddenham as an endowment.[1] Endowments gradually become increasingly numerous as will be exemplified in detail when we deal with the foundation of chantries and other charitable institutions.

(d) Judicial Functions of Schoolmasters.

By the ordinance issued by William the Conqueror, the separation of the civil and the ecclesiastical courts was effected. As a result, it came about that those who were entitled to the " benefit of clergy " claimed that disputes in which they were concerned, should be dealt with in the ecclesiastical courts. Possibly it is by an extension of this principle that it was claimed that cases in which the scholars of a particular school were concerned, should be considered to be under the jurisdiction of the schoolmaster of that school. The evidence available is not sufficient to enable us to decide the extent to which this custom prevailed, but a study of the powers of jurisdiction possessed by the schoolmasters of Salisbury, Cambridge, St. Albans, and Canterbury will assist us to determine its general character.

The respective jurisdiction of the Chancellor and the Sub-dean of Salisbury was decided in 1278 when it was provided that the chancellor " ad cuius officium pertinet scolas regere " should deal with all disputed matters (with the exception of questions of immorality) in which his scholars were implicated, whilst the sub-dean was to exercise jurisdiction in all matters in which the priests of the city were concerned.[2]

A similar decision was arrived at by the Bishop of Ely in 1276, when he sought to define the respective jurisdiction of the " Magister Glomerie," the Chancellor of Cambridge University, and the Archdeacon of Ely.[3] The judicial powers of the Master of St. Albans School were

[1] *S. M. E.*, p. 161.
[2] Rashdall, *Univ.*, II., pt. II., p. 765.
[3] Cooper : *Annals of Cambridge*, I., p. 56.

set out in detail in the school statutes of 1309.[1] It is interesting to note that the master could be assisted " by the secular arm, invoked if need be for the special purpose."

The Canterbury schoolmaster possessed considerable powers of jurisdiction in matters in which his scholars were concerned, and there is evidence that some of these schoolmasters did not hesitate to use their powers when necessity arose. John Everard, " Rector scolarum civitatis Cantuariensis " in 1311, in particular, was keen on asserting his authority. The claim, which he maintained that he possessed, was investigated by a special commission of clerics and laymen, who reported in his favour. To prevent him from exercising his authority, an appeal was made to the Court of King's Bench. The schoolmaster continued vigorously to press the recognition of his powers of jurisdiction and ultimately the authority he claimed was upheld.[2]

We cannot generalise from these instances, but it is unquestionable that some schoolmasters possessed special powers of acting in a judicial capacity in cases in which their pupils were involved.

---

[1] *Reg. Joh. Whethamstede*, II., 305.

[2] *Cant. Cath. Mun.*, X., 4, S. B. 4 : *Ed. Ch.*, pp. 252-267. The Statutes of Ipswich School (1476-7) state that "The grammar schoolmaster shall henceforth have jurisdiction and governance of all scholars within the liberty and precinct of this town, except only petties." *Ipswich Court Bk.*, B. M., MS. Add. 30158, fol. 34.

CHAPTER VI.

THE EDUCATION OF THE SONS OF THE NOBILITY.

It is necessary to consider now the nature of the Education of those whose social position prevented them from sharing in the gratuitous Education, which was offered by the Church and freely accepted by the sons and daughters of "liberi tenentes," or of villeins, cottars, or serfs. These educational facilities thus offered by the Church might possibly be utilised by the children of the manorial officials, the steward, or the bailiff; but they would never be shared by children of gentle birth.

In the Middle Ages, in England as on the continent, youths of noble parentage were not sent to schools for their education, but to the households of great nobles or great ecclesiastics. Thus, as we have seen, Odo, subsequently Archbishop of Canterbury, was taught as a boy in the household of the thane Athelhelm [1]; this custom was consequently already well established in the tenth century. Other instances that may be given are those of Stephen of Blois, who received his education at the court of his uncle, Henry I.; of Henry II., who lived at the house of Duke Robert of Gloucester; and of Henry VI., who was put under the care of Richard Beauchamp, Earl of Warwick. To that noble were also entrusted the heirs of baronies in the Crown's wardship, so that his court practically became "an academy for the young nobility."

Fitzstephen, the biographer of Thomas à Becket, tells

[1] P. 39.

us that "the nobles of England and of the neighbouring kingdoms used to send their sons to serve the Chancellor, whom he trained with honourable bringing-up and learning; and when they had received the knight's belt, sent them back with honour to their fathers and kindred; some he used to keep. The king himself, his master, entrusted to him his son, the heir of the realm, to be brought up; whom he had with him, with many sons of nobles of the same age, and their proper retinue and masters and proper servants in the honour due." [1]

The nature of the education which was given at the houses of the great nobles was determined by an ideal which grew out of the special circumstances of the time. Prominent among the contributory factors to the formation of this ideal were (1) the Feudal System, (2) the Crusades, (3) the Church.

(1) We have already dealt briefly with the origin and development of the Feudal System; hence it will be sufficient to point out here, that the Conquest had succeeded in establishing it more firmly in this country. Each fief now became in practice a separate court under its lord, whose eldest son could naturally look forward to succeeding to the position occupied by his father. It is in this connection that we find one need which the education of the young noble would be expected to meet. It was necessary that he should receive the training which would be of service to him in discharging effectively the position which in the ordinary course of things he would subsequently be called upon to fill.

(2) Without enquiring fully into the causes contributory to the Crusades, we may mention that they arose out of one of those outbursts of energy which in subsequent ages found expression in such movements as the Revival of Learning and the French Revolution. More definitely, the Crusades were the response made by the nobility to the appeal of the East for help against the infidel. This response was given the more readily because it was in

---

[1] *Vita S. Thomas*, pp. 189, 190, ed. Giles, quoted Furnivall, *Forewords*, p. 6.

harmony with the restless love of adventure and with the desire for glory and fame, which manifested themselves during this period.

(3) It is also important to notice that there existed at this time a widespread belief in the efficacy of penitence and ascetism, as a means of gaining religious virtue. This frequently took the form of a pilgrimage, and the Crusades furnished a "stupendous pilgrimage under specially favourable and meritorious conditions." "The first Crusade was the marriage of War and Religion, the consecration by the Church of the military spirit, which was the first step in the creation of Chivalry."[1]

These three factors contributed to the growth of those customs which prevailed among the noble classes in Western Europe during the greater part of the Middle Ages, and to which the term chivalry is usually applied. A certain ideal of the qualities which were essential to a "perfect knight" gradually evolved. Hence it was the business of the household to which the sons of the nobility were sent for training to endeavour, as far as possible, to equip their "pupils" with the knowledge, skill, habits, and qualities which custom had decreed should be possessed before admission to the grade of knighthood was obtained.

It is possible to trace four main elements in the chivalric ideal: (1) military prowess, (2) service and loyalty, (3) the "worship of woman," (4) religion.

Taking each of these points in turn, we note first that the importance of military training at this period is a topic which scarcely calls for elaboration. The age was essentially warlike; the definite objective of the Crusades was one that could only be achieved through military skill. Hence, no slight amount of the training of the future knight was devoted to the acquisition of skill as a horseman and in the use of the weapons of war.

The second element to which we have referred—"service and loyalty"—may be described as the underlying principle of chivalry. The service, however, sprang from pride in the position occupied; no task was considered menial if

---

[1] Cornish, *Chivalry*, p. 24.

it arose out of the service due from the squire to his liege lord. Loyalty is inherent in the idea of chivalry ; it is an inseparable part of the knightly ideal.

Only a passing reference is necessary to the third element—the " worship of women "—even though it played a most important part in the development of the character of the prospective knight by refining his manners, checking coarseness of expression, and tending generally to the growth of the idea of courtesy which is now conceived of as the distinctive mark of a chivalrous man. Here we may simply say that to do the pleasure of ladies was regarded both as the chief solace of the knight and the mainspring of his actions.

The remaining element in the chivalric ideal is that of religion. The Church looms large ; the knight was brought up to use her sacraments, to obey her precepts, and to show reverence to her ministers. " The Crusader, the Hospitaller, and the Knights of Santiago were champions of the Church against the infidel. The knight's conse- cration to chivalry was after the form of a sacrament, and to defend the Church was a part of his initiation. The least religious acknowledged the authority of religion and it was the imputation of impiety rather than of immorality which destroyed the Templar ; for impiety was in those days a worse imputation than immorality." [1]

To summarise the course of preparation for knighthood, it may be pointed out that for the first seven years of training, the aspirants were known as pages, varlets, or damoiseaux. Under their masters and mistresses they performed most humble domestic duties and practised at doing everything they saw done by the knights. After attaining the age of fourteen years, they were promoted to the rank of squire, a promotion that was celebrated by a religious ceremony. The training now became more severe and included ability in all matters relating to the art of warfare, together with duties in connection with the stables and horses, and skill in the art of heraldry.

The intellectual part of the training of the squire involved

[1] Cornish, *op. cit.*, pp. 15, 16.

instruction in " sondry languages " and the acquisition of ability " to pipe, sing, dance " and to play the harp.[1] In the oft-quoted passage from Chaucer it is stated that the squire :—

> " wel cowde ryde,
> He cowde songes wel make and endite,
> Justne and eek daunce, and wel purtray and write."

The actual school curriculum followed by the squire would therefore resemble that of children of lower social grades, to the extent that " song " and " writing " were included in both. Among the " sondry languages," it is certain that Latin would be numbered; in addition he would learn French and (possibly) Italian.

Chivalry began to decline about the middle of the thirteenth century. " Froissart characterises and describes with picturesque detail this tendency to decay which, as time advanced, gradually resulted in a complete transformation, so that the chivalric ideal became lost and the independence of the soldier, once the slave only of his God and of his lady, gave way to the obsequiousness of the courtier, and finally became a selfish and pitiful servility." [2]

What place does chivalric education occupy in the evolution of educational thought and practice ? In the first place, it contributed to the elaboration of the educational ideal. Though, as we have indicated, chivalric education was based on utility, just as was the education of the schools of the cloister or of the church, yet it resulted in a wider connotation being given to the term "education." Chivalric education aimed at fitting a man to live a life in society ; whereas the education given by the monk or priest aimed only at fitting a man to lead a religious life. A change was also made in the estimation of educational values : the intellectual element of education (though not entirely ignored) was yet relegated to a subsidiary position, whilst the care of the body, notoriously absent from the

---

[1] *Liber Niger*, p. 45 ; quoted *Forewords*, p. 11.
[2] Lacroix ; *Military and Religious Life in the Middle Ages*, pp. 137, 138.

ecclesiastical education, was exalted to an important position. It is interesting also to note that the custom of sending boys of good family away from home directly contributed to the practice of sending boys to a residential school, which is characteristic of the present day, especially among parents of good financial means. In addition, we must note that some of the ideals of chivalry have tended to live on in our great public schools of to-day; further, they have influenced our secondary schools and, to a lesser extent, our elementary schools. Admiration for physical prowess, as exemplified on the playing fields, still occupies the highest place in the mind of the schoolboy; the ideal of service survives in the custom of "fagging"; loyalty, honour, courtesy, and deference to external ceremonial continue to be distinctive marks of the "schools of the nobility" of to-day.

There is a danger in assuming that all the ideals of chivalry were equally high, and that the contribution of chivalry to education was greater than it really was. "Chivalry," writes Cornish, "taught the world the duty of noble service willingly rendered. It upheld courage and enterprise in obedience to rule, it consecrated military prowess to the service of the church, glorified the virtues of liberality, good faith, unselfishness, and courtesy, and, above all, courtesy to women. Against these may be set the vices of ostentation, love of bloodshed, contempt of inferiors, and loose manners. Chivalry was an imperfect discipline, but it was a discipline, and one fit for the times. It may have existed in the world too long; it did not come into existence too early; and with all its short-comings, it exercised a great and wholesome influence in lifting the medieval world from barbarism to civilisation."[1]

The practice of sending the sons of the nobility and gentry to the houses of other nobles continued even after "chivalry" itself as a mode of life had died out. Thus, Sir Thomas More was brought up at the house of Cardinal Morton;[2] Cardinal Wolsey had a number of young lords

[1] Op. cit., p. 27.
[2] Roper's Life of More, ed. Singer, p. 3.

residing with him;[1] in the household of the Earl of Northumberland in 1571 were a number of young gentlemen.[2]

For the purpose of teaching these young nobles, it was customary that there should be a "Maistyr of Gramer" as a part of the establishment of the house, who was responsible for the instruction "which is necessary for song and the rules of grammatical construction."[3] Various household books bear testimony to the presence of this tutor.[4] It is not suggested that the education given at the houses of nobles and other great men was very effective from an academic point of view. In fact, the opinion in which letters were generally held at the time was not sufficiently high to serve as an inducement for study to be taken up seriously by young members of the higher social classes.[5] The course of study followed included Latin, French, writing, fencing, accounts, and music,[6] but this enumeration of subjects does not imply that a high standard was attained. A further consideration of this subject will be necessary when the period subsequent to the Reformation is dealt with.

---

[1] Cavendish : *Life of Wolsey*, ed. Singer, vol. I., p. 38.
[2] *Household Book*, p. 254.　　　　[3] *Liber Niger*, p. 51.
[4] *Household Bk.*, Earl of Northumberland, pp. 41, 47, 97, 254.
[5] *Forewords*, p. 13.　　　　[6] Froude, *Hist.* V., pp. 39, 40.

BOOK III.

EDUCATION PASSING OUT OF CHURCH CONTROL.

CHAPTER I.

SOCIAL AND ECONOMIC CHANGES.

During the period we now proceed to consider, the idea gradually developed that education was not a matter which exclusively pertained to the Church. With the rise of the universities, the control of education tended to pass out of the power of the Church; with the social and economic progress of the country, there was a growth of the idea that civic and trade and craft organisations respectively owed a duty to the community, and that this duty included the provision of facilities for education.

This idea of civic or community responsibility for education which began to manifest itself in a tentative manner, was not the outcome of any opposition to the Church, or due to a feeling that the Church had not been sufficiently alive to its responsibilities. On the contrary, the provision for education which was made was, generally speaking, entrusted to the care of the Church, and the teachers of the schools continued to be the priests of the Church. In fact, we may go so far as to assert that the conscious-

124

ness of social responsibility which now developed was, to a
great extent, the outgrowth of religious teaching.

At the same time that we emphasise this general statement, we must admit that there existed certain signs of a
tendency to assert independence of the Church, and various
symptoms began to manifest themselves which were indicative of the fact that school-keeping was ceasing to be
regarded as exclusively a function of the priesthood. The
tendency to independence of the Church showed itself,
among other places, at Coventry, where the corporation
sent a deputation to the Prior of Coventry " wyllyng hym
to occupye a skole of Gramer, fyye he like to teche hys
Brederon and Childerom of the aumbry, and that he wol-
not gruche ne meve the contrai, but that euery mon off
this Cite be at hys ffre chosse to sette hys chylde to
skole to what techer off Gramer that he likyth, as reson
askyth "[1]; and at Bridgenorth, where an ordinance was
passed in 1503, that no priest should keep a school after
a schoolmaster had come to town.[2] As illustrating the
tendency to place schools under the control of organisations other than the Church may be mentioned the school
founded at Farthinghoe in 1443 by John Abbot, a mercer
of London, who placed the school under the control of the
Mercers' Company,[3] and the school founded by Sir Edmund
Sha in 1487, which was put in mortmain " unto his
felliship of the craft of goldsmythes."[4] Two other instances are available. In 1502, Sir John Percyvale founded
a "Fre Gramer Scole" at Macclesfield[5] for "gentil mennes
sonnes and other good menses children in Maxfiled and the
Countre thereabouts." The government of the school was
entrusted to seventeen local laymen who were to act as
trustees. In 1505, Sir Bartholomew Read, who founded
a school at Cromer, made the Goldsmith's Company the
governing body.[6] That school-keeping was ceasing to be

[1] *Coventry Leet Book*, I., 101.
[2] Mrs. Green, *Town Life in the Fifteenth Century*, II., 18.
[3] Chantry Certif., E.S.R., II., 144.
[4] Mrs. Green, *op. cit.*, II., 16.
[5] Carlisle : *Grammar Schools*, I., 117.
[6] *Schools of Medieval England*, p. 246.

regarded as the exclusive function of the priesthood is indicated by the will of the founder of Sevenoaks Grammar
School in 1432, which specified that the schoolmaster was
not to be a priest "in sacris ordinibus minime consti-
tutus,"[1] and by the fact that the names of schoolmasters
are to be found on the rolls of the Freemen of the city of
York.[2]

The growing interest of the laity in education did not
result in apathy on the part of the Church. On the contrary, the Church was stimulated to renewed activity.
Not only did the great churchmen of the day, e.g. Wykeham, Chicheley, and Waynflete, found schools of enduring
magnificence, but a large number of collegiate churches
were established in various parts of the country, and there
exists considerable evidence (which we shall consider in a
subsequent chapter) to show that the majority of these
collegiate churches provided special facilities for education.

The change in the attitude of the nation towards education is the direct outcome of its social and economic
conditions, and if we are properly to understand the educational developments, it is necessary that we should consider briefly the changes in the economic conditions of
England, and the resultant social changes, which manifested themselves in the closing centuries of the Middle
Ages.

The date of the pestilence termed the Black Death will
form a convenient starting point from which we may
consider these changes. The factors contributory to the
results, which we propose to describe, may be traced to an
earlier date, but as we are concerned in this chapter with
general tendencies rather than with minute economic
investigations, the year 1349 will admirably serve our
purpose.

The economic effects of the Black Death were particularly evident in the rural districts. The decay of the
manorial system was accelerated; the system of manorial
farming was thrown into confusion and new methods of

---

[1] Sharpe, *Wills*, II., 484.
[2] *Freemen of York*, vol. I., pp. 1, 77, 98—Sur. Soc., No. 96, 1897.

land tenure became imperative; the existing system of
customary regulation was no longer possible. In the
towns the influence of the pestilence was not so marked.
Though individual towns might suffer, yet the relative
importance of towns in the life of the nation was increased, and the way was prepared for that industrial and
commercial supremacy of towns which began to manifest
itself in the early years of the fifteenth century.[1]

In addition to the economic effects, the Black Death
had important educational effects. The mortality among
the clergy was considerable, and consequently the number
of men who were qualified to act as schoolmasters was
appreciably diminished. The reduction in the number of
priests, as a result of the Black Death, is indicated by a
letter which Pope Clement V. wrote in 1349 to the Archbishop of York, and in which it is stated that " in consequence of the Plague, there are not enough priests to
administer the sacraments." [2] A statute of 1362 also
refers to the fact that " the priests be become so very
scant after the pestilence to the great grievance and
oppression of the people." [3]

This diminution in the number of schoolmasters, for
some reason or other, seems to have continued into the
following century. William Byngham, in the petition
which he submitted to the king in 1439 for the purpose of
obtaining permission to found a college at Cambridge for
the training of teachers for grammar schools throughout
the country, stated that, " on the East of the way between
Hampton and Coventry and no further north than Ripon,
no less than seventy grammar schools had fallen into
desuetude because of the scarcity of teachers." [4]

It is also extremely probable that the Black Death contributed considerably to the almost total disappearance of
the French language from the schools. One effect of the
Norman Conquest had been the gradual growth of French
as the spoken language; after the pestilence period, the

---

[1] Meredith : *Econ. Hist.*, p. 81.

[2] *Historical Papers and Letters from the Northern Registers* (R.S.),
p. 401.   [3] 36, Ed., III., c. 8.

[4] *Muniments of King's College, Cambridge* : *Ed. Ch.*, p. 402.

use of the native tongue of the English nation again became common. This is directly evidenced by statements
contained in John de Trevisa's translation of Higden's
Polychronicon. After showing that French was at one
time very prevalent in this country because it was the
language in common use at schools and that the children
of " gentil men " were taught that language from the time
they were " i-rokked in here cradel," Trevisa states that
after the Black Death the knowledge of French had disappeared to so great an extent that "now children of
gramer scole conneth na more Frensche than can hir lift
heele." [1]

The fifteenth century witnessed important changes in
the economic condition of England. The most important
of these changes was connected with the development of
manufactures. At the close of the fourteenth century,
we learn that wool was " la Sovereigne Marchandise and
Jewel . . . d'Angleterre " [2]; a century later, it is said that
" the makeyng of cloth " was " the grettest occupacion and
lyving of the poor people of the land." [3]

Various enactments of the period testify to the growth
of the woollen industry, and to the efforts which were
made by the government to foster and develop it. But
though the manufacture of cloth was the most important
industry, yet it was not the only form of industrial
occupation. Before the close of the fifteenth century,
the manufacture of silk had been established in London,
coal mining was carried on to a considerable extent, the
manufacture of beer had been instituted, the making of
bricks had been renewed, guns were being made, and
ship-building was making progress. [4]

The development of manufactures naturally brought
about changes in the organisation of industry. Owing to
the operation of the principle of division of labour, new
crafts came into existence, and these, in their turn, were
also sub-divided into other new crafts. Gradually, all the
various classes of the industrial world—the artisan, the

[1] *Op. cit.*, II., 157.   [2] *Rot. Parl.*, II., p. 246.
[3] *Ibid.*, V., p. 274.   [4] Abram : *Social Life in England*, Ch. 1.

manufacturer, the middleman, and the merchant—began to emerge. As a result, the " rude beginnings of a factory system" manifested themselves,[1] and there are even traces of a movement which resembles a modern strike.[2]

These changes in the industrial system necessarily exerted a powerful influence upon the agricultural industry, which previously had been the principal occupation of the people. The Black Death had been responsible for a great diminution in the number of agricultural labourers, and as a result, it was scarcely possible to find sufficient labour for the cultivation of the soil. This scarcity of labour was intensified by the fact that employment in the manufacturing industries proved to many a more attractive form of occupation than service on the land. The Central Government took steps with the object of compelling people to work on the land, and an attempt was even made, as we shall see in a subsequent chapter, to prevent agricultural labourers from sending their children to school. Thus in the reign of Richard II., it was enacted that any person who was engaged on agricultural labour up to twelve years of age, was to be compelled to remain at that occupation during the remainder of his life.[3]   Other Acts of Parliament, with a similar object, were passed in 1406 and 1444.[4] This repressive legislation failed to secure its purpose, as the steady flow of labour from agriculture to manufacture continued.

The increasing scarcity of labour led naturally to the gradual substitution of sheep farming for the cultivation of wheat, a development to which the growth of the cloth industry necessarily contributed. The demand for wool by the English manufacturers of cloth increased to so great an extent that sheep-farming gradually became more profitable than the cultivation of the soil and, as a result, the enclosure movement, which began to set in during the closing years of the fourteenth century, made such progress that, during the fifteenth century, there occurred

[1] Green : *Life in an Old English Town*, p. 278.
[2] Abram : *Social England*, p. 13.
[3] *Rot. Parl.*, III., 501.   [4] *Ibid.*, III., 601-2, V., 113.

" the greatest of those agricultural changes which have in successive ages swept over this country—the transition from arable to pasture farming." [1]

Even more important than the industrial changes were the commercial changes, which occurred during the fifteenth century. These arose out of the development of English foreign trade with its natural effect upon the growth of a shipping industry. The records of the time show that English merchants visited all the civilised maritime countries of Europe, notably Holland, Zealand, Flanders, and the shores of the Baltic. Trade was also carried on with Iceland, Spain, Portugal, the countries of Southern Europe, and, in spite of the Hundred Years' War, with France.

These developments in manufactures, in agriculture, and in commerce naturally necessitated changes in financial matters. In the earlier part of the Middle Ages a system of barter had been common. Such a system could not continue under the new order of things. Not only did the use of money for facilitating international exchange become common, but money began to be employed for capitalistic purposes instead of being hoarded or used for unproductive military purposes.

These various changes could not occur in the economic life without producing important effects in the social life of the community. One of the most important of these resulted from an appreciation of the power of wealth. Formerly, rank and birth had been the main mark of distinction between one man and another. Apart from high birth, the Church had previously been the only avenue by which a man of ability could attain to a position of importance. Under the new condition of things, the possession of wealth proved to be a passport to social recognition, and the old ideas of status and class began rapidly to disappear.

The social standing thus gained by men of wealth naturally hastened the decline of the Feudal System; the failure of the Feudal System involved the decay of

[1] Abram, *op. cit.*, p. 30.

chivalry, which was closely associated with it. Outwardly chivalry continued to flourish, but the tournaments which now took place were held for political purposes on occasions of pomp and show, and not with the object of effecting a training to war.

The closing century of the Middle Ages not only witnessed the rise of the capitalist class, but it also saw the rise of the middle class, which has been described as the "most noteworthy feature in the history of social life in England in the late fourteenth and the early fifteenth century."[1] The various changes in the economic conditions had made it possible to acquire wealth through successful trade, and abundant evidence exists that the merchant class was both numerous and was held in high esteem. Socially, these men seem to have ranked with squires and in consequence " Merchaundes and Franklonz, worship fulle and honourable, they may be set semely at a squyers table."[2]

The educational development of a country is closely connected with its social and economic progress, and it is necessary clearly to bear in mind the economic changes of the fourteenth and fifteenth centuries if we are properly to understand the educational adjustments which resulted.

[1] Abram, *op. cit.*, p. 96.
[2] *Manners and Meals*, p. 189.

CHAPTER II.

THE RISE OF THE UNIVERSITIES. [1]

It is possible to trace a rapid advance in the intellectual life of England after the eleventh century. Among the contributory factors may be mentioned the restoration of social and political order, resulting in the greater security essential for intellectual life, and the influence of the Crusades. The Crusades were not only a sign of the re-awakened energy of Europe but were also a cause of increased intellectual activity and change. Those who took part in the Crusades were brought in contact with new people and new ideas; new interests were created, and a more human conception of the world developed. More-over, the deeds of the Crusades supplied new material for historical literature, and stimulated the romantic element in life and thought. The intellectual effect of the Cru-sades was manifested in every department of literary activity; the number of books written was greatly in-creased; studies of law, medicine, and theology received greater attention; scholastic philosophy manifested itself, and the universities came into being. Of these effects, the development of scholasticism and the rise of the univer-sities are closely connected, and are of special importance for our present purpose.

[1] The subject of the origin and development of the English uni-versities has been so fully treated by other writers, notably by Mr. Bass Mullinger and Dr. Hastings Rashdall, that it has only been dealt with here to the extent strictly necessary for the thesis with which we are concerned.

THE RISE OF THE UNIVERSITIES.   133

The development of that system of thought known as scholasticism may be traced from the subjects taught in the medieval schools. These subjects were the Trivium,[1] and the more advanced Quadrivium.[2] The ordinary text-books of the age (of which the chief were founded on the works of five authors—Orosius, Martianus, Boethius, Cassiodorus, and Isidorus) enable us to estimate what was known of these subjects of instruction. Music included little more than the rules of plain song; arithmetic was discussed chiefly with reference to the mystical interpretation of numbers; geometry consisted of a few propositions from Euclid without demonstrations; astronomy, together with arithmetic, found its way into the curriculum chiefly because these subjects supplied the means of finding Easter.

The Trivium was the real basis of the secular education of the period. Grammar included both the rules formulated by Donatus and Priscian and the study of a few of the classical writers of ancient Rome. " Under the head of rhetoric, the treatises of Cicero, such as the ' De Oratore ' and the pseudo-Ciceronian ' Ad Herennium ' were largely read. The elements of Roman Law were often added, and all schoolboys were exercised in writing prose or what passed for prose."[3] The most prominent and important of the subjects of secular instruction was Dialectic or Logic. The student of this subject had at his disposal richer material than in most other branches of secular knowledge. Rashdall instances the translations by Boethius of the " De Interpretatione " and the " Categoriae," as well as the "Isagoge " of Porphyry.[4] It was this concentration on Dialectic by minds whose chief interest was theology that paved the way to that philosophic system known as scholasticism. From its nature, it is scarcely possible to define scholasticism, but its meaning may be understood by considering the ground on which theological statements were based. For some centuries, such state-

---

[1] Grammar, Rhetoric, Dialectic.
[2] Music, Arithmetic, Geometry, and Astronomy.
[3] Rashdall, *Univ.*, I., p. 36.   [4] *Ibid.*, p. 39.

ments were required to be accepted merely on the authority
of the Church. By the eleventh century, heretical views
had crept in which could scarcely be dealt with so sum-
marily. The stimulation of intellectual interests, due to
the Crusades, made it necessary that theological beliefs
should be carefully formulated and defended by intellectual
weapons.

The history of scholasticism falls into two fairly distinct
periods. Among the great names associated with the first
period are Anselm, "the last of the great monastic
teachers," Roscellinus, William of Champeaux, and Abelard, "the true founder of the Scholastic Theology." [1]
The second period which extended from the beginning of
the thirteenth century to the Renaissance was the period
of the culmination of scholastic thought and its consolida-
tion into a system. The "great schoolmen" include
Albertus Magnus, a Dominican who has been described
as "the great organising intellect of the Middle Ages,"
Thomas Aquinas, famous as the scholar who brought
scholasticism to its highest development by harmonising
Aristotelianism with the doctrines of the Church, and two
Englishmen, both of whom were Franciscan friars, Duns
Scotus, and William of Occam.

The intellectual activity of the schoolmen was connected
mainly with questions of interpretation. Original investigation was scarcely attempted. The form adopted was
that of commenting upon Aristotle or the Church Fathers,
and the method employed was that of discussion and dispute, conducted according to recognised logical methods.
At an early date, a question which was considered of
primary and fundamental significance began to be discussed
—the nature of universals. Stated briefly, the problem is :
have the universals a substantial existence of their own, as
the realists claimed, or, are they merely conceptions in the
mind, as the nominalists maintained ? This philosophical
problem was bound up with such questions as the reality
of the Church, of the State, of the Trinity, of the Sacraments. Was the Church a "reality," or was it merely the

[1] *Ibid.*, p. 42.

name of certain individuals who professed a certain allegiance? Was the State a "reality," or simply a name? Such questions as these serve to illustrate the passionate interest taken in the matter by the medieval world of learning.

It was under the stimulus of this interest in dialectic that certain schools connected with cathedrals or monasteries became famous in the later eleventh century and the beginning of the twelfth. Prominent among these was Paris, as the reputation of its master, William of Champeaux, attracted scholars to it from many parts. Abelard was one of the students who had been drawn to Paris by the fame of its school, but before long he openly combatted the teachings of its masters and determined to open school for himself. On account of the principle of the licensing of schools and of teachers, this was a matter difficult of accomplishment, but the difficulties were temporarily overcome, and Abelard is later found as the deputy master of the Cathedral School. Fresh difficulties arising, Abelard resumed his studies, this time under Anselm at Laon. Later he returned to Paris, and lectured as a duly authorised master in the schools of Notre-Dame. His reputation spread rapidly, and Abelard became supreme in the intellectual capital of Europe. In 1118 occurred his rapid and terrible downfall occasioned by his liaison with Heloise. In every attempt which he made after this to regain his position, he was met by fierce and relentless opposition especially from Bernard of Clairvaux. Twice he was condemned for heresy, in 1121 and 1141; his persecution being due, not so much to definite heretical opinions as to the general spirit and method of his teaching. Abelard may be regarded as the best exponent of his time of that method which applies the test of reason to all established beliefs and opinions. Though he was defeated personally at the Council of Sens, yet the movement which had been associated with his name continued.

Forces that tended to make Paris one of the most important cities of transalpine Europe were in operation at this time; hence the stream of pilgrim students to Paris, which set in in the days of Abelard, continued for at least

one and a half centuries.[1] At this time, too, the tendency
for those who had interests in common to associate in
some form of "gild," was everywhere prevalent. It was,
therefore, only natural that wherever a concourse of
masters or students was found, the necessity soon arose
for some form of organisation, which would serve to pro-
tect their common interests. Though these organisations
came into existence without any express authorisations,
yet from such beginnings the universities of the Middle
Ages originated. The circumstances, which contributed
to the formation of a medieval university were therefore
twofold : (1) the existence of a cathedral school, or monastic school, which had attained eminence, and (2) the
formation of a gild, either of masters, or of students, or
of both. Special circumstances led to the selection of the
original university centres. One of these circumstances
was the specialisation of the learning of the time. A mass
of learning and tradition on subjects of interest to man
and essential to his welfare, had grown up in a particular
locality. Students who desired to possess themselves of
this knowledge were attracted to the place. Thus, the
schools at Bologna developed into specialised law schools
about 1100 to 1130 ; Salerno became famous for the study
of medicine ; Paris became celebrated as the main centre
of scholastic philosophy.

It must be noted, however, that the term "universitas"
was not the common appellation for one of the higher
schools ; the earliest specialised name was "studium" or
"studium generale"—a term that Denifle has traced back
as far as 1233. At the outset, no restriction upon the
establishment anywhere of a "studium generale" existed,
but by the latter half of the thirteenth century this unre-
stricted liberty came to an end. The idea gradually grew
that the erection of new "studia generalia" was a papal
or imperial prerogative ; hence in 1224 the Emperor
Frederick II. founded a "studium generale" at Naples ;
in 1229 Gregory IX. established one at Toulouse, whilst
in 1244 or 1245 Innocent III. founded a "studium

[1] Rashdall, *Univ.*, II., p. 60.

generale " in the Pontifical Court itself.[1]   In 1292 even
the old universities—Bologna and Paris—received formal
recognition of their existence by Bulls of Nicholas IV.
" From this time, the notion gradually gained ground that
the ' jus ubique docendi ' was of the essence of a ' studium
generale,' and that no school which did not possess this
privilege could obtain it without a Bull from Emperor or
Pope."[2]

Turning to the question of the origin of the University
of Oxford, it may be noted that though many mythical
origins trace the existence of the university to a very early
time in the history of the country, yet, in fact, Oxford did
not become known as a centre of learning until the twelfth
century.   The earliest definite reference, which has been
traced so far to the existence of any school at Oxford, dates
to some time in the decade 1110-1120, when Theobald of
Etampes is described as a "Master of Arts at Oxford."[3]
Apparently, Thurstan, Archbishop of Canterbury, had referred to Theobald the question whether monks could
legally impropriate churches and tithe.   His reply was in
the negative on the ground that the monk was one who
had retired from the world, and " by choosing the monastic
habit and putting the world aside had judged himself unworthy of the dignity of an ecclesiastic."[4]   This provoked
an anonymous reply which incidentally contains the statements that Theobald held a scholastic post of some importance.   " You, yourself, a nobody, are you not said to
have taught as a master sixty or one hundred clerks, more
or less?[5]"   This statement supports an hypothesis that
the schools at Oxford must have been flourishing at the
time.

A new era in the development of Oxford may be traced
from C. 1135 when Robert Pullen, a theologian, lectured
there.[6]   Then, at a date between 1145 and 1150, the jurist
Vacarius, " a Lombard by birth, an upright man and a law-
yer," was teaching Roman Law somewhere in England.[7]

[1] Rashdall, *Univ.*, I., p. 10.   [2] *Ibid.*, p. 72.
[3] *Oxford Historical Society : Collectanea*, II., p. 153.
[4] *Ibid.*, p. 105.   [5] *Ibid.*, p. 156.   [6] *Ibid.*, p. 159.
[7] *Rob. de Monte, Chron. ed. Migne*, Vol. CLX., p. 466.

At some time or other he also taught at Oxford and is stated to have been the first to teach Roman Law in that city.[1] The university must be regarded as being fully in existence by 1189, as Giraldus Cambrensis lectured there about that date on "Ireland" to "all the doctors of the different faculties and such of their pupils as were of greater fame or note" on one day, and to the "rest of the scholars" on another.[2] After this date, the references are numerous and conclusive.

Two main theories have been advanced to account for the rise of a "studium generale" at Oxford. One group of writers[3] connects its origin with some one or other of the conventual schools at Oxford. By analogy with the origin of the European universities which are considered "primary," they suggest that the Church was the foster-mother of the university, and that the earliest schools were those in connection with St. Frideswide and the abbeys of Oseney and Eynesham. The other theory (advanced by Rashdall) connects the rise of a university at Oxford with a migration from Paris, which is supposed to have occurred in or about the year 1167. In support of this hypothesis it is pointed out that about that date Henry II. (who was then engaged in a conflict with his Archbishop, Thomas Becket) required "that all scholars be compelled to return to their country or be deprived of their benefices."[4] Rashdall also points out that from this time onwards we hear of sermons being preached expressly for "clerkes from various parts of England."[5]

Both of these theories are open to objections. The evidence in favour of a migration is based upon a series of assumptions; if a migration of this character really occurred it is difficult to account for the silence of all the English chroniclers on an event which must have appealed to the imagination; no record is available of any clerk

---

[1] *Gervasius Cantuar., Actus Pontificum Cant.*, ed. Stubbs, Vol. II., p. 384.

[2] *Giraldus Cambrensis:* ed. Brewer, Vol. I., pp. 72, 73.

[3] Mullinger, pp. 80, 81, Brodrick, p. 3, Laurie, p. 236.

[4] *Materials for the Life of Becket,* ed. Robertson, VII., p. 146.

[5] Rashdall, *Univ.*, vol. II., p. 342.

who left Paris on account of the edict, or of any clerk going from Paris to Oxford. On the other hand, it must be admitted that the theory of gradual development is also open to objection. It is vague and indefinite as to details of the growth of the " studium generale "; no authoritative explanation is given for the independent position of the early Oxford masters, and for their freedom from all immediate ecclesiastical control.

The question of the relationship of the university to the Church needs careful consideration. A great deal depends upon the account of the origin of the university which is accepted. If it is maintained, that from the time of its origin, it was under ecclesiastical supervision, then it is difficult to account for the spirit of independence which was manifested during the period that immediately preceded the Legatine Ordinance of 1214. However, by that ordinance ecclesiastical control was definitely asserted; the scholars were made subject to the jurisdiction of the Church, and the position of chancellor was established—probably to mark the subjection of the masters to episcopal control.[1]

The chancellor of the university was, at first, merely the representative of the bishop possessing only such powers as were delegated to him. As long as Robert Grosseteste was Bishop of Lincoln, the relationship between the university and the bishop was most harmonious. Soon after his death, however, disputes began to arise between the two authorities.[2] The details of the conflict may be omitted here; the fact that needs to be noticed is, that in connection with the dispute, the chancellor (though in theory a representative of the bishop) becomes identified with the interests of the university. Four years later we find the chancellor exercising the power of excommunication on his own responsibility, a power which was subsequently confirmed by the Archbishop of Canterbury.[3] The Archbishop also took the part of the chancellor in a

[1] *Munimenta Academica* (R. S.), I., 2.
[2] See Rashdall, *Univ.*, II., 419-421.
[3] *Munimenta Academica* : I., 39, 40.

dispute with reference to the exercise of certain privileges, which arose between the university and the bishop in 1280; the bishop was practically compelled to yield on all the points in dispute. From that time onwards, the chancellor was in practice independent of the bishop.[1] The last phase of the struggle between the bishop and the university is concerned with questions arising out of the confirmation of the election of the chancellor. The dispute first arose in 1288 and recurred with successive elections. The question was finally settled in 1368 when the Pope decreed that the confirmation of the chancellorship by the Bishop of Lincoln might be dispensed with.[2] Ever since that date, the university of Oxford has enjoyed the power of electing and confirming its highest honour without reference to any ecclesiastical authority.

An important event in the history of the university occurred in 1209. The murder of a woman by a scholar led to two or three of the scholars being hanged by the townsmen with the tacit consent of the king. "On this nearly 3,000 clerks, masters, and scholars alike, left Oxford, not a single one of the whole university remaining. Some of them went to study the liberal arts at Cambridge, some to Reading, but the town of Oxford was left empty."[3] Oxford remained practically destitute of scholars till 1213 when the townsmen humbled themselves, an event contributed to by King John's submission to the pope. Rashdall states that the ordinances issued by the papal legate in 1214 constituted the first official recognition of the university which has come down to us.[4]

By this time Oxford had become a recognised centre of learning and had attained to such importance that its opinion on disputed matters was highly esteemed. Thus, in 1252, Henry III. submitted to the university the question in dispute between Raleigh, Bishop of Norwich, and himself; Archbishop Boniface of Canterbury went to Oxford

---

[1] Rashdall, *Univ.*, II., 424.
[2] *Munimenta Academica* (R. S.), I., 228, 229.
[3] *Chron: Roger of Wendover* (R. S.), II., p. 51.
[4] See also *Munimenta Academica*, pp. 1-4.

in 1252 in order to make known to the university the conduct of the Bishop of Winchester, so that through the influence of the university the news might be spread throughout the world of learning.

Passing next to the university of Cambridge, we find that its origin also is a matter of doubt. Here, again, two theories have been advanced—one which upholds the idea of gradual development, the other which bases the origin of the university on a migration from Oxford.

The earliest extant reference to a university at Cambridge dates from 1231. In that year Henry III. sent a communication to the sheriff of Cambridge, authorising him to take action in the case of " divers disorderly and incorrigible clerks " . . . and also " divers criminals in the guise of clerks pretending to be what they are not." [1]   Evidence also exists to show, that in 1276, the Bishop of Ely defined the jurisdiction of the Chancellor of Cambridge University, the Archdeacon of Ely, and the Grammar Schoolmaster.[2]

The early history of the university of Cambridge, like that of its sister university, is largely a history of disputes, of feuds between the townsmen and the burgesses, of quarrels between the opposing "nations," of disputes arising out of disorders on the part of the students, and of the struggles for independence of ecclesiastical control. The last of these is the only one which concerns us here, but as the matter is so fully dealt with elsewhere [3] it will suffice to point out here that the growth of freedom from episcopal supervision was slower at Cambridge than at Oxford. It was not until the close of the fourteenth century that the power of the Bishop of Ely to decide internal disputes between the chancellor and the masters, and between the various faculties and to hear appeals from the chancellor, was dispensed with, and it was not until 1432 that the university was entirely independent of the direct control of the Church.

In this chapter we have given the various hypotheses

[1] *Cal. Close Rolls*, 15 Hen. III., p. 586 ; *Ed. Ch.*, p. 149.
[2] Cooper : *Annals of Cambridge*, I., 56.
[3] Mullinger, 288, 290 ; Rashdall, II., 549, 550.

which have been advanced, to account for the origin of the English universities. Whichever hypothesis we accept, the important fact is that a class of teachers gradually grew up in this country, and that these teachers, influenced by the gild spirit which was particularly strong in the twelfth century, ultimately formed themselves into a gild which became strong enough to gain recognition. It is impossible to point to any definite charter or document by which this was effected; it is not until the university was in actual being and admitting to its degrees those teachers whom it considered qualified for admission, that we have any real evidence of its existence.

The development of the universities had three important effects, so far as the special subject of this investigation is concerned.

(1) The licensing of teachers passed out of the hands of the Church and was undertaken by the universities. With the general recognition of the universities, the licence to teach which was considered valuable was the licence granted by the university and not that of bishop or cathedral chancellor. It is interesting to note that the power of conferring degrees now possessed by the Archbishop of Canterbury is a relic of the power which he formerly exercised of granting recognition to teachers in the diocese of Canterbury.

(2) The theological schools of the chancellor gradually ceased to exist, as the theological teaching at the universities began to develop. Since specialised teaching centred itself at the universities, and as the demands upon the time of the chancellor became more insistent with the increasing work of the cathedral and diocese, together with the fact that the teaching function of the chancellor was gradually being lost sight of, so it came about that the theological schools of the chancellor became of less and less note until at last it is impossible to trace any real signs of their existence.

(3) The universities, and not the Church, became recognised as the centre of the intellectual activity of the country. As we have shown, the Church was originally regarded as the custodian of all interests which might be

conceived of as intellectual. "Religion and letters" were considered to be identical; gradually the principle of division of labour manifested itself, and the Church was left to concern itself with its spiritual functions, leaving to others the care of those matters which may be considered as exclusively relating to the development of the intellectual well-being of man.

CHAPTER III.

GILDS AND VOLUNTARY ASSOCIATIONS.

At an early stage in the development of the English nation there became manifest a tendency for persons who possessed certain interests in common, to organise themselves into a species of club or association. To such associations the term "gild" has been applied. Mr. Toulmin Smith maintains that the early English gilds came into existence for the purpose of joining all classes together, for assisting the needy and promoting objects of common welfare. These gilds were inspired by religious motives, and were closely associated with the Church.[1] The first three English gilds of which records are now available, are those of Abbotsbury,[2] Exeter, and Cambridge. The earliest available statement of the purposes of gilds appears to date from 858, when the Archbishop of Rheims, in giving particulars of the gilds of that date in France states that they "unite for offerings, for mutual assistance, for funeral services for the dead, for alms, and for other deeds of piety."[3] The number of these associations rapidly increased. Brentano states that at one time during the Middle Ages, there were twelve gilds in Norwich and Lynn respectively. Gallienus counts 80 gilds in Cologne, Melle about 70 at Lübeck, and Staphorst over 100 at Hamburg.[4] Gilds were so very numerous and so marked a characteristic of the social life of the period that it is not to be

---

[1] Toulmin Smith : *English Guilds*, p. XIV.
[2] Dates from the eleventh century.
[3] *English Guilds*, p. lxxxi.   [4] *Ibid.*, p. lxxxiii.

wondered at if exaggerated statements were made as to
their number. "In Norfolk, the most densely populated
county of England, Taylor is said to have counted no less
than 909 gilds, and in Lyme Regis alone 75." [1]

It is important to remember that the most prominent
characteristic of gilds was the religious element. As a
matter of fact it is impossible to conceive of any social
organisation which was entirely divorced from religion,
existing at this time. Hartshorn states "No matter what
the specific *raison d'être* was of any gild, it necessarily had
a religious aspect. Each had its patron, in whose honour
candles were burnt. Some had as their object the aid of
poor scholars, the maintenance of schools or the payment
of schoolmasters, the presentation of religious plays, as
even to-day that of Oberammergau in South Bavaria, or
the repair of roads and bridges. The Frith Gilds had rules
for helping the gild-brothers in every need. The statutes
of the English gilds frequently mention loans made to
needy brothers with but one condition, that it be repaid
when there was no more need of it." [2]

Before proceeding to consider the educational significance
of the gilds, we may refer here, for the sake of convenience,
to two subsequent developments of the gild movement—
the gild-merchant and the craft gild.

In the years which immediately followed the Conquest
the more important towns of England suffered greatly,
partly on account of the chances of war and partly on
account of the policy of castle-building associated with the
English kings of the Norman period. However, as soon as
the Norman rule was firmly established, an internal peace,
such as had not been previously enjoyed , was secured for
this country ; the towns, consequently, made rapid progress,
and in one commercial centre after another a gild-merchant
was set up. [3]

A gild-merchant came into existence for reasons similar
to those which brought into being the religious and social

[1] *Two Thousand Years of Gild Life*, p. 106.
[2] Hartshorn : *Study of Voluntary Associations in Europe*, 1100-
1700, p. 12.   [3] Ashley : *Econ. Hist.*, I., p. 70.

gilds. There was a consciousness of a community of interest, and a common object which could be secured more effectively through co-operation. It is foreign to our purpose to attempt to examine critically the origin of gilds-merchant, and so it must suffice for us simply to state that their history has been traced back to corporations of merchants and artisans, which existed in Rome under Numa Pompilius, and which were termed "collegia" or "corpora opificum et artificium." [1] In France, the first gild-merchant was formed in 1070, and came into existence for the purpose of protecting the free townsmen against the oppression of the nobility. Gradually their number increased, and with the growth in their number their purposes became more clearly defined, and the custom developed that the gild should receive formal recognition from recognised authority. Thus the traders of Paris formed the "Hanse des marchandes de L'eau" and the privileges they claimed were confirmed by Louis VII. in 1170.

The first purposive mention of a gild-merchant in England dates from C. 1093.[2] The general line of development seems to have been that such associations gradually came into existence at various centres; they defined their purposes, their claims, and the exclusive privileges they desired. When a favourable opportunity presented itself, they secured from the king or other lords the grant of a charter which was necessary for legal recognition. Henry I. seems to have been the first king who systematically granted these charters; during the reign of Henry II., charters were obtained by many of the principal towns of the country, notably Bristol, Durham, Lincoln, Carlisle, Oxford, Salisbury, and Southampton; in each of these charters the recognition of a gild-merchant was an important feature.[3] Ashley writes: "In spite of the paucity of evidence, the existence of a merchant gild can be definitely proved in 92 towns out of the 160 represented at one time or other in the parliaments of Edward I. No considerable

---

[1] Gasquet: *Précis des Institutions de l'Ancienne France*, II., 233-243.   [2] Gross, *Gild Merchant*, p. 32. n. 1.   [3] *Ibid.*, pp. 37 *seq.*

name—with two exceptions, namely London and the Cinque Ports—is wanting from the list. It is impossible not to conclude that every town, down to those that were not much more than villages, had its merchant gild. This fact of itself is enough to prove the great part it must have played in the town life of the time." [1]

A third type of gild—the craft gild—begins to appear early in the twelfth century. These gilds become more numerous as the century advances. In the thirteenth century they are a common feature of industrial life. The circumstances which gave rise to the origin of gilds of this character are still in dispute. The popular view is that the gilds-merchant came into existence, first of all, in order to secure protection against the feudal lords. Gradually they became exclusive and so rendered necessary the formation of craft gilds for the protection of the common interest of those who were engaged in crafts in opposition to the interests of those who were concerned in the sale of the commodities produced.

Ashley points out the difficulties involved in this theory,[2] and suggests an alternative hypothesis. He states that originally membership of the town assembly was bound up with the possession of land within the town boundaries, and that membership of the gild-merchant was practically identical with citizenship. In course of time, there came into existence a class of landless inhabitants of the town, who consequently could not be regarded as burgesses, and therefore could not be admitted into the gild-merchant without the payment of fees. Some of these people would turn to handicrafts. The same spirit of community of interest which produced the religious gilds and the gilds-merchant respectively would also operate to induce the craftsmen to form a guild of their own.[3]

The first craft gilds which come into notice, were those of the weavers; the weavers of London date their charter from the reign of Henry I. There were also gilds of weavers in London, Lincoln, and Oxford in existence before 1130.[4]

---

[1] Ashley, *Econ. Hist. I.*, p. 72. [2] *Ibid.*, p. 79.
[3] *Ibid.*, p. 80. [4] *Ibid.*, p. 81.

Just as the gild-merchants obtained a legal recognition of their existence, so the craft gilds also in course of time received recognition from the king, whilst those gilds which were not authorised were amerced as " adulterine." No attempt, however, seems to have been made forcibly to dissolve the adulterine gilds.

The only definite provision contained in these charters of recognition was, that no one within the specified area should follow the craft unless he were a member of the gild. This provision, however, involved the imposition of conditions of membership, and a general power of supervision over the members of the craft.

We are concerned in this thesis only with the educational significance of the gilds ; hence we need not discuss further their economic aspects. It is, however, interesting to note that the social value of these gilds survived their economic functions. Judged from an economic standpoint, they began to degenerate during the fourteenth century. They had come into existence in response to the impulse arising out of a vague sense of the value of association of membership in a corporate body ; against this spirit, the sense of individualism, which particularly manifested itself at the time of the Reformation, asserted itself and ultimately triumphed.

The gild system was of considerable importance from the point of view of education. We may note that the gild spirit manifested itself among teachers. They organised themselves into a form of association. Gradually, they laid down the conditions of membership of their body. In course of time, legal recognition was received from pope or emperor or king, and the embryo university gradually obtains general recognition. "The rise of the universities," says Rashdall, "was merely a wave of that great movement towards association which began to sweep over the cities of Europe in the course of the eleventh century."

We may next note that the gilds we have described proved to be the means by which the growing social consciousness of the nation evinced an interest in education. The term " social consciousness " is vague, and is capable of being variously defined.   The origin of the phenomenon may be traced to the gregarious instinct, when the resulting consciousness is merely the "consciousness of kind," to use Professor Giddings' phrase.   A higher stage of development is reached when an individual member of a group recognises the relationship in which he stands to the other members of the group, together with a realisation of the duties which such relationship involves.   A still higher degree of development of the social consciousness results when the group as a whole recognises that it possesses social duties and responsibilities.

We may trace roughly four stages in the growth of a national social consciousness.   First, there is the stage at which the individual cares only for himself, a second stage is attained when family claims are recognised, a still higher stage when a duty to a social group is perceived, a fourth stage is reached when social organisations are formed for discharging more effectively social duties.

The earliest of these social organisations in point of time—and the most important from the standpoint of education—were the social gilds.   These gilds, as we have shown, were essentially religious.   They were a manifestation of what may be described as a "democratic religious impulse."   The term is admittedly clumsy, but it denotes a desire proceeding from the people to carry out religious duties apart from the official requirements of the Church.   On a large scale we can see this force at work in the movements initiated by St. Francis of Assisi and St. Dominic respectively, or, to take a more recent example, in the Methodist revival in the Church of England.   To return to our period, we find that men and women, impelled by a spirit of association, formed themselves into a gild in order to carry out more effectively their religious and social responsibilities.   We particularly wish to note that, in some cases, these responsibilities included the making of provision for the education of the young.

It is not possible yet to indicate the full extent to which these social gilds made such provision, but it is probable that they did much more for education than is commonly

conceived.   Our chief means of discovering what was
accomplished, is by an examination of the returns which
were made when the gilds were being dissolved.   From an
examination of these records, we are led to the conclusion
that, after an association or gild had been formed for
specified purposes the general method of procedure was,
that the members of the gild made certain payments to
secure the services of one or more priests, who were to
devote themselves to carrying out such objects as the gild
had in view.   These aims frequently included the keeping
of a school.

We can find this illustrated by a consideration of the
information available[1] with regard to the Gild of Kalendars,
Bristol.   In 1318 the Bishop of Gloucester issued an in-
quisition as to the rights and privileges of this gild.   The
report of the commissioners states that " the beginning of
the fraternity exceeds the memory of man," and it was
established that it existed before the Conquest.   The gild
was formerly called the " Gild or Brotherhood of the
Community of the clergy and people of Bristol " and
received a licence from the Cardinal-legate Gualo in 1216.
Among other works carried out by this association is
mentioned the maintenance of " a school for Jewes and
other strangers, to be brought up and instructed in chris-
tianitie under the said fraternitie."[2] Here then is established the fact that gilds, as apart from churches,
conceived themselves as responsible for education at least
as early as the thirteenth century.

We may also consider the Palmers Gild which was
founded in 1284.   This gild supported a " warden, 7
priestes, 4 singyng men, twoo deacons, syx Queristers, . . .
32 pore Almes people " as well as a schoolmaster to teach
Latin.[3]

As additional instances of schools which were established
through the agency of gilds we may enumerate the school
at Maldon which is supposed to have been founded by the

---

[1] *Bristol Little Red Book*, fol. 82-3.   Ed. by W. B. Bickley for
the Corporation of Bristol.

[2] Toulmin Smith, *op. cit.*, p. 280.   [3] T. Smith, *op. cit.*, p. 198.

Fraternity of the Assumption of the Virgin,[1] and the school at Raleigh, which was founded by the Trinity Gild in 1388-9.[2] The chantry certificate relating to this gild states that " lands were put in feoffement by diverse and sundry persons to ffinde a prieste . . . to teach a fre schole their to instruct youth. Which seide town of Raleigh is a very greate and populous towne." [3] These instances readily demonstrate the democratic appreciation of education, and that among the purposes for which people joined themselves together in voluntary association was the provision of facilities for education.

We pass to an important topic when we consider the work of the gilds-merchant and the craft gilds. If we can trace any educational activities on the part of these associations then we can trace the origin of the interest taken by the civic communities and by organised labour respectively in education.

Though it is an error to conceive of the gild-merchant as identical with the municipal authority yet as Gross points out the distinction between them was barely perceptible. Now, if we can show that the gilds-merchant in some cases supported schools, then we have shown the interest of the civic community (as apart from the work of the Church) in educational matters. The only specific case of a gild-merchant taking an interest in education which we have been able to find is that of the gild-merchant of York. The chantry certificate of the city

---

[1] Maldon Court Rolls, Dr. Andrew Clark in *Essex Rev.* XV., p. 146.

[2] *Gild Certif.*, 57.

[3] Other instances are Prittlewell, *Cal. of Pat.* 1476-85, p. 34 ; Thaxted, *ibid.*, p. 227 ; Finchingley, *Chantry Certif.*, XIX., 13 ; XX., 19 ; XXX., 17. The connection of a grammar school at Ipswich with the Corpus Christi Gild is shown by the *Ipswich Court Bk.*, Brit. Mus. Ad. MS., 30158 fol. 34; at Winchester with the Corpus Christi Gild, Brit. Mus. Ad. MS. 24435 fol. 153 b. ; at Louth with St. Mary's Gild, Church-wardens' Accounts of the Parish Church, 1533 in R. W. Goulding's Court Rolls of the Manor of Louth. The gild of the Blessed Mary founded a school at Wellingborough in 1392 (Pat. 16, R. II., pt. ii., m. 29, 30). See also p. 161 infra. ; gilds and chantries are so closely connected that it is difficult to draw a definite line of demarcation in some cases.

of York states that "the governour and kepers of the mysterye of merchauntes of the cytie of York," co-operated in the foundation of a hospital which had as one of its objects the maintenance of "two poore scolers." [1]

Our difficulty in dealing with this topic arises from the fact that the "founder" of schools mentioned in the available documents is so very frequently not the real founder. It is for this reason that Edward VI., Queen Mary, Queen Elizabeth, and others have been regarded as the founders of schools which cannot in any real sense be attributed to them. In the case of gilds, we find the names of certain persons mentioned as the founders of various charitable trusts without a distinct statement of the fact that they were acting simply as representatives of an association.

We are, therefore, driven to consider the full objects of the charitable trust under discussion. If the objects mentioned are mainly religious or eleemosynary, then it is probable that the trust created was ecclesiastical in its origin, but if these characteristics are not definitely present, or if the purposes specified by the trust include duties which should form a part of the duty of the municipality, then we consider that the gild should be classed under the municipal gilds.

With this object in view, we may examine the chantry certificate for the town of Wisbech, one of the fullest and most complete of the chantry certificates and one which would have well served as a model to others who had the duty of drawing up these returns. In answer to the question of the founder of the gild, the certificate states the gild was founded in the reign of Richard II. by certain clerks whose names are specified "with other mo." This last phrase is significant as it supports the inference that the gild was formed by the citizens of the town, but that the clergy, as the natural leaders of the community, would append their names first to the document.

[1] *E. S. R.*, II., 283, 284.

The objects of the gild, which are specified in this return may be briefly summarised—

(1) The maintenance of Divine service.
(2) Prayer for the souls of the faithful departed.
(3) Maintenance of a Grammar School.
(4) Relief of the Poor.
(5) Maintenance of almshouses.
(6) Repair of the church.
(7) Maintenance of dykes " for the sauftie bothe of the sayd towne and 14 other towns." [1]

Here we have an effective enumeration of the duties of a municipal authority, and when the date of the founding of the gild and the absence of any legislation which compelled the carrying out of such tasks are considered, then the duties specified point to a high degree of social responsibility having been attained at Wisbech at this date. We may, therefore, conclude that the gild at Wisbech was not simply a religious association for purely spiritual purposes, but was an association of the civil community for municipal purposes. That these purposes included certain religious functions is not a matter of surprise. Religion in the Middle Ages was more closely interwoven with the life of the people than it is to-day.

The gild existing at Stratford-on-Avon seems also to have been a citizen gild. Its origin can be traced to a date earlier than 1295. In the return made to the sheriff's proclamation in 1389, it was stated that the gild was begun at a time beyond the memory of man. The affairs of the gild were administered by two wardens who were elected by the members. The main objects of the gild seem to have been the maintenance of priests to celebrate divine service and the keeping of a grammar school. [2]

The chantry certificate of the city of Worcester further supports the contention that the municipal authority provided a school. The certificate referred to was signed by the master of the gild, two bailiffs of the city, an alderman, a citizen, and two stewards of the gild. It is notable that not a single ecclesiastic signs the return. The school,

[1] *E. S. R.*, II., pp. 20-22.   [2] Toulmin Smith, *English Gilds*, p. 221.

moreover, was kept in the Gild Hall of the city, and was
apparently a successful one, as there were over 100 scholars
who attended it.   This return, coupled with the fact that
Worcester was a cathedral city, raises several points of
interest which it is hoped that future research will eluci-
date.   From whom was the necessary authority to establish
the school derived ?   Was the school the outcome of a dispute between the civic and the ecclesiastical authorities, as
was the school at Exeter in the seventeenth century ?
Prima facie, facts certainly point in that direction.[1]

We have quoted the case of these three gilds to support
the contention that it had begun to be realised that it was
the duty of the municipal authorities to make provision for
education.   A full investigation into this subject can only
gradually be made, as the various municipal documents are
examined. with this object in view.   We may, however,
note here that the " Gilds of Holy Trinity and St. George "
in Warwick were responsible for the continuance of Warwick School,[2] that the burgesses of Coventry seem to have
maintained a school,[3] that a grammar school at Ipswich
was founded by the municipality,[4] that the civic authorities
at Bridgenorth were in charge of the schools,[5] and that the
school at Plymouth was founded by the corporation.[6]

The work of the craft gilds for education still remains
to be considered.   We find that at Shrewsbury, the
Drapers' Gild, the Mercers' Gild, the Shermen Gild, the
Shoemakers' Gild, the Tailors' Gild, and the Weavers'
Gild, each supported a chantry priest at either the church
of St. Mary, or St. Chad, or St. Julian.   By analogy with
other cases, we assume that these chantry priests acted as
schoolmasters to the children of the members of the craft
gilds.[7]

A new departure was instituted when a successful member of a craft gild bequeathed money to it for the purpose of endowing a school at a specified place.   Thus, in

---

[1] *Ibid.*, pp. 203-205; *E. S. R.*, 267-268.
[2] *Hist. of Warwick Sch.*, p. 95.   [3] *Coventry Leet Book*, I., 101.
[4] Redstone, *Trans. Royal Hist. Soc.*, N.S., XVI., p. 166.
[5] *Hist. MS.*, Com. X., App. IV., 425 ; *Ed. Ch.*, 439.
[6] Carlisle : *Endowed Gr. Schs.*, I., 335.   [7] *E. S. R.*, II., 180-184.

1443, John Abbot made the Mercers' Craft the trustees of a school to be founded at Farthinghoe in Northampton-shire.[1] A school at Lancaster was founded in 1469 by John Gardyner, burgess and probably miller, of Lancaster.[2] In 1487, Sir Edmund Shaw or Sha "cytezen goldsmyth and alderman and late mayer of the citee of London" devised money to the Goldsmiths' Company for the purpose of establishing and maintaining a grammar school at Stockport.[3] Then, in 1505, another Lord Mayor, Sir Bartholomew Read, founded by will a school at Cromer and also appointed the Goldsmiths' Company as trustees.

The general conclusion we seem to be justified in drawing from these instances is, that the value of education was being more and more realised, and that the duty of making provision for education ceased to be regarded as exclusively the function of the Church. This does not mean that there existed an idea that education was not still regarded as something which should be closely associated with the Church, but rather, that the idea had originated and developed that organisations which represented the municipality and handicrafts respectively, also possessed a responsibility in making provision for the education of the young.

In addition to making provision for schools, the gilds were important educative forces in other directions. They constituted one of the most important agencies for breaking down social exclusiveness and "in transmitting social manners and ideals from a narrower to a wider circle." As the gilds had increased in number, so they increased in wealth and importance. They built halls which were the external testimony to the position they occupied. At times they entertained kings and other magnates of the realm and admitted persons of standing to honorary membership. Music and the drama were also fostered by the gilds. Several gilds existed in England[5] with the object of developing an interest in music. The performance of

[1] P.C.C., 34 Luffenham, p. 269.
[2] Copy of will in *Duchy of Lancaster Misc. Bks.*, 25 fol. 19.
[3] *E. S. R.*, II., 144.   [4] *E. S. R.*, II., 144.
[5] *E.g.* Douze Gild, Feste du Pin.

dramatic representations was a common feature of the gilds.

Membership of the gilds also proved to be a training for the performance of the duties of citizenship and of society, as the members of such organisations were brought into intimate relation with a wider circle than their own individual interests would furnish, and they would be required to take part in the transactions of the business of the gild. It is noteworthy that gilds were organised on a social basis, and that women were admitted to the membership of the merchant and craft gilds, as well as to that of the social and religious gilds. Thus at Kingston, the Gild of the Blessed Virgin Mary was founded in 1357 by 10 men and 13 women,[1] and the Gild of Corpus Christi founded in the same town in 1338 included 18 women among its 43 founders.[2] The sons and daughters of these founders might be admitted to membership of the gilds without initiatory payment.[3] Again, at Coventry, the names of women as well as men are mentioned in the Charter of the gild merchant.[4]

One other point may be mentioned, a point which has been described as "the most important educational service of the gilds." This service was the growth of the system of apprenticeship. Originally, apprenticeship was merely a private contract between an individual and his prospective master. With the development of gilds, regulations specifying the conditions of such apprenticeship began to be issued, e.g. the master craftsman might teach his art to as many members of his family as he pleased, but he could only have one other apprentice. Moreover, from the outset, the apprentice was under the special protection of the gild which was practically a court of appeal in the event of any serious complaint on the part of the apprentice. Important, however, as this topic is, a further consideration of it would lead us beyond the special limits of our investigation.

---

[1] Toulmin Smith : *English Gilds*, p. 115.
[2] *Ibid.*, p. 155.   [3] *Ibid.*, p. 160.
[4] *Ibid.*, p. 226. For other instances see pp. 179, 194, 287, and Hartshorn, *op. cit.*, p. 15.

CHAPTER IV.

CHANTRIES.

One of the characteristics of the ecclesiastical life of this country during the fourteenth and fifteenth centuries was the institution of chantries; altogether upwards of 2,000 of them are known to have been founded during the period. As chantry priests played an important part in connection with the provision of educational facilities in England, the topic of chantries calls for careful consideration.

A chantry may be defined as a foundation for the purpose of providing a priest who shall pray daily, primarily for the soul of the founder, and secondly for the souls of all Christian people. The earliest instances of chantries definitely recognised as such, date from the latter part of the thirteenth century. The "Taxatio of Pope Nicholas" only mentions two; one which was founded by Hugh of Lincoln, who died in 1225, and the other which existed at Hatherton in the county of Warwick. The custom gradually grew, but did not become common until the fifteenth century, the period in which the number of such institutions largely increased.[1]

The idea of offering prayers for the souls of the faithful departed was not a new one. The practice is at least as old as the institution of the Christian faith, and is a custom which is perfectly natural to those who believe in the immortality of the soul, and a state of future personal existence. It had also been a custom, " from time im-

---

[1] Cf. Page, *Yorkshire Chantries*, Surtees Society.

memorial," that prayers for the souls of the founders were
regularly offered up in religious houses and other ecclesiastical foundations.   A list of donors and benefactors was
carefully preserved, and prayers for their good estate were
offered up for them while they were living, and for the
repose of their soul after death.   Thus, the "Catalogus
Benefactorum" of St. Albans Monastery, with its detailed
account of every benefaction, is still preserved in the
British Museum.[1]   The distinctive mark of a chantry was,
that it was expressly founded for the apparently selfish
purpose of making financial provision to secure the
prayers of others for the future well-being of the soul of
the founder.

But though this selfish and personal purpose may have
been the dominating thought in the case of some foundations, yet it is probable that it was not the only purpose
of the majority of these institutions.   The primary point
to be remembered is that it is a laudable desire to wish to
perpetuate one's memory, especially if the memorial should
take a form which will benefit the social community.   In
the fourteenth and fifteenth centuries, the prevailing
method of doing this was by establishing a chantry.

In attempting to investigate the reasons why chantries
were founded, we are faced from the outset with a difficulty.   The licence in mortmain, by which permission to
assign lands for the support of the chantry priest was
effected, scarcely ever mentions any other object for the
memorial except the chantry itself, whilst the foundation
statutes, which enumerate more specifically the purpose of
the founder, are very rarely forthcoming.

An example will make this clear.   In 1414 Langley,
Bishop of Durham, issues to himself an episcopal licence
empowering the founding of the chantry he wished to
endow.   In the same year he, in his temporal capacity as
Earl of a County Palatine, grants a licence in mortmain,
authorising the chantry to hold lands and to make the
chantry priest a corporation.[2]   Both these records are

---

[1] See also *Liber Vitae* of Durham, Surtees Society.
[2] *E. S. R.*, I., 53.

available, but in neither of them is there any reference to the *real* objects for which the chantry was to be instituted. Consequently, if further information was not forthcoming, we would assume that all that the Bishop of Durham had done was to evince, in some tangible manner, his belief in the efficacy of masses for the departed.

Fortunately, however, there still survives a lengthy deed,[1] dated the day after the licences to which we have referred were granted. This deed specifies that the priests appointed to the chantry were to keep schools of grammar and of song respectively, in addition to offering prayers for the souls of the departed, and that a certain sum of money out of the proceeds of the chantry was to be used for the purpose of distribution to the poor.[2]

Strangely enough, we are dependent for information as to the purposes of chantries, on the instrument which brought about their destruction. In 1545 was passed the Chantries' Act of Henry VIII. This Act began by reciting that many people had been appropriating the endowments of "Colleges, Freechapelles, Chantries, Hospitalles, Fraternities, Brotherhoods, Guilds and Stipendarie Priests," and that the expenses of the war with France and Scotland had been heavy, and then proceeded to give authority to the king to send out commissioners to investigate the nature of these endowments and afterwards to take such action as he thought fit.

· "Apparently, Henry had a fit of reaction after the Chantries' Act was passed. He is reported to have dissolved Parliament with a speech in which he said he was going to reform chantries, not destroy them."[3]

A new Chantries' Act was passed in the first parliament of Edward VI.[4] The object of this Act was essentially different from that of its predecessor. The preamble to the Act specified that it was thought that "a great part of superstition and errors in Christian religion has been brought into the minds and estimation of men, by reason

---

[1] See *V. C. H.*, Durham, I., p. 371.   [2] *E. S. R.*, II., 60.
[3] *Ibid.*, p. 65.
[4] *Stat. of the Realm*, IV., pt. I., p. 24.

'of their ignorance of the very true and perfect Salvation
through Christ Jesus, and by devising and fancying vain
'opinions of purgatory and masses satisfactory to be done
for them which be departed, the which doctrine and vain
'opinion by nothing more is maintained and upholden than
by the abuse of trentals, chantries, and other provisions
made for the continuance of the said blindness and
ignorance."

The Act proceeded to vest in the Crown " all Colleges,
Free Chapels and Chantries "; " all Lands given for the
finding of a Stipendiary Priest for ever "; " all payments
made by corporations, gilds, fraternities, companies, or
fellowships, of mysteries or crafts."

A commission was to be issued, under the Great Seal,
to investigate the origin and purpose of the various
chantries, etc., to arrange for the continuance of such
charitable objects as they deemed necessary, and to
assign pensions to the incumbents whose office was
abolished.

It is to the returns that were made to these commissioners that we are mainly indebted for a knowledge of
the objects and purposes for which the chantries were
provided. The purposes, which are most frequently mentioned, are:—

  1. Provision of a priest to teach children freely.
  2. Assistance of the parish priest.
  3. Care of bridges.
  4. Relief of the poor.
  5. Provision of almshouses.
  6. Repairing the parish church.
  7. Equipping soldiers.
  8. Repairing the sea walls.
  9. Provision of lamps.
  10. Provision of dowries.

Of these purposes, the most important was probably the
provision of an endowment to enable a priest to keep a
school. Mr. Leach, who was the first writer to realise
fully the significance of the chantries in relation to the
provision of facilities for education, states that " in all

259 schools appear in these records."[1] Two or three examples will serve to make clear the nature of the provision for education made by the chantry bequests.

"Wymborne.

Cantaria Margarite Comitisse Rychemond et Derbie matris Domini Regis Henrici Septimi.

Memorandum that this was foundyd to the intent that the incumbent thereof should say masse for the solles of the founders and to be a Scolemaster, to teche frely almanner of childern Gramer within the said College."[2]

"The Parish of Newland.

Gryndoures chauntrye.

Foundyd to Fynde a preste and a gramer scole half free for ever and to kepe a scoller suffi:ientt to teche under hym contynually."[3]

"Towcester.

The Colledg or Spones Chauntree.

Founded to mayntene 2 Prestes, beyng men of good knoweledg. The one to preach the Worde of God. And the other to kepe a Grammar Scole."[4]

Our task is now that of attempting to interpret the reasons why the chantries were founded.

We must give due weight to the ostensible object, which must be also regarded as the primary one. A widespread belief in the efficacy of prayers for the departed existed; unfortunately, there also prevailed, apparently, a belief in the value of hired prayers. It must be clearly realised that it was for the purpose of securing prayer for the

---

[1] *Eng. Schs. at Ref.*, p. 91.   [2] *E. S. R.*, II., 56.

[3] *Chant. Certif.* XXI., No. 24, Trans. Bristol and Glouc. Archael. Soc. VI.

[4] *Chantry Certif.*, No. 36. This chantry was founded by Letters Patent. (Pat. 27, Henry VI., pt. 1, m. 27). Further Letters Patent were granted in 1451. (P. C. C. Luffenham, p. 278). The chantry patent does not say anything about the school. See also *E. S. R.*, II., 146.

welfare of the living and the repose of the departed soul'
that these chantries were founded.

But, side by side with this main object, there also existed
in the minds of the majority of the founders a desire to
benefit the community. We have already enumerated the
main directions in which it was proposed to effect the
benefit. The remarkable fact is, that, in as many as 259
cases, education was regarded as of such importance that
specific arrangements were made to provide for it.

In a large number of cases, it is specified that the
proceeds of the chantry are to be devoted to the support
of a priest to assist the parish priest. We venture to
suggest that there is to be found here a clue to the
explanation of many of the unspecified trusts and particularly of those in which it is expressly laid down that it
was a purpose of the chantry to provide a priest for
educational purposes. We have previously shown that
it was a recognised duty of the parish priest to keep a
school. The growth in the duties of a parish priest would
make it difficult for him effectively to discharge this
function; possibly, in some cases, he might be incapable
of doing so; moreover, the progress of the universities
had caused the profession of a teacher to be a definite one.
Our analysis of the social structure[1] has enabled us to
realise that the increasing complexity of our industrial
system and the social and economic changes which occurred,
had caused education to be more necessary and to be
esteemed more highly. The "Paston Letters" show that
the dependents and servants of great households were able
to read and write.[2] Thorold Rogers states that the accounts
of bailiffs afford proof that they were not illiterate, and he
also evidences that artisans were able to write out an
account.[3] We must not, however, assume that a knowledge of reading and writing, though probably widespread,
was universal. It is interesting to note that, of the twenty
witnesses who were examined in connection with the enquiry touching Sir John Fastolf's will in 1446, eleven

[1] Bk. III., Ch. 1.   [2] *Paston Letters*, V., 21.
[3] *Work and Wages*, p. 165.

were described as "illiterate"; they consisted of five husbandmen, one gentleman, one smith, one cook, one roper, one tailor, and one mariner. The description "literatus" was applied to seven persons, two husbandmen, two merchants, and one whose occupation was not specified.[1] The two remaining witnesses could both read and write.

Our hypothesis is, that the founder of the chantry desired to be of assistance, both to the parish priest himself, and to the children of the parish. He sought to accomplish this by leaving lands to provide an endowment to support a priest who would relieve the parish priest of his duties as a teacher. This hypothesis would also help to explain the gradual disappearance of the parish priest as the responsible master of the parochial school, a disappearance which would be accelerated by the increasing recognition of the fact that teaching was a specialist function, to be entrusted to a person expressly appointed for that purpose.

A most important and noteworthy feature of some chantries is, that in certain parishes they were founded by the inhabitants themselves, for the express purpose of providing educational facilities. We do not imply that the religious element was lacking, or that the doctrine of the efficacy of prayer for the departed was lightly held. In all probability, the religious motive was a strong impelling force. For our present purpose, the significant fact is, that in certain communities some of the inhabitants founded chantries with the provision of facilities for education as the expressed object. We have been able to trace the origin of the following schools to the action of the inhabitants, but it is not claimed that the list is exhaustive.

Aldeborough.	Wragby.
Basingstoke.	Bridgenorth.
Deritend.	East Retford.
Eccleshall.	Lancaster.

---

[1] *Paston Letters*, IV., 237-44; Abram: *Social Life in England*, p. 189.

Eye.	Truro.
Gargrave.	Coggeshall.
Northallerton.	Thaxted.
Odiham.	Prittlewell.
Staunton.	Berkhampstead.
Thirsk.	

We may now consider the establishment of typical cases.

BASINGSTOKE.

The school at Basingstoke was founded "by the decision of the inhabitantes at the begynnyng."[1] Apparently, the inhabitants of the town had formed themselves into a gild called the "Brotherhood of the Holy Ghost" for this special purpose. Their school can be traced back to 1244, and is the earliest school of which at present we have any knowledge, whose origin may be attributed to the enterprise of the inhabitants.

NORTHALLERTON.

This school existed before 1321, as is evidenced by the fact that in that year the master was appointed to the school by the prior of Durham.[2] It was founded by "certen well disposed persones—for the better bringinge up of the children of the towne."[3]

DERITEND.

The existence of this school can be traced back as far as 1448, and is due to the enterprise of "the inhabitans of the same hamlet cauled Deretende."[4]

LANCASTER.

The first available reference to a school at Lancaster occurs in a deed in the priory chartulary which dates from the reign of Henry III.[5] The school was "ordeyned and founded by the Mayor and burgesses of Lancaster."[6]

[1] *E. S. R.*, II., p. 89.
[2] *Yorkshire Schools*, II., pp. 60, 61.
[3] *E. S. R.*, II., p. 286.
[4] *E. S. R.*, II., p. 228.
[5] *S. M. E.*, p. 177.
[6] *E. S. R.*, II., p. 123.

Aldeborough.

" Having no foundacion but presented by certain feoffees of severall landes gyven by syndry persons of the said paroch." [1]

Eccleshall.

"The enhabitants of Eccleshall did among themselfes, without incorporacion, erect two Gyylds . . . and one of the same priestes have alwais kept a scole and taught pore mens children of the same parishe freely." [2]

East Retford.

" Founded by the predecessors of the bailiffs, burgesses, and Commywalts of the said towne." [3]

Gargrave.

" Founded by the inhabitants there." [4]

Odeham.

" Founded of the devocion of the inhabitantes . . . to the intente to teche children gramer." [5]

Staunton.

"Founded by the parishenours there upon theyr Devocion." It was the purpose of this chantry that the priest appointed should assist the incumbent " in his necessitie"; apparently this assistance included the teaching of "many pore mens chylderne." [6]

Wragby.

"There is no foundacion of the same but certen landes and tenementes purchased by the parishioners to th'entente . . . to teach chyldren in the saide paroche." [7]

[1] *E. S. R.*, II., p. 297.   [2] *E. S. R.*, II., p. 201.
[3] *E. S. R.*, II.. p. 160.   [4] *E. S. R.*, II., p. 302.
[5] *E. S. R.*, II., p. 89.   [6] *E. S. R.*, II., p. 100.
[7] *E. S. R.*, II., p. 297.

TRURO.

"Of the Benyvolence of the Mayer and burges of the saide Towne to fynde a preste for ever to mynyster in the parish churche and to kepe a scole there."[1]

As we have stated, these instances we have quoted cannot claim to be exhaustive. They are examples which are available, and they serve to indicate the noteworthy fact that a consciousness of the value of education existed among the inhabitants of many towns and villages in England in the Middle Ages. The question is sometimes raised, whether these schools were elementary or secondary schools, or whether some of them might be classed as elementary and others as secondary.[2] The question is quite irrelevant. The distinction between elementary and secondary education is entirely a modern one. In fact, it is difficult, even now, to determine the meaning of these terms. If we regard the elementary school as one in which the chief academic aim is to teach the children to read and write English, and to work elementary problems in arithmetic, and a secondary school as one in which the classical languages form an important part of the curriculum, then we have set out the difference between two types of schools which were prevalent during the greater part of the eighteenth and nineteenth century; but this distinction is inapplicable to the fourteenth and fifteenth centuries. The chantry school did not attempt to teach English, but Latin, as Latin still continued to be the language of the Church of this country. Of the 259 instances of chantry schools which Mr. Leach has collected, 193 of them he regards as grammar schools; the remaining schools he classes either as song schools or as elementary schools.[3] The distinction is quite unnecessary. The chantry schools were simply the parochial church schools, which were now supported by a separate endowment, and taught by a priest who was practically able to devote his whole time to the work, instead of being

---

[1] *E. S. R.*, II., p. 39.   [2] Cf. Leach, *E. S. R.*, I., p. 91.
[3] *E. S. R.*, I., pp. 91, 92.

under the control of the parish priest who, in many cases, would scarcely be able to set aside a definite part of each day for the work of teaching.

We have pointed out that the child who attended these church schools was required previously to have obtained a knowledge of the alphabet at least. If Colet was setting out the current practice in the statutes which he drew up for St. Paul's School, even more knowledge was required antecedent to admission, as he states that "the master shall admit these children as they be offirid from tyme to tyme; but first se that they can saye the catechyzon, and also that he can rede and write competently, else let him not be admitted."

In the case of some of the chantry schools, express arrangements were made for elementary teaching. Thus, the bell ringer at Glasney was required to teach the ABC as a part of his duty[1] at Brecon; at Chumleigh it was expressly stipulated that the ABC was to be taught by the chaplain;[2] at Launceston it was stipulated that an old man chosen by the mayor was to teach the alphabet.[3] Then, the chantry priest at Newland was required to provide "meate, dryncke, clothe and all other necessaries" to one of his scholars who, in return, was to assist with the teaching of the little ones.[4]

The provision of exhibitions to assist in supporting poor scholars at schools and universities was also a purpose of some chantries. Thus, at Brecon, twenty poor scholars were to receive 24/- each annually:[5] at Chumleigh, a part of the proceeds of the chantry was employed to support "a lyttle childe who goythe to scole, and hathe no other profyttes towardes his fynding and sustentacion"[6]; at Eton "70 scollers, 13 poore children and 10 choristours" were to be supported:[7] at Stamford "the Revenues and proffyttes thereof hathe byn convertyd only to the use of . . . an infant of the age of 13 or 14 yeres, towards his exhibicion at Schole."[8] Other instances of the provision of

[1] *E. S. R.*, II., p. 31.   [2] *E. S. R.*, II., p. 317.   [3] *E. S. R.*, II., p. 34.
[4] *E. S. R.*, II., p. 78.   [5] *E. S. R.*, II., p. 317.   [6] *E. S. R.*, II., p. 47.
[7] *E. S. R.*, II., p. 15.   [8] *E. S R.*, II., p. 152.

school exhibitions are to be found in the chantry certificates
relating to Houghton, Hull, Lincoln, Lyme Regis, Newland, Rotherham, Sullington, Thornton, Winchester, and
Wotton-under-Edge.

Turning next to the chantries which were employed for
the purpose of supporting students at the universities, we
find that the return to the chantry commissioners, which
relates to the chantry of North Wroxall, states that: "the
sayd Incumbent is a student in Oxforde, but no prieste;
and, ferthermore, a verey pore man, havynge no parentis,
or any other lyvinge to kepe hym to scole." [1] In the return
for the chantry at Norton are given the names of 8 men,
among whom the proceeds of the chantry are shared, so as
to enable them "to studye at the universite." [2] Other
instances of chantry foundations for the purpose of supporting university students are those of Asserton, Calne,
Crediton, Denton, Dorchester, Holbeach, etc.

The analysis of the chantry foundations we have given,
serves to illustrate our contention that, not only was there
a growing appreciation of education but that there also
existed a growing sense of the responsibility of the community, or of representative members of the community,
to make provision for education, and that the responsibility
for making this provision did not rest on the Church
alone. At the same time, the Church was alive to the
necessity of emphasising the duty of the clergy to interest
themselves in education, as is evidenced by the canon
promulgated at the Convocation of Canterbury in 1529
which intimated to the "rectors, vicars and chantry priests
that when divine service is done, they shall be employed in
study, prayer, lectures or other proper business, becoming
their profession: namely, teaching boys the alphabet,
reading, singing, or grammar; and on three days in the
week, for three or at least two hours a day, shall, in the
absence of some lawful hindrance, occupy themselves in
reading Holy Scriptures or some approved doctor. And
the ordinaries shall make diligent inquiry about this in
their visitations, to the end that they may severely chastise

[1] *E. S. R.*, II., p. 258.   [2] *E. S. R.*, II., p. 320.

and punish lazy priests, or those who spend their time badly." [1]

This canon was practically reiterated by the Royal Injunctions of 1547, which prescribed that "all chauntery priests shall exercise themselves in teaching youth to read and write, and bring them up in good manners and other vertuous exercises." [2]

The practical effect of the Chantries' Act of 1547 was that it put an end to the educational provision which the founders of the chantries had made This was not contemplated by the Act. On the contrary, the Act gave to the commissioners "full power and authoritie to assigne and shall appoynte, in every place where guylde fraternitye, the Preist or Incumbent of anny Chauntrye in Esse . . . oughte to have kepte a gramer scoole or a preacher" for the continuance of such school.[3] The usual practice of the commissioners was to vest the chantry lands in the Crown, and to make a Crown charge of a certain annual sum, equivalent to the stipend which the teacher of the grammar school was then receiving. But as the value of money has now decreased to so considerable an extent, and the value of land has so enormously increased, the practical effect of this legislation, as we have indicated, was the disendowment of the educational provision which had been made by the founders of gilds, colleges, and chantries.

[1] Wilkins, *Concilia*, III., p. 722 ; *Ed. Ch.*, pp. 444-6.
[2] Wilkins, *Concilia*, IV., p. 3.
[3] *Statutes of the Realm*, IV., pt. 1, p. 24.

CHAPTER V.

MONASTICISM AND EDUCATION IN THE LATER MIDDLE AGES.

The problem of the relation of monasteries to education in the later Middle Ages is an obscure one. On the one hand, there is the popular opinion (which is followed, generally, by uncritical writers) that the monasteries afforded the main means of education at this time; on the other hand, the tendency of modern research into the nature of the educational work of the monasteries is to maintain that no general work for education was accomplished by them.[1] Effectively to set out the work of the monastic orders for education, it is advisable to consider separately: (I.) schools in connection with monasteries, (II.) almonry schools, (III.) the education of girls, (IV.) the education of the novices, (V.) the monks and university education, (VI.) education and the mendicant orders.

I. Schools in connection with Monasteries.

As a general principle, it may be assumed that a school existed in connection with every large monastery. The connection consisted in the fact that these schools were maintained by the monasteries, and that the master was appointed by the monastic authorities. These schools

---

[1] Cf. Coulton: *Monastic Schools of the Middle Ages.* Leach: "*Monasteries and Education*" in *Cyclopaedia of Education.*

fall into one or other of two classes: they were either founded by the monasteries, or they were handed over to the monasteries, which acted as trustees for their maintenance, by their real founders. It is not easy in every case to determine whether the school was the property of the monastery or was merely held on trust by them. The commissioners, entrusted with the task of securing the dissolution of all the monasteries, did not attempt to do so. The property held by the monastery was confiscated, regardless of whether the property was held on trust for other purposes, or was indisputably the possession of the monastery. Among the earliest of the schools which we know of, as being connected with monasteries are St. Albans, c. 1100;[1] Christ Church, Hants, c. 1100;[2] Thetford, c. 1114;[3] Huntingdon, c. 1127;[4] Dunstable, c. 1131;[5] Reading, c. 1135;[6] Gloucester, c. 1137;[7] Derby, c. 1150;[8] and Bedford, c. 1160.[9] We know that Bourne School was in connection with the monastery, because the Abbot of Bourne possessed the patronage of the school.[10] For a similar reason, it can be shown that the school at Bury St. Edmunds was monastic.[11]

Passing next to give instances of the schools which were held by monasteries as trustees, we may mention Lewes Grammar School, which was founded in 1512 by the will of Agnes Morley, who provided that the appointment of the schoolmaster should be vested in the prior of Lewes.[12] We note, too, that Peter of Blockesley gave possessions to the prior and convent of Coventry in trust for the school.[13] The school at Bruton may also be quoted as

[1] *Gesta Abbatum Mon. S. Albani*, I., p. 72.
[2] *V. C. H., Hants.*, II., p. 251. [3] *V. C. H., Suffolk*, II., p. 303.
[4] *P. R. O.*, antiq. H., No. 8.
[5] Charter Roll, 2 Henry III., pt. 1, m. 27.
[6] *V. C. H., Berks.*, II., p. 245. [7] *Rot. Chart*, p. 7.
[8] *V. C. H., Derbyshire*, II., p. 209.
[9] *V. C. H., Bedfordshire*, II., p. 152.
[10] *V. C. H., Lincs.*, II., p. 450.
[11] *Statutes of the Abbey of Bury St. Edmunds*, Harl. MSS. 1005, fol. 95 b. The list of schools in connection with monasteries does not profess to be exhaustive. [12] *V. C. H., Sussex*, p. 413.
[13] Exch. K. R. Misc. Bks. (P. R. O.), fol. 21, 168, 178, 180. *V. C. H.*, Wars, II., p. 319.

illustrative. By an endowment deed of 1519,[1] various possessions were given to the Abbot of Bruton, subject to the condition that he should provide a schoolhouse and house for the master, and also pay him £10 a year. The returns to the chantry commissioners from Bruton[2] state that, after the dissolution, the schoolmaster was no longer called upon to work, but as he had had a pension assigned him, he was able "to lyve licentiously at will than to travaile in good education of yewthe" "to the greate Decaye as well of vertuous bringing uppe of yewthe of the saide shire in all good lernyng, as also of the inhabitants of the Kinges said town of Brewton."

II. ALMONRY SCHOOLS.

An essential duty discharged by the inmates of a monastery was the offering of divine worship. Effectively to discharge this duty, the voices of boys were required in addition to those of the men. It is difficult to determine when this custom originated; probably it was adopted first of all in the collegiate churches, and then subsequently imitated by the monasteries. The earliest available reference to an almonry school in this country is in connection with St. Paul's Cathedral. A statute which dates c. 1190 refers to the boys of the almonry, and informs us that they lived on alms.[3] Lincoln, York, and Salisbury are three other secular cathedrals, at which choristers, who were boarded and lodged together, were maintained.

The boys, who acted as choristers in the monasteries, were lodged at the outer gate; they were clothed, fed, and educated at the expense of the monks. The earliest reference available to almonry boys in monasteries dates from 1320, when it was provided that "no scholar shall be taken into the almonry unless he can read, and sing in the chapel, and is ten years old."[1] The earliest statutes which set forth the work of the almonry are those of St.

---

[1] See *Somerset and Dorset Notes and Queries*, III., p. 241.
[2] *Chant. Certif.*, 42, No. 172.
[3] Sparrow Simpson, *Registrum Statutorum*, pt. VIII., ch. 6.
[4] *Ed. Ch.*, p. xxxii.

Albans, and date from 1339. They include the following regulations.

(1) " Let the boys be admitted to live there for a term of five years at the most, to whom this period suffices for becoming proficient in grammar.

(2) No poor scholar shall absent himself from the Almonry without the licence of the sub-Almoner, under the penalty of expulsion until reconciliation.

(3) Whosoever is convicted or notorious for being incontinent, a night walker, noisy, disorderly, shall be wholly expelled.

(4) Immediately on admission, the scholars shall shave an ample tonsure, after the manner of choristers, and shall cut their hair as becomes clerks.

(5) Every scholar shall say daily the matins of Our Lady for himself, and on every festival day the Seven Psalms for the convent and our founders." [1]

In the schedule of the almoner's duties at St. Albans [2] it is stated that the almoner is responsible for the repair of the studies of the monks, and of the grammar schoolhouse in the town. He has also the right of appointing the master of grammar, subject to the approval of the archdeacon. He is entrusted with the general care and supervision of the boys, and for the payment of the stipend of the schoolmaster.

A description of the almonry school at Durham is given in the "Rites of Durham." [3] This account states that "there were certain poor children called children of the Almery, who only were maintained with learning and relieved with the alms and benevolence of the whole house, having their meat and drink in a loft, on the north side of the abbey gate. And the said poor children went daily to school at the Farmary School, without the abbey gates; which school was founded by the prior of the said abbey, and at the charges of the said house."

[1] Reg. Whethamstede, (R. S.), II., 315, trans. Gibbs: *Hist Rec. of St. Albans.*
[2] B. M. Landsdowne, MS., 375, see *V. C. H., Herts.*, II., p. 315.
[3] Surtees Society publication, p. 91.

There is also a reference to this school in the *Valor Ecclesiasticus*[1] which mentions "De magno solario supra tenebatur scola." The same authority tells us that there were thirty poor scholars who attended this school.

The duties commonly undertaken by the schoolmaster of the almonry boys may be gathered from the agreement entered into in 1515, between the abbot of the monastery of Gloucester and the schoolmaster he appointed. The agreement specified that the master was to "teach the art of grammar to all the youthful brethren of the monastery sent to him by the abbot, and thirteen boys of the clerk's chambers; and shall teach and inform five or six or seven boys apt and ready to learn in plain song, divided or broken song and discant, sufficiently and diligently." In addition, the schoolmaster was to sing and play the organ at the monastery services.[2]

Besides the almonry schools in connection with the monasteries at St. Albans, Durham, and Gloucester, to which we have referred, almonry schools have also been traced at Canterbury,[3] Reading,[4] Westminster,[5] Winchester,[6] Bardney,[7] Worcester,[8] St. Mary's Abbey, York,[9] the Carthusian Monastery, Coventry,[10] Coventry Priory.[11]

The examples given support the probability that every monastery supported an almonry school. Admission to these schools was in some cases regarded as a valuable scholarship. This is evidenced by a letter which Queen Philippa wrote to the prior of Canterbury in 1332, and in which she asks for a boy to be admitted into the almonry "to be maintained like other poor scholars of his estate."[12]

It would be an idle task to attempt to estimate the

---

[1] *Op. cit.*, V., pp. 302-3.   [2] *Hist. Mon. Glouc.*, III., p. 290.
[3] *Lit. Cantuar* (R. S. 85), II., p. 464.
[4] *B. M. Add. Chart*, 19641, *V. C. H., Berks.*, p. 243.
[5] *Journal of Educ.*, Jan. 1905. *Ed. Ch.*, p. 306.   [6] *S. M. E.*, p. 220.
[7] *Ibid.*, p. 221.   [8] *Ibid.*, p. 221.
[9] *Early Yorkshire Schools*, I., p. 31.
[10] Sharpe : *Hist. and Antiq. Coventry*, p. 154 n.
[11] Valor. Eccl. (R. C.), III., p. 51. Among the remaining almonry schools were those of Sherborne Abbey, Thornton, Ixworth, Norwich, Ely, Evesham, Furness, Bristol, Tewkesbury, Winchcombe, and Winchester.   [12] *S. M. E.*, p. 218.

value of these almonry schools for national education. We do not possess any definite information as to the number of boys who were educated in this way at each monastery, neither do we know for certain the number of monasteries which provided these facilities. All we can really assert is, that a large majority of the chief monasteries provided board and residence and education for a number of children, who would otherwise be unable to obtain any education. These children would learn to sing and read, and would also master grammar to the extent necessary to proceed to the universities if they desired to do so.

Mr. G. C. Coulton warns us that there was a great temptation for the monastic authorities to neglect the almonry schools. He points out that, in 1520, the visitors found that Norwich Cathedral Priory had cut down its almonry scholars from thirteen to eight, and that in 1526 it was noted at Rushworth that " pueri in collegio non continue aluntur sumptibus collegii sed custodiunt pecora parentum nonnunquam." [1]

III. THE EDUCATION OF GIRLS.

When Robert Aske, in 1536, was endeavouring to justify his rebellion against the action of Henry VIII. in suppressing the monasteries, he stated as one of the good works of these institutions that " in nunneries their daughters (were) brought up in virtue." [2] The education of girls of the higher classes was one of the duties undertaken by some of the convents, but it is difficult to estimate the extent to which this was done. The available refer-

---

[1] Mon. Schs. in Mid. Ages. *Contemp. Rev.*, June 1913. Appendix. As to the number of children in the almonry schools, we may note that there were only three boys at St. Swithun's in 1381-2, five in 1400-1, eight in 1469-70, and none at all in 1484-5. Compotus Rolls . . . of St. Swithun's, 204 n. See also Abram : *English Life and Manners*, p. 207. Leach considers that the total number of boys educated in the almonry schools was 1,000. *S. M. E.*, p. 230.

[2] *Letters and Papers of Henry VIII.*, ed. Gairdner, Vol. XII., p. 405. Coulton, Monastic Schools, *Contemp. Rev.*, June 1913.

ences to the education of girls at convents may be readily
summarised : at the time of the dissolution, there were
from thirty to forty girls being educated at Pollesworth
Nunnery, who were described as "gentylmen's children" [1];
at St. Mary's Nunnery, Winchester, there were twenty-six
girls who are similarly described.[2] A claim has also been
made [3] that girls were educated at Carrow Abbey, Norfolk,
but Mr. Coulton shows that "among all the 280 persons
who are recorded to have boarded with the nuns of Carrow
during forty-six years (an average of six a year), not one
can be clearly shown to be a schoolgirl." [4] The point that
needs to be emphasised is that the question of a nunnery
school, as Mr. Coulton indicates, was at bottom a financial
one.   Convents which were not well endowed found it
necessary to have recourse to some means of increasing
their revenues, and teaching was one of the possible means
of doing so. The early references to schoolgirls in episcopal
registers show that an effort was made either to restrict or
prohibit the practice. The reason of this episcopal opposition was the fear that the institution of a school would
break down the discipline of the convent, and distract the
attention of the nuns. Thus, at Elstow in 1359, Bishop
Gynwell would only allow girls under ten and boys under
six to remain there, because, "by the living together of
secular women and nuns, the contemplation of religion is
withdrawn and scandal is engendered." [5] Very few other
references to the education of girls in monasteries have
been traced so far. Dr. Abram tells us that "In the
Chancery Proceedings it is recorded that 'Lawrens Knyght,
gentleman,' arranged that the Prioress of Cornworthy,
Devon, should have his two daughters, aged respectively
seven and ten, 'to scole' and he agreed to pay her twenty
pence weekly for their meat and drink." [6] In English
literature, the only instance we have been able to discover
is the well-known reference of Chaucer to the Miller's wife.

---

[1] *Dugd. Mon.*, II., p. 363.   [2] *Ibid.*, II., p. 457.
[3] *Ibid.*, IV., p. 69.   [4] Coulton, *Mon. Sch.*, p. 7.
[5] *V. C. H., Beds.*, I., p. 356.
[6] *Social Life*, p. 216.   See also *Early Chanc. Proceed.*, 44/227.

IV. The Education of the Novices.

Abbot Gasquet has written a careful and interesting account of the life of a novice in a claustral school of the fifteenth century.[1] Dealing with St. Peter's Abbey, Westminster, he says, "The western walk was sacred to the novices, whose master took the first place, with the youngest nearest to him. Their method of sitting was peculiar : they were placed one behind the other, so that the face of one looked on the back of his neighbour. And this was always the case, except when there was general conversation in the cloister. The only fixed seats were those of the abbot, prior, and master of novices; the rest were placed according to the disposition of the prior, sub-prior, or novice-master, to whom the care and due order of the cloister were specially committed. There, in the morning after the chapter, and at other intervals during the day, the novices attended to their tasks, and one by one took their books to their master, who either heard their reading himself, or sent them to some other senior for help or instruction."[2]

The "Rites of Durham"[3] also gives us a description of a novices' school. It is there stated that the school was held both in the morning and in the afternoon in the "weast ally" of the cloisters. Boys began to attend these schools when they were seven years of age, and the eldest learned monk acted as their tutor. The novices were fed, clothed, and educated gratuitously. If they were "apt to lernynge . . . and had a pregnant wyt withall" they were afterwards sent to Oxford to study divinity; otherwise, they were kept at their books till they could understand their service and the scriptures, and then became candidates for ordination to the priesthood.

Incidental references to the school of the novices occur in various monastic records. Thus, we learn that when Richard II. held his first parliament in 1378, at Gloucester,

---

[1] *Downside Rev.*, Vol. X., p. 31, *seq.*
[2] *The Old English Bible and other Essays*, p. 227.
[3] Surtees Society, 107, ed. Canon Fowler, p. 91.

he and his court were lodged in the abbey, with the result
that the monks were obliged to have their meals " in the
schoolhouse."[1]   The same chronicler also laments the
destruction of turf in the cloisters, which " was so worn by
the exercises of the wrestlers and ball players there that
no traces of green were left on it."[2]

The Benedictine Statutes of 1334 emphasised the importance of study, and in order that monks might subsequently be fitted to proceed to the universities, it was
decreed and ordained that " in all monastic cathedral
churches, priories or other conventual and solemn places of
sufficient means belonging to such order or vows, there
shall henceforth be kept a master to teach the monks such
elementary sciences, viz. grammar, logic and philosophy."[3]
If, however, a competent teaching monk could not be found
in the monastery, a secular priest was to be appointed for
the purpose who, in addition to his residence, food and
clothing, was to receive £20 a year—a large salary for the
time.[4]

Some records are still available of agreements to teach
between the prior of a monastery and a secular priest. As
an example may be quoted the one made between the prior
of Durham and a priest who covenanted to teach " the
monks of Durham and eight secular boys."   He was
especially to teach " plain song, accompanied song, singing
plain prick note, faburdon, discant square note and counter-
point," and to play on the organ at the monastic services.[5]

Enquiry was also made from time to time to ascertain
whether sufficient attention was being paid to the education of the novices.   Thus, at the visitation of the priory
of St. Peter's, Ipswich, in 1514, the complaint was made
that there was no schoolmaster at the monastery;[6] in 1526,
the monastery was required to provide a master to teach
the novices grammar.[7]

[1] *Hist. Mon. Glouc.*, I., 53.   [2] *Ibid.*
[3] B. M. Cott. Faust., VI. (Durham Priory Register): *Ed. Ch.*,
p. 290.   [4] *Ibid.*
[5] Roger Prior's *Reg.*,V., 261 b.   [6] "Non habeant ludimagistrum."
[7] *Visitations of Dioc. of Norwich* (Camd. Soc.) 1888, ed. Jessop,
pp. 137, 221.

Similarly, among the defects noted by William Warham, Archbishop of Canterbury, at his visitation of the monastery in 1511, was the lack of a " skilled teacher of grammar . . . to teach the novices and other youths grammar." The archbishop emphasised his point by stating that " in default of such instruction it happens that most of the monks celebrating mass and performing other divine service are wholly ignorant of what they read, to the great scandal and disgrace both of religion in general and the monastery in particular." [1] It is interesting to note that a statement is appended to this criticism, intimating that " one of the brethren is deputed to that work and has already begun to do it, and teaches the younger monks daily." [2]

V. THE MONKS AND THE UNIVERSITIES.

Originally, we have seen, the monasteries were the centres of the intellectual activities of this country. The progress of the universities caused a change in this respect, with the result that Oxford and Cambridge gradually became the chief places of theological, as well as other branches of academic study. It then became necessary that the monks should adapt themselves to the new order of things, and arrange that those of their number who showed ability should avail themselves of the opportunities of advanced study which the new centres of learning afforded.

It is not possible to state when monks first went to either Oxford or Cambridge for the purpose of study, but it must have been at a comparatively early date in the thirteenth century, because at a general chapter of the Southern Benedictines held at Abingdon in 1275, it was decided to erect a house at Oxford in which " the brethren of our order who are to be sent from the various monasteries may live properly." [3] It was further resolved that each Benedictine house in the province of Canterbury should contribute for the first year " twopence in every

---

[1] Brit. Mus. MSS., Arundel, f. 69, *Ed. Ch.*, p. 445.   [2] *Ibid.*
[3] *Worcester College*, by C. H. Daniel and W. R. Barker, p. 3.

mark of all their spiritual and temporal possessions according to the assessment of the former lord of Norwich . . .
and in the following years shall contribute a penny a mark
to provide for the said places and other things in the said
chapter."[1] It was also enacted, at the same time, that a
theological lecturer to instruct the monks should be
appointed in every monastery, as quickly as possible.

The first definite mention of monastic students at Oxford
occurs in a letter written by Bishop Giffard of Worcester
to the Chancellor of the University, requesting that " a
doctor in the divine page " might be nominated to instruct
the monks who were in residence.[2] In 1287, a site for the
erection of a college for the monks, which was known as
Gloucester College (now Worcester), was conveyed to the
abbot and convent of Gloucester.[3]

This was not the only college for monks which was established at Oxford. In 1286, the prior and convent of
Durham had purchased land there (which is now the site
of Trinity College) for the purpose of securing further
education for the monks of Durham.[4]

In addition to these institutions, the monks of Christ
Church, Oxford, had a hall of their own as early as 1331.[5]
This they sold to the monks of Westminster, after acquiring a regularly endowed college of their own known as
Canterbury Hall. Canterbury Hall, which was founded
by Simon Islip, Archbishop of Canterbury, in 1362, was at
first intended to be used both by seculars and regulars.
This policy did not prove a success ; .the college was then
used by the regular clergy only, and continued to be used
by them until the dissolution.[6] Other monastic educational establishments at Oxford were the Cistercian Abbey
of Rewley, St. Bernard's College, and St. Mary's College.[7]

Returning to Gloucester College—the most important
of the monastic colleges—we note that the first of the

---

[1] *Chron. Petroburgense* (Camd. Soc., 1849), p. 31, *Ed. Ch.*, p. 197.
[2] Worc. Epis. Reg. Giffard, fol. 206, *Ed. Ch.*, p. 199.
[3] Worc. Ep. Reg. Giffard, f. 429, *Ed. Ch.*, 198.
[4] *Some Durham College Rolls* (Oxon. Hist. Soc., 1896); *Collectanea*, III., 7.   [5] Rashdall, *Univ.*, II., p. 498.
[6] *Ibid.*, p. 499.   [7] *Ibid.*, pp. 478-480.

Benedictine monks to obtain the D.D. degree at Oxford
was William Brock, who achieved that honour in 1298.
The occasion was regarded as important, and a feast,
which was attended by the leading English members of
the order, was held to commemorate it.[1]

A difference of opinion exists as to the normal number
of monastic students who were in residence at Gloucester
College. The editors of " Worcester College" estimate
that there were from one hundred to two hundred students
as a general rule at the college.[2] Mr. Leach denies this,
and considers that the usual number of monks to be
found at the college would be about sixty.[3] In 1537, there
were thirty-two students there.[4] The importance of university education for Benedictine monks was emphasised
by the Benedictine statutes of 1334, which enacted that
"the cathedral churches, monasteries, priories, and other
such places, each of them . . . shall be bound to send out
of every twenty monks one who is fit to acquire the fruit
of greater learning to a university, and to provide each
one so sent with the yearly pension underwritten."[5]

Whether or not this decree was systematically complied
with, we have no means of determining. It is interesting
to note that further action was subsequently necessary,
because, in 1504, John Islip, Abbot of Westminster, complained that " for lakke of grounded lerned men in the
lawes of God, vertue emonges religious men is little used,
religion is greatly confounded, and fewe or noo hable
persones founde in dyvers houses of religion, lakking
lerned men to be the heddes of the same houses to the
high displeasure of God and great subversion of
religion."[6]

In order to deal with this ignorance on the part of the
monks, Henry VII. conveyed lands for the endowment of
three chantry priests at Westminster Abbey. It was
resolved that "the said Abbot, Prior, and Convent and

[1] *Hist. Mon. Glouc.* (R. S.), I., 34.   [2] *Op. cit.*, p. 26.
[3] *V. C. H. Glouc.*, II., p. 341.   [4] *Worcester Coll.*, p. 27.
[5] B. M. Cott. Faust, VI. (Durham Priory Reg.), *Ed. Ch.*, p. 293.
[6] Brit. Mus. MS. Harl., 1498. *Ed. Ch.*, p. 440.

their successours shall provide encrease have and fynd
three moo monkes of the said monastery over and above
the said three monkes contynually and perpetually to be
and contynue scolers in the said Universitie of Oxonford
there to studye in the science of Divinitie." [1]

Dr. Rashdall does not consider that the monastic colleges
were of great importance, either in the history of learning
or of education.   He maintains that the aim of these
colleges was simple and practical, viz. the preparation of a
few instructed theologians who were able to preach an
occasional sermon, and to give an elementary theological
education to the novices.   In addition, a supply of men
capable of transacting the legal business of the convent
was also necessary.[2]   The real services of the monks to
literature lay in the realm of medieval history.   " The
Benedictine monks of this period were, above all things,
men of the world : their point of honour was a devotion
to the interests of the House ; their intellectual interests
lay in its history and traditions." [3]

VI. The Mendicant Orders and Education.

Reference must also be made to the part played in
education by the Mendicant Orders.   St. Francis of Assisi
was a devout and earnest believer in Christianity. Impelled
by a force working in him, he renounced all material and
worldly possessions, and accepted for himself the task of
building up the Church, through the conversion of the
souls of men.   In 1207 he received formal recognition from
Pope Innocent III. ; a band of enthusiastic converts soon
gathered around him, with the single aim of preaching
and ministering to the poor.   " To the poor by the poor.
Those masses, those dreadful masses, crawling, sweltering
in the foul hovels, in many a southern town with never a
roof to cover them, huddling in groups under a dry arch
alive with vermin ; gibbering cretins with the ghastly
wens ; lepers too shocking for mothers to gaze at and
therefore driven to curse and howl in the lazar house out-

---

[1] *Ibid.*   [2] Rashdall : *Univ.* II., p. 480.   [3] *Ibid.*

side the walls, there stretching out their bony hands to clutch the frightened almsgiver's dole, or, failing that, to pick up shreds of offal from the heaps of garbage—to those, St. Francis came." [1]

The Franciscan movement was originally a movement of piety only, and did not contain within itself any intellectual elements. In fact, learning was distinctly discouraged. " Must I part with my books ? " said the scholar with a sinking heart. " Carry nothing with you for your journey " was the inexorable answer. " Not a Breviary ? Not even the Psalms of David ? " " Get them in your heart of hearts, and provide yourself with a treasure in the heavens. Whoever heard of Christ reading books save when He opened the book in the synagogue and then *closed* it and went forth to teach the world for ever." [2]

Almost simultaneously with the founding of the Franciscan movement, St. Dominic realised the necessity of bringing about a moral reformation. His method, however, differed appreciably from that adopted by St Francis. To St Dominic, ignorance and vice were the great evils to be contended against : hence, he formed a community whose purpose it was to instruct the unlearned and to confute the heretic, through the agency of the pulpit. [3] To this community, Innocent III. gave his formal sanction in 1215.

Study was not regarded in the same way by the Friar as it was by the monk. To the monk, study or labour was enjoined as a means for bringing about a subjugation of human passions, or as an occupation for hours that would otherwise be spent in idleness ; the extent to which they became teachers arose out of the exigencies of the times. " Officium monachi non docentis sed plangentis." The aim of the monk was simply the salvation of his own soul ; for the outside world he disclaimed duty or responsibility.

[1] Jessop : *Coming of the Friars*, p. 21.   [2] *Ibid.*, p. 22.
[3] See Denifle : *Constitutiones des Predeger*—Ordene vom Jahre, 1228—in Archiv. fur Litt. und Kirchenges des Mittelalters, 1885, p. 194.

Seclusion and separation from all but the members of his own community, were regarded as the great instruments by which his object was to be achieved. To the friar christianity appeared as a means by which the regeneration of society could be effected. Hence the cause of the difference in the attitude towards education. It was not an occupation for idle hours, or a prophylactic against temptation, but a means by which a power to influence the minds of men could be acquired. Particularly was this true of the Dominicans. The immediate purpose of their Order was resistance to the Albigensian heresy. " Hence it was natural that Dominic should have looked to the universities as the most suitable recruiting ground for his Order; to secure for his preachers the highest theological training that the age afforded, was an essential element of the new monastic ideal." [1]   It was not, however, long before the Franciscans also found it necessary to go to the universities for additions to their ranks. Within thirty-five years of the death of their founder, the Franciscans had become as conspicuous for intellectual activity as the Dominicans, and, for the next two hundred years, the intellectual history of Europe is bound up with the divergent views of these great Orders.

In 1224 the Franciscans opened a school at Oxford, which served as a centre from which teachers went all over England; in the following year, they also opened a school at Cambridge. It is stated that, prior to the Reformation, there were sixty-seven Franciscan professors at Oxford, and seventy-three at Cambridge. [2]

Mr. A. G. Little has investigated the educational organisation of the Mendicant Friars in this country. [3]   He points out that the absence of authentic materials will probably make it for ever impossible accurately to give the history of the Mendicant Orders in England. The available sources consist only of " a few chronicles, a few letters, the general constitution of the Orders, the Acts of the General

[1] Rashdall : *Univ.*, vol. I., p. 348.
[2] *Cyclopaedia of Educ.*, Art. Franciscans.
[3] *Trans. Roy. Hist. Soc.*, VIII., N.S. May, 1894.

Chapters, the registers of the general masters, and the Acts of the provincial chapters of other provinces."[1]

The general system of education in vogue among the Mendicant Orders was developed before 1305.[2] This was established in England in 1335, when the General Chapter held at London in that year decreed that provincial priors and chapters in their respective provinces should provide "de studiis theologie, philosophie, naturalium et artium."[3]

At the basis of the educational organisation of these Orders would be the grammar schools. Novices were not accepted unless they had attained to a certain standard of education. The Dominican statutes of the thirteenth and fourteenth centuries required candidates to be examined "in moribus et scientia," and they were rejected if they were deficient in either.[4] Consequently, the instruction to be given by the master of the novices was mainly moral.[5]

For the next grades of instruction, the convents were combined into groups. Common schools for special studies were established in one or more convents of each group.[6]

The first of these grades was the "studium artium." At one time the study of arts was discouraged. "Students shall not study in the books of the Gentiles and philosophers though they may look into them occasionally."[7] The statutes of 1259 and 1261 indicate a different attitude. "Quot fratres juniores et docibiles in logicalibus instruantur."[8] "No student was to be sent to a "studium artium" until he had been two years in the Order.[9] The

---

[1] Little : *Op. cit.*, p. 49.

[2] *Acta Selecta Capitulorum Generalium Ord. Praed.*, ed. Martene and Durand, IV., pp. 1899-1900.

[3] Douais : *Essai sur l'Organisation des Etudes dans l'Ordre des Frères Precheurs en Provence et Toulouse*, p. 53. Little points out that "philosophy is generally equivalent to arts, and is sometimes applied to natural philosophy. So one may take 'naturalium et artium' as interpretative of 'philosophie,' " *op. cit.*, p. 50.

[4] *Constitutiones antique ordinis Predicatorum*, ed. Denifle, I., p. 202.

[5] *Ibid.*, I., p. 201.   [6] Little : *op. cit.*, p. 50.

[7] Denifle: *op. cit.*, I., p. 222.   [8] Douais : *op. cit.*, p. 3.

[9] Little : *op. cit.*, p. 53.

next grade was the " studium naturalium." The period of study at this stage extended over two years at least.[1] The " studia naturalium " were less numerous than the " studia artium." There seem to be few traces of the existence of these in England, but Mr. Little has established that there was one at Lynn in 1397.[2]

The " studium theologie " was the third grade. In these schools a period of three years might be spent, but the usual stay was for two. Mr. Little raises the question where such "studia " were to be found in England and considers that they may possibly have existed at Thetford in 1395, at Lincoln in 1390, at Norwich in 1398, at Ipswich in 1397, at Newcastle-on-Tyne in 1397, at Guildford in 1397, and at London in 1475.[3]

The convents of Oxford and Cambridge stood at the head of the educational system. The statute of 1305 enacted that " No one shall be sent to a ' studium generale,' either in his province or out of it, unless in the order mentioned he has made sufficient progress in logic and natural philosophy, and has attended lectures on the ' Sentences ' for two years in some ' studium particulare ' and unless the testimony of the lector, cursor, and master of the students gives good hope that he will be fit for the office of lector." [4]

Mr. Little also deals with the appointment and qualifications of students and lecturers, and shows that, generally speaking, their selection was in the hands of the provincial prior and the provincial chapter, who were bound to make diligent enquiry each year for promising friars.[5] In this way, the most capable and efficient members of the order attained to the positions of the greatest importance. Learning was always most highly esteemed among the Dominicans, and the prosecution of studies regarded as a religious occupation worthy of being ranked with the divine services properly so called.[6] Important privileges were allowed to students and lectors, and care was taken that

---

[1] Douais : *Op. cit.*, p. 58.   [2] Little : *op. cit.*, p. 53.   [3] *Op. cit.*, p. 54.
[4] Martene *op. cit.*, IV., p. 1900.   [5] *Op. cit.*, p. 56.
[6] Denifle : *op. cit.*, pp. 190-1.

every possible facility was available for those who were desirous of continuing their education.

Neither the history of the Mendicant Orders, nor the causes which contributed to their degeneracy, concern us here. It will be sufficient to mention two ways in which they influenced educational development. The first arises out of the connection of the friars with the universities. For a time they captured the intellectual centres of the country, and dominated its literary activities. The leading men of learning of the time were friars. Among them may be mentioned Alexander of Hales, John Peckham, Richard of Middleton, Duns Scotus, and William of Ockham. The second arises from the relationship between the friars and the secular clergy. This relationship was not a friendly one, as the seculars were jealous of the intrusion of the mendicants into their parishes. We suggest that the friar movement served to accustom the people of the country to the thought that the National Church was not the only spiritual agency, and thus incidentally contributed to the development of those forces which were causing the control of education to pass out of the power of the Church.

CHAPTER VI.

THE ORIGIN OF THE GREAT PUBLIC SCHOOLS.

The Chantries' Act of 1547, which we have previously described, expressly stipulated that its provisions should not apply either to the universities, or to the cathedral churches, or to "the Colledg called St. Marye Colledg of Winchester of the foundation of Bishopp Wikeham: nor to the College of Eton." [1] It is these two latter schools with which we are now concerned, and more particularly with the questions relating to their origin and purpose.

A great deal of the current misconception of the origin and purpose of these schools may be removed if we reconstruct for ourselves the special ecclesiastical and educational features of the time. Our starting point in this connection must be the Black Death which, as we have shown,[2] caused so great a scarcity of priests and of candidates for the priesthood. William of Wykeham, desiring to give thanks to Almighty God because He had "enriched us, though unworthy, with ample honours and beyond our deserts raised us to divers degrees and dignities," [3] founded "a perpetual college of seventy poor scholars, clerks, to study theology, canon and civil law and arts in the university of Oxford." [4] In erecting this college, Wykeham was only following the example which was already well

---

[1] *Stat. of the Realm*, IV., pt. 1, p. 24.   [2] Bk. I., Ch. 1.
[3] Foundation deed, Winchester College in Hist. *Winchester Coll.*, p. 66.   [4] *Ibid.*

established at the universities, since several colleges had previously been established both at Oxford and at Cambridge. Experience soon convinced him that to found a college was one thing; to obtain a supply of students, who were qualified to profit by the proposed course was quite another; especially as, "through default of good teaching and sufficient learning in grammar, (they) often fall into the danger of failing, where they had set before themselves the desire of success." [1]

Nor was a lack of knowledge of Latin the only difficulty. A greater obstacle was the poverty of the prospective student of the period. Wykeham refers to this, "There are and will be, hereafter, many poor scholars suffering from want of money and poverty, whose means barely suffice or will suffice in the future to allow them to continue and profit in the aforesaid art of Grammar." Neither was this poverty a relative poverty, a mere "façon de parler," as some would maintain. The university itself was poor, and had scarcely any funds available for general purposes.[2] "The university students of the Middle Ages were drawn from every class of society, excluding probably as a rule the very lowest, though not excluding the very poorest." [3] We also note that poor students received from the chancellor a licence to beg.[4]

The writer of *Piers Plowman* illustrates the contemporary opinion of the social standing of many of those who proceeded to the priesthood.

> " Now might each sowter his son setten to schole,
> And each beggar's brat in the book learne,
> And worth to a writer and with a lorde dwell,
> Or falsely to a frere the fiend for to serven,
> So of that beggar's brat a Bishop that worthen,
> Among the peers of the land presse to sythen ;
> And lordes sons lowly to the lorde's loute,
> Knyghtes crooked hem to, and coucheth ful lowe,
> And his sire a sowtor y-soiled with grees,
> His teeth with toyling of lether battered as a sawe."

[1] *Ibid.*   [2] Lyte : *Hist. Univ. Oxford*, p. 97.
[3] Rashdall, *Univ.*, II., p. 656.
[4] *Munimenta Academica*, II., p. 684.

The "Norwich Corporation Records" contain an account which, even if not typical, is certainly illustrative of the way in which, the sons of many poor men found their way to the priesthood. The account to which we refer is the story of his life which was given by "Sir William Green" when undergoing examination on the charge of being a spy. He stated that he was the son of a labouring man living at Boston, Lincolnshire, and that he "lerned gramer by the space of 2 yeres." For about five or six years he was engaged in manual occupation with his father; next, he is at school again "by the space of 2 yeres and in that time receyved benet and accolet in the freres Austen in Boston of one frere Gaunt, then beyng suffragan of the diocese of Lincoln." Subsequently he is found at Cambridge, where he enters upon his studies, and supports himself, partly by labour, partly by "going to the colleges, and gate his mete and drynke of almes." After an interval, he "obteyned a licence for one year of Mr. Capper, than being deputee to the Chancellor of the said univ'sitie, under his seal of office whereby . . . . (he) gathered toguether in Cambridgeshire releaff toward their exhibicion to scole." [1]

We need not follow the fortunes or misfortunes of this pretended priest any further. The record gives the names of three men who were of the lowest social grade, and who were evidently unscrupulous, as they not only forged begging licences, but also forged letters of ordination. Though we do not claim that the case is typical of the social class from which students come, yet, on the other hand, it should not be regarded as entirely exceptional; in other words, the class of person who received the licence to beg as an accredited student of the university must have been a commonly recognised one. We must remember, at the same time, as Dr. Hastings Rashdall points out, that the example of the Friars had made mendicity comparatively respectable. "Many a man who would have been ashamed to dig was not ashamed to beg; and the begging scholar

[1] *Norwich Corporation Records.   Session Book of 12th Hen. VIII.* Norfolk Archaeol., IV., p. 342.

was invested with something like the sacredness of the begging Friar."[1]

Realising that it was necessary that prospective priests should study grammar before they proceeded to the universities, and assuming that these embryo scholars were literally poor, and could not afford even to attend the local grammar schools, which, as we have seen, were common in medieval England, we ask what action would a man such as William of Wykeham, who was desirous of perpetuating a memorial to himself and of being of service to the Church generally, naturally take ?

The answer to this question depends partly on the nature of the models available for imitation. We have previously shown that imitation has played a large part in English educational development. The first obvious model for imitation was the ordinary one of providing a master who should teach grammar freely to all boys who might care to come to him. This plan naturally commended itself at first to William of Wykeham, and was adopted by him. In 1373 he made an agreement with Master Richard Herton, Grammarian, that he " should instruct and teach faithfully and diligently in Grammar the poor scholars whom the said Father keeps and shall keep at his own expense; and shall receive no others without the licence of the said Father."[2]

This arrangement would scarcely meet the purpose which Wykeham had in mind. He wished to provide for suitable poor youths in all parts of the country, and not only for those whose homes were in the locality of Winchester.

Again we ask, what models were available ? Provision for the feeding of poor scholars had been made, two centuries previously, in connection with the Hospital of St. Cross, about a mile distant from the city of Winchester, by Bishop Henry of Blois. At this hospital thirteen poor and infirm men were lodged and boarded, and, in addition, one hundred of the poor of the city were provided with

[1] *Univ.*, II., p. 657.
[2] Quoted in Moberly's *Life of William of Wykeham*, p. 108.

a dinner each day. Among these one hundred poor were to be included, "thirteen poor scholars of the city school," who were to be sent there " by the Master of the High Grammar School of the city of Winchester."

A similar custom had prevailed " from time immemorial " at the Hospital of St. Nicholas where forty loaves were to be provided each week for the scholars who attended Pontefract School.[1]

Then too, the provision of a house for the lodging of scholars was a form of charity whose origin could be traced back to the twelfth century at least. About 1150, Walchelin, the moneyer of Derby, and Goda, his wife, bequeathed certain property to the abbey of Derby " on this trust that the hall shall be for a school of clerks and the chambers shall be for the house of a master and clerks for ever."[2].

A more immediate example for Wykeham in his desire to make provision for the maintenance and education of " pauperes et indigentes clericii " was Bishop Stapledon of Exeter. He wished to provide for the "maintenance of boys studying grammar and receiving instruction in morals and life " in connection with the Hospital of St. John at Exeter. The accomplishment of this purpose was prevented by his death, but Bishop Grandisson, his successor, arranged in 1332 that the master and brethren of the hospital were to provide accommodation and all other necessaries for a master of grammar and fourteen boys. Prior to admission, the boys were to know their psalter and to be familiar with plain song.[3]

Several similar instances may be quoted. Thus, about the close of the twelfth century, the Archdeacon of Durham, of the time, provided an endowment for the purpose of supplying three scholars of Durham School with food and lodging at the almonry[4] In 1262 Bishop Giles of Salisbury founded a hostel in that city " for the perpetual

---

[1] *Yorkshire Schools*, II., p. 4.
[2] Cott. MSS. Titus, c. IX., f. 58 ; *Ed. Ch.*, p. 110.
[3] *Grandisson's Register*, II., p. 666.
[4] *Durham Cathedral Muniments, Liber Elemosinarii*, fol. 12 r. ; *Ed. Ch.*, p. 124.

reception and maintenance of a warden, two chaplains and twenty poor, needy, well-behaved and teachable scholars." [1] In 1364, Walter de Merton, Chancellor of England, gave certain manors " for the perpetual maintenance of twenty scholars living in the schools at Oxford or elsewhere." [2] About 1387, Bishop Burghersh of Lincoln provided that the chantry founded by him should maintain six poor boys who were " professing the art of Grammar."

In addition to these models, there existed the models furnished by the collegiate churches and the monasteries. The collegiate churches were under the control of a dean or provost and a small number of officials ; generally speaking, a master of grammar was also attached to the Church. These colleges were non-resident. The priests attached to the church lived in their own homes. A monastery was presided over by an abbot or prior, the monks were resident, and a small number of choir boys were also attached.

It does not require any great stretch of the imagination to conceive of William of Wykeham pondering over all these possibilities. In the end, the monastic idea seems to have triumphed with this important distinction that, for the adult monks, were substituted " scholares pauperes et indigentes."

A study of an illustration of Winchester School serves to support this conception. The most prominent feature of the college buildings was the church. Divine worship was to be effectively rendered daily. Grouped round the church were the cloisters and the chambers, the dwelling places for the poor scholar clerks. The more closely the building is examined, the more clearly is its relation to the monastic ideal realised.

The influence of the monastic ideal is even more evident in connection with the foundation of Eton College, the second of our great public schools in respect of date of origin. The foundation charter of this school was sealed on October 11th, 1440. In this charter, Henry VI., the founder of the college, who was then eighteen years of age,

---

[1] *Sarum Church and Diocese* (R. S.), p. 334.
[2] *Stat. Coll. Oxon.*, I, ; *Ed. Ch.*, p. 171.

declared his intention to establish a college[1] " in the
honour and for the support of our great and most holy
mother in the parish church of Eton by Windsor, which is
not far removed from the place of our birth." [2]

This college, as originally planned, was to consist of a
" provost and ten priests, four clerks, and six chorister
boys whose duty it shall be to serve divine worship there
daily, and twenty-five poor and needy scholars whose duty
it shall be to learn grammar and moreover twenty-five poor
and weakly men whose duty it shall be always to pray in
the same place for our good estate while we live and for
our soul when we have passed from this light . . . also of a
master or teacher in grammar, whose duty it shall be to
teach the said needy scholars and all others whatsoever and
whencesoever of our realm of England coming to the said
college, the rudiments of grammar gratis without exacting
money or anything else." [3]

The monastic conception is brought out prominently.
At the head of the institution were the provost and ten
priests, corresponding to the abbot and the obedientaries
of a convent, next we find the chorister boys who correspond
to the boys of the almonry school who assisted in divine
worship, next comes the support of poor and weakly men,
a common feature of many monasteries, finally there are
the " poor and needy scholars " to take the place ordinarily
occupied by monks.

In 1441 Henry VI. founded a college in Cambridge
University by the name of King's College of St. Nicholas.
At first, there was no connection between Eton and King's
College, but in 1443, new statutes were made which enlarged
the number of students who could be admitted there and
also arranged for the admission of " commensales " who
were to pay for their board.   The addition of " commensales " accentuates still further the influence of the monastic
model.   From early times, it had been customary for the

---

[1] Strictly speaking, Winchester and Eton were examples of the
collegiate churches we are describing in the next chapter.   In their
turn, the collegiate churches of the fourteenth and fifteenth centuries
were chantries on a large scale.

[2] *Rot. Parl.*, V., 45.   [3] *Ibid.*

heads of monasteries to receive a kind of " parlour boarder " and it would be particularly fitting that, in an institution which was primarily educational and not merely devotional, arrangements should be made for the reception of those scholars who were able and willing to pay.

Henry showed his interest in the school by his issue of a warrant in 1446, in which, after reciting that he had founded a college at Eton for " seventy scholars whose duty it is to learn the science of grammar and sixteen choristers whose duty likewise it shall be, when they have been sufficiently instructed in singing, to learn grammar, also a master teacher in grammar and an usher to teach the aforesaid boys, scholars and choristers, " [1] he proceeded to declare that " it shall not be lawful for anyone, of whatever authority he may be, at any time to presume to keep, set up, or found any such public grammar school in the town of Windsor or elsewhere within the space of ten English miles from our said Royal College." [2]

This warrant is specially significant in two respects. One is, that it shows that the institution, founded by Henry VI., was not intended to differ in any essential respect from the other local grammar schools which existed in various parts of the country. On the contrary, steps were taken to prevent opposition. There was a real danger that the gratuitous character of the instruction given at Eton might tempt masters to open fee paying schools, with the inevitable result that the social prestige of the school would be lowered. The other significant fact arises from the use of the phrase " public grammar school." This is the first use of the term in this sense which we have been able to trace, and it is probable that we have here the first occasion on which the word is employed as an alternative for " free," which denotes, as we have explained, that the school was open to all comers.

It is not necessary that we should consider any further the history of the public schools. This subject has already been fully treated by others, notably by Mr. Leach in his

---

[1] Chancery Warrants, Series I., file 1439 : *Ed. Ch.*, p. 413.
[2] *Ibid.*

History of. Winchester College, and by Sir H. C. Maxwell Lyte in his *History of Eton College.*

We may, however, note three respects in which Winchester first, and subsequently Eton differed from the scholastic institutions, which had previously been established.

1. The scale on which Winchester College was carried out, clearly differentiates it from all earlier foundations. The number of scholars for whom Wykeham provided, and the value of the endowments attached to the school, mark a considerable advance on what had been attempted previously.

2. It was a new idea to associate a school in a district remote from a university centre with a college at Oxford. Rashdall points out that Robert Egglesfield, the founder of Queen's College, had hoped to have had at Oxford a school of boys in connection with his college. This proposal was not carried out. That which Egglesfield simply proposed for Oxford, Wykeham actually accomplished at Winchester.[1]

3. Winchester College is the first example of a boarding school, pure and simple. Collegiate churches had previously provided for the gratuitous instruction of scholars, but the real object of the establishment of a collegiate church was that divine worship should be rendered in an effective and dignified manner. Endowments had previously been provided for the feeding and lodging of scholars, but this was to be effected in connection with an existing charitable institution. At Winchester, for the first time, an institution was established for the combined purpose of teaching and of maintaining scholars, and for those purposes alone. "The really important new departure was taken, a real step in advance made, when Wykeham made his school a separate and distinct foundation. . . . The corporate name of 'Warden and scholars, clerks' stamped the school and the schoolboys as the aim and object of the foundation."[2]

One other question must be considered The great public schools to-day are attended by the sons of wealthy

[1] *Univ.* II., p. 500.   [2] *Winchester College,* pp. 88, 89.

parents : were these schools founded originally for children of the social grade who now attend them ? The foundation deeds state explicitly that they were established for " pauperes et indigentes scolares."

Mr. Leach writes vehemently on the subject. " A great deal of discussion has taken place, and much excellent eloquence run to waste on the qualification of 'poor and needy.' It was alleged . . . that there had been a robbery of the poor in the matter of endowed schools ; that the persons entitled, under the founder's statutes, to the benefits of Winchester College, were the poor in the sense of the poor law, the destitute poor, the gutter poor, or, at least, the poor labouring classes. There is not, I believe, a title or a shred of justification for any such allegation in the case of any public or endowed grammar school founded before 1627."[1]

The following arguments are advanced by Mr. Leach in support of the views he enunciates :—

(1) He urges that the test of poverty from the school point of view, was the oath which every scholar had to take on reaching fifteen years of age : " I have nothing whereby I know I can spend beyond five marks a year."[2] Now, as there were at this date sixty-seven livings in the diocese of Winchester below this value, and as £1 6s. 8d. was the pay of a skilled artisan of that date, Mr. Leach maintains that the possession of £3 6s. 8d. was a very considerable income for a boy.

In reply it may be pointed out that the oath would provide for extreme cases only. In this connection, it may be mentioned that it was proposed, towards the close of the reign of Henry VIII., to establish a free grammar school in connection with Exeter Cathedral. Forty of the scholars of this school were to be admitted without making any payment for their instruction and, in addition, they were to receive a shilling a week for the purpose of paying for " their commons within the citie." Now, the test of poverty to qualify the candidates for this position was, that their parents were not to be in receipt of a higher

[1] *Winchester School*, p. 92.   [2] *Ibid.*

income than £300 a year, possibly equal to £5,000 to-day.[1]
If we assume that the money payments of the opening
years of the twentieth century were forty times the value
of such payments in the fourteenth century, even then the
extreme limit of the income of a candidate for admission
to Winchester was £133 6s. 8d. of modern money.   It is,
therefore, obvious that the class of boy for which Winchester College was intended must have been of a lower
social scale than that for which the proposed cathedral
grammar school at Exeter was to be established.

(2) By a clause which forms a postscript to Rubric
XVI., it was provided that " sons of noble and powerful
persons . . . to the number of ten *might* be instructed
and informed in grammar within the college, without charge
to the college."   This clause Mr. Leach describes as containing the " germ " of the public school system, and he
claims that he has traced among the early commoners of
the college " young noblemen, scions of county families and
relations of judges and chancery officials."

We contend that this does not apply to the case at all,
inasmuch as " parlour boarders," as Mr. Leach himself
points out,[2] had frequently been received in monastic
houses.   Even apart from the fact that the details which
he gives are meagre, and that his conclusions are by no
means demonstrated, it may be maintained that the
presence of wealthy boys at school, under special circumstances, does not invalidate the contention that the boys
normally found there were the " poor and needy."   Thus
Dr. Hastings Rashdall, in speaking of the students at the
university, states that " there was the scion of the princely
or noble house who lived in the style to which he was
accustomed at home, in a hostel of his own with a numerous ' familia ' including poorer but well born youths who
dressed like him. . . . At the other end of the social ladder
there was the poor scholar, reduced to beg for his living,
or to become the servitor of a college, or of a master or
well-to-do student."[3]   If the poor, in the sense of those

---

[1] Whiston : *Cathedral Trusts*, p. 12.
[2] *S. M. E.*, p. 119.   [3] *Univ.*, II., p. 656.

who had to beg for a living or earn it, whilst they were at college, by manual labour, were not excluded from the university, why should it be assumed that they did not rank among the "pauperes et indigentes scolares" for whom Winchester College was expressly founded?

We may also point out that it was not customary, at this time, for boys of good family, or even the sons of wealthy and prosperous merchants and tradesmen, to be educated by being sent to school. The instances which may be given are few and inconclusive. The usual practice adopted for the education of these young people, as we have shown, was either by sending them to a great household or, at a later date, by having a private tutor in the house. Evidence may also be adduced to show that youths of good social standing rarely proceeded to the universities at this time. Thus Dr. Furnivall points out that, up to the close of the sixteenth century, only three names of noblemen and nine of sons of knights are mentioned in Cooper's *Athenae Cantabrigienses* and only nineteen men of noble or knightly birth in Wood's *Athenae Oxonienses*.[1]

We may next pass to consider the evidence for the contention which we advance, that, when Wykeham built his college, he intended it for those who were too poor to pay for an education, irrespective of their social position, and that the term "poor" did not exclude the children of men who were members of the labouring classes of the community.

(1) As we have reiterated so frequently, the actual term used in the foundation deed is "pauperes et indigentes." Mr. Leach maintains that this simply means the "relatively poor," the poor relations of the nobility, or the children of prosperous merchants. His contention seems to be an unwarranted extension of the meaning of the phrase, and it will not be possible to quote from any charter or document of the time in which this special meaning is assigned to the term.

[1] *Forewords*, XXXI.-XXXVI.

(2) Even sixty years later, at the foundation of Eton College, when the character of Winchester School would be definitely fixed, when King Henry VI. desired to establish a foundation which should exceed that of Wykeham, he associated with the school an almshouse for " twenty-five poor and weakly men." The associating of an almshouse with the school marks the purpose of the school as a charitable endowment for the lower classes of the community.

(3) The middle class of the fifteenth century was a wealthy class. In the eleventh century, there were only two social grades in England, the nobility and the various classes of tenants. The middle class, which gradually grew up, won its way through its wealth. Wealthy and prosperous merchants would seek to emulate the nobility of the land, and send their sons to the houses of nobles for their education or—at the least—to provide them with a tutor. It may also be added that the clergy of the period, who were practically the professional class, were celibates.

(4) Mr. Leach himself, undesignedly, applies examples to show that the sons of serfs attended schools. He instances that in 1295, Walter, the son of Reginald the carpenter, " was licensed to attend school " subject to the payment of a fine.[1] Similarly, in 1344, a villein at Coggeshall in Essex was fined for sending his son to school without license. At Harrow in 1384, a villein was deprived of his horse for sending his son to school without license. Mr. Leach continues " the fourteenth century manor rolls all over the country are dotted with fines for sending boys, ' ad scolas clericales,' to schools to become clerks." [2] Now, it would appear to us obvious, that if some serfs sent their sons to schools after paying a license, others would attempt to do so without payment and would probably succeed in doing so. But the point which is established, without doubt, is that it was customary for children of parents of the lowest social grade to attend school.

[1] *S. M. E.*, p. 206.
[2] *Ibid.*, p. 207.

When these arguments are fairly considered, it is claimed that the institutions of Eton and Winchester were originally intended for boys whose parents were "poor and needy"—and not simply for scions of the nobility or the sons of prosperous merchants. The only condition of admission, practically, was that these boys would subsequently proceed to the universities, in order that their course of preparation for the priesthood might be completed.

CHAPTER VII.

UNIVERSITY COLLEGES, COLLEGES AND COLLEGIATE CHURCHES IN THE LATER MIDDLE AGES.

In the early chapters of this work, we have shown that the work of evangelising England was simultaneously the work of the regular and of the secular clergy. The regular clergy were those who had taken certain vows and who shared a common institutional life. The secular clergy fall into one or other of two classes. In the one class, we place those who worked in the various parishes of which they were placed in charge; in the other class, were certain bodies of clergy who were organised into communities, termed colleges, and who served a church in common.

About the beginning of the twelfth century, there was in this country a general movement towards monasticism. Some of the existing secular cathedrals and collegiate churches were made monastic, and, in addition, there was a great increase in the number of monasteries. This practice continued until about the middle of the thirteenth century, when the beginning of the collegiate system at the universities manifested itself. The tendency to build new monasteries gradually ceased. Henceforth, we read of the establishment of colleges and collegiate churches.

One of the earliest instances of the building of a university college is that of the " College de Dix-huit " which was established at Paris, in 1180, by Joisey of London on his way home from a pilgrimage to Jerusalem. His sole object was that of making some provision for the scholar clerks who were studying at Paris.[1]

In England, the earliest instance of a university college was the one established at Salisbury by Bishop Giles of Bridport. Ever since 1209, there had been a university at Salisbury, which was augmented by a migration from Oxford in 1238.[2] In connection with this university, Bishop Giles, in 1262, set up a hostel for " the perpetual reception and maintenance of a warden, for the time being, two chaplains and twenty poor, needy, well behaved and teachable scholars serving God and the Blessed Nicholas there, and there living, studying and becoming proficient in the Holy Scriptures and the liberal arts." [3]

The origin and development of the university colleges in connection with the universities of Oxford and Cambridge has been so fully dealt with by various writers that little more than a passing reference is necessary here. Dr. Hastings Rashdall describes Walter de Merton as " the true founder " of the English college system. In 1264,[4] he founded at Maldon " The House of Merton's Scholars " " for the perpetual maintenance of twenty scholars living in the schools at Oxford, or elsewhere where a university might happen to flourish and for the maintenance of two or three ministers of the altar of Christ living in the same house." [5] The idea of this founder, originally, was the provision of funds for the education of his nephews or the descendants of his parents, or (failing a sufficient number of these) of other " honest and capable young men." [6] The men supported by these funds were to hire a hall and live together as a community in the university. In 1274, a new code of statutes for the control and regulation of the foundation was issued. Here, in the first of the English colleges, the monastic institutions form the model which

---

[1] Lebeuf : *Histoire de la Ville et tout le Diocese de Paris*, II., pp. 129, 130.

[2] Walsingham : *Ypodigma Neustriae* (R. S.), p. 141.

[3] Sarum Ch. and Dioc. (R. S.), p. 334.

[4] Or 1263; *Univ.*, II., p. 481.

[5] *Stat. Coll. Oxford*, I. ; *Ed. Ch.*, p. 171.   [6] *Univ.*, II., p. 482.

was imitated. At the head of the institution was an official corresponding to the abbot, next come certain officials who resembled the various officers of a monastery; these include the "Vicenarii" who were placed over every twenty scholars, and the "Decani" over every ten scholars. The scholars corresponded to the monastic novices. The scheme for the control of the boys (because some of the scholars might often be only thirteen or fourteen years of age)[1] resembles in its general spirit the regulations of Lanfranc for the oblates and novices school at Canterbury.[2]

The similarity between a monastery and Merton's foundations manifests itself still more clearly when we realise that he even provided for a class which would correspond to the oblates. He enacted that "if any little ones of the kindred aforesaid becoming orphans or otherwise through their parents poverty want maintenance while they are receiving primary instruction in the rudiments, then the warden shall have them educated in the house aforesaid."[3]

The example set by Walter de Merton was followed by Bishop Balsham of Ely in his foundation of the first college at Cambridge in 1280. He placed some poor scholars in the Hospital of St. John "to live together and to study in the university of Cambridge according to the rule of the scholars of Oxford who are called Merton's."[4] The experiment did not prove a success because "in process of time from various causes, matter of dissension had often arisen between the brethren of the same house and the scholars aforesaid,"[5] as a result of which the scholars were moved outside the town "and translated to the inns by St. Peter's Church"[6] which was appropriated to them, and in consequence the college received the name of Peterhouse by which it is still known.

We must leave here the subject of the establishment of university colleges and pass to consider the colleges of secular canons which were rapidly founded in all parts

---

[1] *Univ.*, II., p. 485.   [2] Wilkins, *Concilia*, I., pp. 3, 55 *seq.*
[3] Statutes, cap. 40 ; *Ed. Ch.*, p. 185.
[4] Pat. Roll, 9 Edw., I., m. 28 ; *Ed. Ch.*, p. 224.
[5] Charter Roll, 13 Edw., I., m. 28 ; *Ed. Ch.*, p. 226.   [6] *Ibid.*

of the country. The *Monasticon*[1] gives a list of twenty-six establishments, described as collegiate churches, and of one hundred and sixty-five, which are described simply as colleges, exclusive of the cathedral churches. We are underestimating the number when we state that, outside the universities, there were two hundred colleges or collegiate churches in this country. The term "college" or "collegiate church" may be used indifferently; both imply an organisation of secular priests or of secular priests and scholars founded for the purpose "ad orandum et studiendum."

One of the first of the collegiate churches to be established subsequent to the Conquest was that of Howden in Yorkshire. The church was intended at one time to form the endowment of a monastery,[2] but in 1266 Bishop Robert of Durham caused it to become a college of secular priests.[3] The remaining records of this church are meagre and relate mainly to the endowments which it gradually received.

Howden Collegiate Church serves to illustrate the difficulties in connection with tracing the educational history of this country, and also the educational significance of the collegiate churches. As we have just remarked, the records of this church are extremely meagre, and if we were dependent upon them alone we would naturally conclude that no educational interest was attached to this institution. A different interpretation is put upon the matter when we examine a Durham register of the period.[4] Here we find records of scholastic appointments to this church, e.g. to a song school in 1393, to a grammar school in the same year, to a reading and song school in 1394, to a reading and song school in 1401, to a reading and song school in 1402, to a grammar school in 1403, to a grammar and reading school in 1409, to a song and reading school in 1412, separate appointments for reading and song in

---

[1] Ed. Caley, Ellis and Bandinel.
[2] Wharton: *Anglia Sacra*, I., p. 740.   [3] *Mon.*, VI., p. 1473.
[4] Brit. Mus. *Cott. MSS. Faustina*, A., VI. f. 104, reprinted in *Early Yorkshire Schools*, Vol. II., pp. 84-86; *Registrum Parvum*, f. 11, reprinted *Yorkshire Schools*, pp. 86-88.

1426, whilst the last record is that of J. Armandson, B.A., who was appointed " ad informandum pueros in lectura et grammatica " during the good pleasure of the prior.

We have given these various references to the appointments because they show that the collegiate churches, as a general rule, regarded it as one of their definite functions to provide educational facilities for those who cared to avail themselves of them. For the purpose of demonstrating this statement more fully, we now proceed to give a series of examples of the establishment of collegiate churches.

In 1267 the collegiate church of St. Thomas the Martyr was founded at Glasney near Penrhyn, in Cornwall, by Bishop Bromescomb of Exeter.[1] We should not know anything about the educational work carried on at this church were it not for the return made to the commissioners under the Chantries' Act of 1547. The Continuation Certificate stated that a school was to continue at Glasney because it had previously been kept by " one of the said vicars scolemaster . . . for the which the people maketh great lamentacione and it is mete to have another lerned man, for there is muche youthe in the same Towne."[2] This college is particularly interesting, as it is one of the few places of which records are available where provision was made for teaching the first rudiments of learning. It is stated that :—

" John Pownde, bell rynger there, of the age of 30 yeres, hathe for his salarye ther 40/-, as well for teachynge of pore mens children there ABC as for ryngynge the Bells 40/-."[3]

Passing next to the college founded in 1337-8 at Ottery St. Mary in Devonshire by Bishop Grandison, we find the first instance of a collegiate church where the charters of the institution provide that the establishment should include " a Master of Music " and a " Master of Grammar."[4] The chantry return stated that " Syr John Chubbe preste,

[1] *Mon.*, VI., p. 1344.   [2] *E. S. R.*, II., p. 40.   [3] *E. S. R.*, II., p. 31.
[4] *Mon.*, VI., p. 1346.

beyng scholemaster ther" received an annual stipend of £10.[1]

A college of secular priests was founded at Raveningham in Norfolk in 1350; this was moved to Mettingham Castle in 1382. This college also made the usual provision for education.[2] For a time the boys associated with this college seem to have attended the grammar school at Beccles.[3]

A foundation, which was quasi-collegiate, but which may be considered as the precursor of the non-residential grammar schools which subsequently became common, dates from 1384. It was founded at Wotton-under-Edge by Katherine, Lady Berkeley, who gave certain lands for the provision of a schoolhouse and the maintenance of "a master and two poor scholars clerks living college-wise therein." [4] The priest-schoolmaster was to act as chaplain at the Manor house of the foundress, and to celebrate "for the healthy estate of us . . . and for our souls when we shall have passed from this light." [5] Arrangements were made for the appointment of the master of the school as vacancies arose. It was also required that the master " shall kindly receive all scholars whatsoever, howsoever and whencesoever coming for instructions in the said art of grammar, and duly instruct them in the said art, without exacting, claiming or taking from them any advantage for their labour in the name of stipend or salary, so that the masters aforesaid could not be accused of solicitation." [6] The regulations relating to the scholars provide that they " shall not be set by the master for the time being to do any office or service, but shall be compelled continually to devote their time to learning and study." [7]

Another similar small college was that of Bredgar in Kent which was founded in 1393 by eight persons, chief among whom was Robert de Bredgar. The licence to found the college,[8] merely states the usual purpose of praying for the good estate of the founders while living,

[1] *E. S. R.*, II., p. 54.   [2] *Mon.*, VI , p. 1459.   [3] *S. M. E.*, p. 210.
[4] *Reg. Ep. Worcester*, H. Wakefield, p. 72, *Ed. Ch.*, pp. 330-334.
[5] *Ibid.*   [6] *Ibid.*   [7] *Ibid.*   [8] Pat. 16, Ric. II., p. 1, m. 24.

and for their souls, when they have passed from this light,
and also for the souls " omnium fidelium defunctorum."
We obtain further knowledge of the intentions of the
founders from a study of the " Statuta et Ordinationes pro
meliori Gubernatione ejusdem." [1] It is not necessary for
us to consider these statutes in detail here, though they
emphasise considerably the educational aspect of the
foundation. One of these statutes runs :—

"Volo et ordino, quod nullus capellanus ad capellanium dicti
collegi admittatur nisi tunc sciat bene legere, bene construere, et
bene cantare ; nu'lu⁴ praeficiatur clericus scolaris dicti collegii, nisi
tempore praesentationis hujusmodi bene legere et competenter cantare sciat."

The same year in which Bredgar College was founded
witnessed the establishment of a college at Pleshy, in Essex,
by Thomas, Duke of Gloucester. The foundation was to
consist of a master, eight secular priests, two clerks, and
two choristers.[2] The licences for the foundation of the
college do not, as usual, mention anything about teaching,
but the return to the chantry commissioners, 1547-8, states
that a priest, who kept a free grammar school, was attached
to the college.[3] William Courtney, Archbishop of Canterbury, founded in 1396 a college of secular priests on a
large scale at Maidstone in Kent. A hospital, which
had been founded in 1260 by a previous Archbishop of
Canterbury, was taken to form the nucleus of the new
college. The parish church was utilised as the collegiate
church. The various licences, which authorised the foundation of the college,[4] do not refer to education, but we
know that provision for teaching was made because at the
dissolution of the college, the town council bought from
Edward VI. the right to keep school.[5]

The church of Hemmingborough, in Yorkshire, was
made collegiate in 1426, with a provost or warden, three

[1] Reg. principale D. Archiep. Cantuar, fol. 124 a, reprinted *Mon.*
VI., p. 1391.   [2] *Mon.*, VI., p. 1393.
[3] Duchy of Lanc. Cert. of Colleges, No. 4, Ch ınt. Certif. XX., 43.
[4] Reprıı ted *Mon.*, VI., pp. 1394-1395.
[5] *S. M. E.*, p. 209,

prebendaries, six vicars choral and six clerks.[1] The king's licence for the foundation gives the usual reason for its establishment stating that there was to be in the church "quoddam collegium de uno praeposito sive custode et caeteris prebendaris, vicariis, clericis, et ministris, qui divina in dicta ecclesia celebrent, pro salubri statu nostro, dum vivimus, et pro anima nostra, cum ab hac luce subtracti fuerimus."[2] There is a record of the prior of Durham appointing a master to the school in 1394,[3] so that in all probability educational facilities were provided by the college.

A college which calls for special mention is that of Tonge in Shropshire, which was founded in 1410 by the widow of Sir Fulk Penbridge.[4] The complete foundation consisted of a warden, four secular priests as chaplains, two clerks, and an almshouse for thirteen persons.[5] We are fortunate in possessing the "Statuta et Ordinationes pro Gubernatione ejusdem,"[6] as these make it clear that these colleges commonly conceived it their duty to provide for education. The clause runs, "Statuimus etiam et ordinamus, quod unus e capellanis praedictis, vel alius clericus dicti collegii, si capellanus in hac parte habere non poterit in lectura, cantu, et grammatica competenter instructus, qui pro dispositione custodis, et sanioris partis dicti collegii, clericos et alios ministros collegii, et ultra eosdem pauperes juvenes ejusdem villae, seu de vicinis villis, teneatur diligenter instruere."[7]

It is important to note that a collegiate foundation provided for education even in such a small place as Tonge.

In 1415, the College of Stoke-next-Clare was founded by Edmund Mortimer, Earl of March. There had existed here previously an alien priory, which was afterwards converted into a college of secular priests. The Earl of March augmented its revenues, so as to provide for a dean, six prebendaries, eight vicars, four clerks, six choristers,

---

[1] *Mon.*, VI., p. 1375.   [2] *Pat.* 5, Hen. VI., p. m. 19.
[3] *S. M. E.*, p. 211.   [4] *Mon.*, VI., p. 1401.
[5] *Pat.* 12, Hen. IV., *pars unica*, m. 20.
[6] *Pat.* 3, Hen. V., pt. 1, m. 6, reprinted Mon., VI., pp. 1404-1411.
[7] *Ibid.*, p. 1407.

officers and servants.[1] From the statutes and ordinances
for the government of this college, [2] we learn that a schoolmaster was to be appointed to teach the boys of the
college reading, plain song, and descant.[3]

"A noble college"[4] was founded at Fotheringhay in
1412 by Edward, Duke of York. The college consisted of
a master, twelve chaplains or fellows, eight clerks, and
thirteen choristers. The statutes of the college were largely
based on those of Winchester and New College, and provided for the appointment of one master to teach grammar,
and of another to teach song to the choristers.[5]

Henry Chicheley, Archbishop of Canterbury, founded a
college at Higham Ferrers, his birthplace, in the last year
of King Henry V., for a master, six secular chaplains, four
clerks, and six choristers; of these, " unus eorundem capell-
anorum sive clericorum ad grammaticam, et alius capellanus
sive clericus de eisdem capellanis sive clericis ad cantum
instruendum et docendum ibidem deputetur et assignetur."[6]
The act of Chicheley in making his schoolmasters an
integral part of the foundation marks an advance on
Wykeham, who made them stipendiary officers only.[7]

An institution, which was of the nature of a hospital
rather than a college, was founded in 1432, at Ewelme, by
the Earl of Suffolk. It consisted of an almshouse for two
chaplains and thirteen poor men, [8] and to the almshouse a
grammar school was attached. The school statutes provide
that the schoolmaster was to be " a well disposed man, apte
and able to techyng of grammar to whose office it shall
long and perteyne diligently to teche and inform chylder in
the faculte of gramer, provyded that all the chylder of our
chapelle, of the tenauntes of our lordshyp of Ewelme and
of the lordshypes perteyning to the said Almesse Howse,

---

[1] *Mon.*, VI., p. 1415.

[2] MS. in Libl .o..on, fol. 8, reprinted in *Mon.*, VI., pp. 1417-
1423.

[3] See als *Chant. Certif.*, 45, No. 47.   [4] *Mon.*, VI., p. 1411.

[5] Cf. *E. S. R.*, II., pp. 153, 154, 155, 280; P.R.O., Aug. Off. Misc.
Bks., 147.

[6] *Pat.* 10, Hen. V., m. 3, reprinted *Mon.*, VI., pp. 1425-6.

[7] Cp. *S. M. E.*, p. 254.   [8] *Mon.*, VI., p. 716.

now present and at alle tymes to com, frely be tawt without exaccion of any scole-hir." [1]

In 1432, John Kempe, at that time Archbishop of York
and afterwards Cardinal, obtained a licence from Henry
VI., to establish a college for celebrating divine service
and for the education of the youth in the parish of Wye.[2]
The college was to consist of "a maister and six priests,
two clerks and two queristers and over that a maister of
grammar that shal frely teche withoutyn anything takyng
of hem al thos that wol come to his techyng." [3]

At Tattershall, in Lincolnshire, a college was founded
and endowed by Sir Ralph Cromwell, in 1439. It consisted of a warden, six priests, six clerks, six choristers, and
an almshouse for thirteen poor persons. The existence at
this college of a master of grammar and of a master of the
choristers can be traced.[4]

We now pass to consider the two chief colleges which
were founded prior to the Act of 1547 which brought
about their dissolution—Acaster College and Rotherham
College.

The original documents of the foundations of Acaster
College do not appear to be extant. No reference to the
college is made in the *Monasticon*. A private Act of
Parliament passed in 1483 for the purpose of settling a
dispute relating to a question of enclosure, which had
arisen, recites that the college was founded [5] by Stillington,
Bishop of Bath and Wells, and that this foundation included "three dyvers Maisters and Informatours in the
faculteies underwritten; that is to witt; oon of theym to
teche Gramer, another to teche Musyk and Song, and the
third to teche to Write, and all suche thing as belonged to
Scrivener Craft, to all maner of persons of whatsoever
Cuntre they be within the Reame of Englond . . . openly,
and freely without exaction of money or other thyngs of
any of their suche Scholars and Disciples." [6]

---

[1] Carlisle, *Endowed Gr. Schools*, II., p. 301.   [2] *Mon.*, VI., p. 1430.
[3] *S. M. E.*, p. 255.   [4] *S. M. E.*, p. 256.   [5] Probably about 1470.
[6] *Rot. Parl.*, V., p. 256; reprinted *Yorkshire Schools*, II.,
pp. 89-91.

The chantry certificate relating to this college stated that :—

" There ys a provost and three fellows being all preistes whereof one dothe kepe a free scole of grammar according to the foundacion." [1]

Full information is available of the foundation of a college at Rotherham, by Thomas Rotherham, Archbishop of York, under licence of Jan. 22nd, 1483. [2]

In the college statutes [3] the founder stated that he would have grown up " unlearned, unlettered, and rude," if by chance a " vir in gramatica doctus " had not come to the neighbourhood and thus made it possible for those who were desirous of doing so, to learn the elements of grammar. In order, therefore, to provide for the youth of the future, he had established a college to consist of a provost, three fellows, and six scholar-choristers.

The provost was to exercise a general supervision over the establishment, to guide the studies of the fellows and all others who wished to avail themselves of his services, and to preach in the diocese of York, especially in specified churches. [4]

The first fellow was to give instruction in grammar under the direction and supervision of the provost. The second fellow was to teach the art of music [5] " especially in plain and broken chant, in all the moods and forms of the art," to scholars desirous of learning coming from any part of England and especially from the diocese of York. [6] The third fellow was to be learned in the art of writing and in the keeping of accounts. Archbishop Rotherham states that he founded this third fellowship because he desired to assist those who did not wish to attain to the " high dignity " of the priesthood, to fit themselves "for the mechanical arts and other worldly concerns." [7] All these fellows of the college were diligently to teach " with-

---

[1] *E. S. R.*, II., p. 298.

[2] *Mon.*, VI., pp. 1441-1443 ; *Yorkshire Schools*, II., pp. 101-141.

[3] Reprinted *Yorkshire Schools*, II., 109-130, from MS. at Sydney Sussex Coll., Camb.

[4] *Ib.*, pp. 113, 114.   [5] *Ib.*, p. 115.   [6] *Ib.*, p. 116.   [7] *Ib.*, p. 110.

out exaction of money or anything else in the schools and houses assigned for the purpose in the college." [1]

Before proceeding to consider the data we have collected in this chapter, we may refer briefly to the educational provision made in connection with hospitals. In addition to the educational aspect of the charitable foundation at Ewelme, to which we have already referred,[2] we note that in 1231 a Jewish synagogue existed in the parish of St. Bennet Fink. This was given to the brethren of St. Anthony of Vienne in France by Henry III. A hospital consisting of a master, two priests, a schoolmaster, twelve poor brethren, and various officers was established by them.[3] A further development occurred in 1441 when John Carpenter, who held the position of master of St. Anthony's Hospital at that time, obtained from the Bishop of London the revenues of a rectory adjoining the hospital for the maintenance of "a master or fit Informer in the faculty of grammar . . . to keep a grammar school in the precinct of the hospital or some fit house close by, to teach, instruct and inform gratis all boys and others whatsoever wishing to learn and become scholars." [4] The school, thus founded, made considerable progress and for about 200 years was the chief school in London.

We may also mention the foundation of Heytesbury Hospital in Wiltshire. Licence was granted [5] in 1472 to Lady Hungerford to found an almshouse to consist of a master and twelve poor brethren. The statutes for the government of the institution show that the master was to be able to teach grammar, that the chancellor of Salisbury was to present "an able keeper and a sufficient teacher of grammar at every avoidance," and that it was the duty of the master "to teach and inform all such children and all other persons that shall come to the place which is ordained and deputed to teach them in within Heytesbury and . . . . shall teach them from the beginning of learning until such season as they learn sufficient . . . . of grammar ; no school hire take of no person or take (except from)

---

[1] *Ibid.*, p. 116.   [2] p. 210.   [3] *Mon.*, VI., p. 766.   [4] *S. M. E.*, p. 261.
[5] Pat., II., Ed. IV., p. 2., m. 15, *Mon.*, VI., p. 725.

such as their friends may spend £10 or above, or else that will give freely."[1]

Our treatment of the problem with which we are concerned in this thesis, has differed in this chapter from that adopted in other chapters. We have here collected together a mass of evidence illustrative of the part taken by collegiate churches in education. The evidence is not exhaustive. We can readily adduce evidence of the education provided by the collegiate churches at Ledbury, at Llangadock, at Brecon, at St. David's, at Crediton, and probably further research would enable additional examples to be obtained.

The question is: what general principles arise as a result of a consideration of these examples?

(1) The Church considered it one of her primary works of charity to provide for education. The charitable aspect becomes particularly evident when we consider the association of almshouses and schools as at Eton, Ewelme, Heytesbury, and St. Anthony's. Though, as we have tried to show in preceding chapters, the rise of a social consciousness had led various community organisations to realise that they had a duty to discharge in the provision of educational facilities, yet the fact that other authorities were stirring themselves in the matter did not involve that the Church was to be apathetic. On the contrary, the examples we have adduced indicate considerable activity.

(2) Each of the collegiate churches was normally regarded as a centre of educational work. This fact seems to have been so generally known that it is rarely expressed in the licences authorising the foundation. It is only some special circumstances, *e.g.* the existence of the statutes or the return to the chantry commissioners, which enables the teaching work of these colleges definitely to be known. Since the educational aspect of the work of these colleges was not a matter of enactment[2] it must have been due to tradition. This tradition must date back to the earliest days of the establishment of such colleges and here

---

[1] Cf. *S. M. E.*, p. 272.
[2] Canon Law of 1179 and 1215 did not initiate the custom.

we go back to the time of the introduction of Christianity to this country. In fact, a definite connection between collegiate churches and education can be traced back to the days of St. Augustine of Hippo.[1]

(3) A change is gradually observable in the relationship of these collegiate churches to education. At first the master of grammar and of song was merely a hireling, a clerk, probably, who was attached in some subordinate capacity to the institution. The foundation deed of Winchester College, for example, makes no mention of a master of grammar, the foundation charter of Eton College refers to a " magister sive informator in grammatica," but, whilst other appointments are definitely mentioned, the appointment of a schoolmaster was apparently of secondary consideration. Gradually the position of the master improves until we see in the last instance of the establishment of a college prior to the Reformation, and which we have given in this chapter, the foundation of Rotherham College, that the establishment consisting of a provost and three fellows, each of whom was engaged in educational work, was one in which the scholastic aspect took precedence over all other aspects.

[1] See Bk. I., Ch. II.

CHAPTER VIII.

CURRICULUM AND METHOD.

The conventional view of the curriculum of the schools of the Middle Ages regards it as consisting of the trivium [1] and the quadrivium; [2] under these two terms was substantially included all the learning of the time. To investigate here the contents of the "Seven Liberal Arts" would involve us in an unnecessary digression, especially as the extent to which these subjects actually formed part of the school curriculum is still a matter of considerable doubt. [3]

Having now paid our homage to the generally accepted view, we note, however, when we turn to examine the actual sources now available for the study of medieval education, that the terms which occur most frequently in the records, as indicative of what was taught in the schools, are "grammar" and "song." They are reiterated time after time; a master is appointed "ad informandum pueros in grammatica" or "in cantu"; or, in the chantry returns, "to teche frely almanner of childern Gramer; [4] to "teache gramer and plane songe." [5] Any student who enters upon an investigation of the subjects of the curriculum of the schools of the Middle Ages, without any preconception of

---

[1] Grammar, rhetoric, and dialectic.
[2] Geometry, arithmetic, music, and astronomy.
[3] On the general subject, see Abelson, *The Seven Liberal Arts*, Parker, "The Seven Liberal Arts," *Eng. Hist. Rev.*, V., pp. 417-461, July 1890; Rashdall, *Univ.*, I., pp. 33-37; West, *Alcuin* pp. 4-27.
[4] *E. S. R.*, II., p. 56.   [5] *E. S. R.*, II., p. 117.

what was taught in the schools, and who diligently reads through the documents of the period now available, would unhesitatingly state that the curriculum consisted of grammar and song.

We have previously considered [1] what these terms denoted in a general sense. Our next task is to consider whether any details are available of the school curricula during the period with which we are concerned. As these are comparatively meagre, it will be possible for us to gather together an account of most of the sources which enable us to reconstruct the curriculum of the schools of medieval England.

The most systematic account we possess of medieval education is derived from the writings of John of Salisbury. The main facts of his life are readily given. After spending about fifteen years on the continent undergoing a course of study, he returned to this country and became secretary to Archbishop Theobald, by whom he was entrusted with important diplomatic missions both at home and abroad. Subsequently he became the friend and adviser of Thomas à Beckett, at whose death he was present. For the last four years of his life John was Bishop of Chartres. We may here anticipate an objection which will probably be forthcoming. The education of John of Salisbury took place mainly in France, and as this thesis professes to deal with English education, the question arises : is not the section irrelevant ? The answer is that John of Salisbury was an Englishman, and one of the greatest scholars of the Middle Ages. The education he obtained was the education possible to an Englishman of his period. Further, the account of John of Salisbury's education is the best account available for a study of the curriculum of medieval times.

John tells us that whilst he was a boy he was placed under the charge of a priest, along with some other boys "ut psalmos addiscerem." [2] Incidentally, it may be mentioned that this priest seems to have been interested in

---

[1] Bk. II., ch. II.   [2] *Polycraticus*, II., 28.

magic, and to have employed his pupils to assist him.
However, as John proved a disturbing influence, his services were not made use of after the first occasion.

In his *Metalogicus*,[1] John gives an account of his further
education. He crossed over to France to study when he
was quite a young man.[2] There he studied under Abelard, from whom he received his first lessons in logic.
Subsequently he was instructed by Alberic, the successor
of Abelard, whom he describes as "a greatly esteemed
dialectician and the bitterest assailant of the nominal
sect." He also was taught by Robert of Melun, an
Englishman, who later became Bishop of Hereford. John
remained under these masters for about two years. Both
of them, he says, possessed considerable ability as logicians
and in disputations, though their methods differed. One
of them was scrupulous to the least detail, and discussed
fully the slightest difficulty in connection with the problem
under consideration; the other was prompt in reply, and
never avoided a question that was proposed, "but by
multiplicity of words would show that a simple answer
could not be given."

By these teachers only logic was taught, and the cultivation of "a sharp and nimble wit with an acute intellect"
seems to have been the only goal aimed at. At this subject John became so expert that "in the commonplace rules
and other rudimentary principles which boys study, and
in which the aforesaid masters were most weighty, I seemed
to myself to know them as well as my nail and fingers.
One thing certainly I had attained to, namely, to estimate
my knowledge much higher than it deserved. I fancied
myself a young scholar, because I was quick in what I had
been taught."

John, however, became conscious of an intellectual
appetite which the formal routine of logic did not satisfy;
consequently, he determined to enter upon the study of
grammar, and for this purpose he left Paris for Chartres,

---

[1] Bk. II., ch. X.
[2] "Quum primum adolescens admodum, studiorum causa migrassem in Gallias."

to study under the Grammarian, William of Conches. The cathedral school at Chartres had long been famous as a centre of learning. One of the most famous masters of the school was Bernard Sylvester, described by John of Salisbury as "in modern times the most abounding spring of letters in France."[1]   Poole gives an account of this school under Bernard :—

"The pupil went through all the routine of metaplasm, schematism, and figures of speech ; but this was only the groundwork As soon as possible he was introduced to the classical texts themselves and in order to create a living interest in the study, Bernard used not merely to treat these grammatically, but also to comment freely upon them. . . . Nor did he confine himself to the form of what was being read ; he was still more anxious to impress upon his pupils its meaning.   It was a principle with him that the wider and more copious the master's knowledge, the more fully will he perceive the elegancy of his authors and the more clearly will he teach them."[2]

Among the teaching methods adopted by Bernard, and by his successors in the school, Richard the Bishop, and William of Conches, were those of requiring exercises daily in prose and verse composition.   By way of preparation for these exercises, the pupils were shown the qualities in the classical writers which were deemed worthy of adoption.   The pupils passed round their exercises to one another for comment and criticism, and in this way emulation was stimulated.   In addition to composition, the pupils had a good deal to commit to memory ; they were every day required to keep a record of the lessons they had received.   John of Salisbury writes of Richard the Bishop that he was a man "who was master of every kind of learning and who had more heart even than speech, more learning than eloquence, more truth than vanity, more virtue than ostentation ; the things I had learnt from others, I reviewed from him, besides certain things which I now learnt for the first time relating to the Quadrivium . . . I also again studied Rhetoric, which previously I had scarcely understood when it was first treated of superficially

[1] *Metal.*, I., 24.
[2] *Illustrations of Medieval Thought*, p. 121.

by Master Theodoric." [1]   John also studied rhetoric from
Peter Helias, "a grammarian of high repute."

Apparently John was obliged to maintain himself during this period, as he had no parents or relatives who could
support him.   Consequently, we find that he taught the
"children of noble persons."   He did not consider the
time he spent in teaching the young as wasted, because it
forced him to revise that which he had previously learnt
himself.   Whilst engaged in the task of teaching, John
became acquainted with Adam du Petit Pont, an Englishman who subsequently became Bishop of St. Asaph.   John
describes Adam as a man "of much learning who had
given special study to Aristotle."   John is careful to point
out that he was never a pupil of Adam, yet Adam seems
to have been well disposed to John, and to have assisted
him in various ways.

In order to apply himself to the study of theology, John
returned to Paris.   His course was interrupted by his
poverty; during the necessary interval he again acted as
tutor.   At the end of three years, he was once again in
Paris, where his studies were continued, first under Robert
Pullus and afterwards under Simon of Poissy—"a trusty
lecturer but dull in disputations."

In the conclusion of the record of his school studies,
John gives an account of a visit he paid to the school of
logic at Paris attended by him whilst a youth.   He states
that his purpose in doing so was to endeavour to estimate
the relative progress made by the schools of logic, and by
himself.   He writes :—

"I found them as before and where they were before ; nor did
they appear to have reached the goal in unravelling the old questions, nor had they added one jot of a proposition.   The aims that
once inspired them, inspired them still ; they only had progressed
in one point, they had unlearned moderation, they knew not
modesty.   And thus experience taught me a manifest conclusion
that, whereas dialectic furthers other studies, so if it remain by
itself it lies bloodless and barren, nor does it quicken the soul to
yield fruit of philosophy, except the same conceive from elsewhere." [2]

[1] Johannis Saresberiensis, *Opera*, ed. Giles, Vol. V., pp. 79, 80.
[2] *Metal.*, II., 10 : trans. by Poole.

We also obtain a certain amount of educational biography from the writings of Alexander Neckham, who was at one time the master of the school at Dunstable.[1] Neckham tells us that, when he was a boy, he attended the school at St. Albans; then he passed over to Paris, where he studied theology, medicine, canon and civil law.[2]

A third account needs to be referred to before we can consider what conclusions we can draw with regard to the curriculum of the twelfth century.

William Fitzstephen, (d. 1190), was employed by Thomas à Beckett. He witnessed the murder of his master and wrote his biography. This work contains an interesting account of London in the twelfth century and, incidentally, describes an important occasion in schoolboy life. He states :—

" On feast days, the masters celebrate assemblies at the churches, *en fête*. The scholars hold disputations, some declaiming, others by way of question and answer. These roll out euthymemes, these use the better form of perfect syllogisms. Some dispute merely for show as they do at collections ; others for truth, which is the grace of perfection. The sophists using the Socratic irony are pronounced happy because of the mass and volume of their words ; others play upon words. Those learning rhetoric, with rhetorical speeches, speak to the point with a view to persuasion, being careful to observe the precepts of their art, and to leave out nothing that belongs to it. The boys of the different schools vie with each other in verses : or dispute ; or dispute on the principles of grammar, or the rules of preterites and supines."

Fitzstephen concludes with a quotation from Persius :—

" multum ridere parati
Ingeminant tremulos naso crispante cachinnos." [3]

We may also note, from the same work, the reference which Fitzstephen gives to the education of Beckett. He tells us that the future archbishop was first brought up " in religiosa domo canonicorum Meritoniae," then he passed the years of " infantiae, pueritiae, et pubertatis " in the home of his father and " in scholis urbis." When he became a young man, Thomas proceeded to Paris to study.[4]

[1] *Gesta. Abb. Mon. S. Albani.*, I., 72.   [2] *Ed. Ch.*, p. 116.
[3] *Life of Thomas à Beckett* (R. S.), III., p. 3.   [4] *Ibid.*, p. 14.

These accounts we have given of the education of John of Salisbury, Alexander Neckham, and Thomas à Beckett are noteworthy. They show that education in the twelfth century was much more general, and much more advanced, than we usually think. The audiences, assembled at the school festivities, were able to understand, and thoroughly to appreciate dialectical disputations carried on in Latin. So too, we learn elsewhere, that when Giraldus Cambrensis was giving addresses, he was everywhere understood when he spoke in Latin.

Taking these three accounts together, we are justified in distinguishing four stages of education during the twelfth century.

I. The Grade of Elementary Instruction.—At this stage, the children would learn from the horn book and primer,[1] and would also commit certain psalms to memory.

II. The Grammar Grade.—The object of the instruction at this stage would be to give the student a working knowledge of the Latin language. The chief grammars used were those of Donatus and Priscian; these would be supplemented by a study of various compilations of proverbs, fables, and dialogues, *e.g.* Cato's "Distichs." Song was studied concurrently with grammar.

III. The Logic Grade.—This would be the study of the boys who had made satisfactory progress with grammar. It consisted of formal logic only. The writings of Boethius were the sources from which the early Middle Ages drew their knowledge of logic.

IV. The University Grade.—This term we use to denote the advanced studies of the period, whether pursued at Paris or Oxford, or at any other famous centre of intellectual activity. The examples we have given, of the studies carried on by John of Salisbury and Alexander Neckham, will serve to illustrate the character of the work which was being done at this stage.

---

[1] For description see Drane : *Christian Schools and Scholars*, pp 230-2 ; Foster Watson, *Grammar Schools*, pp. 32-37.

In the thirteenth century the only educational reference which throws light on the school curriculum, outside the university of Oxford, which we have been able to trace, is an extract from the Chapter Act Book of Southwell Minster, which states that, in 1248, "non teneantur Scole de Grammatica vel Logica infra prebendas Canonicorum, nisi secundum consuetudinem Ebor."[1] This passage serves to illustrate the continued existence of the three grades of educational instruction we have enumerated.

The statutes of Merton College, Oxford, which date from the thirteenth century, refer to the study of grammar, which is to be undertaken both by the scholars and the boys. The grammarian is to talk Latin with the boys whenever it shall be to their benefit, or he may talk to them in "idiomate vulgari" (*i.e.* French). The same chapter gives the studies of the scholars as consisting of "arts, philosophy, canon law, or theology."

Further insight into the conditions of medieval education can be obtained from a study of some of the writings of Roger Bacon. Of his life scarcely anything is known: "Born, studied at Oxford, went to Paris, studied, experimented; is at Oxford again, and a Franciscan; studies, teaches, becomes suspect to his Order, is sent back to Paris, kept under surveillance, receives a letter from the Pope, writes, writes, writes—his three best-known works; is again in trouble, confined for many years, released and dead, so very dead, body and fame alike, until partly unearthed after five centuries."[2]

Whilst at Oxford, Bacon studied under two teachers whose names he gives—Robert Grosseteste, who "knew the sciences better than any other man,"[3] and Adam Marsh, whom he links with Grosseteste as "perfect in divine and human wisdom." From Oxford Bacon went to Paris, where he not only continued his studies but also engaged in teaching. He writes, "I caused youth to be

[1] *Mem. of Southwell Minster*, p. 205.
[2] Taylor: *Medieval Mind*, vol. II., p. 516.
[3] Bacon: *Opera Inedita*, ed. Brewer, Rolls Series, p. lix.

instructed in languages and geometric figures, in numbers and tables and instruments, and many needful matters." [1]

Interest in education was apparently spreading about this time. "Never," writes Bacon, "has there been such a show of wisdom, nor such prosecution of study through so many regions as in the last forty years. Doctors are spread everywhere, especially in theology, in every city, castle, and burgh, chiefly through the two student orders." [2] In spite of this general interest Bacon complains that "never was there so much ignorance and so much error." Four causes are enumerated by him to account for this ignorance—"the example of frail and unworthy authority, long established custom, the sense of the ignorant crowd and the hiding of one's own ignorance under the show of Wisdom." [3] The fourth cause, especially, is arraigned by Bacon: "This is a lone and savage beast, which devours and destroys all reason—this desire of seeming wise, with which every man is born."

In addition to this general attack upon the causes of the prevalent ignorance, Bacon specifies seven distinct charges against the teachers of his day. [4]

(1) Though theology is the queen of the sciences, yet philosophy is allowed to dominate.

(2) Theologians do not study sufficiently the "best sciences." By the "best sciences," Bacon meant "the grammar of the foreign tongues, from which all theology comes. Of even more value are mathematics, optics, moral sciences, experimental science, and alchemy." The "common sciences" (scientiae viles) include "grammar, logic, natural philosophy in its baser part, and a certain side of metaphysic."

(3) Scholars are ignorant of Greek and Hebrew and Arabic, and consequently they are ignorant of what is contained in the books written in these languages.

(4) They lecture on the "Sentences" of Peter Lombard, instead of on the text of Scripture.

(5) The copy of the Vulgate Scripture at Paris is very corrupt.

[1] *Ibid.*, p. 59.   [2] *Ibid.*, p. 398.
[3] *Opus Major*, par. 1.   [4] See Brewer's ed., p. 322, *seq.*

(6) Through the corrupt condition of the text, both the literal interpretation and the spiritual interpretation of the Scripture is full of error.

The text of the *Opus Minus* is broken off at this point, so that no information is forthcoming as to the seventh criticism that Bacon desired to offer.[1]

In order to remedy the educational shortcomings, Bacon suggests additions to the usual subjects of study. Special attention, he thinks, should be paid to languages, particularly to Latin and Greek; in addition, Bacon was anxious that Hebrew, Chaldee, and Arabic should be studied. It is noteworthy that Bacon desired these languages to be studied for the sake of their knowledge-matter, and not for the literature they embodied. Next to languages, Bacon placed the study of mathematics. " I hold mathematics necessary in the second place, to the end that we may know what may be known. It is not planted in us by nature, yet is closest to inborn knowledge, of all the sciences which we know through discovery and learning. For its study is easier than all other sciences, and boys learn its branches easily. Besides, the laity can make diagrams, and calculate and sing, and use musical instruments. These are the ' opera ' of mathematics." [2]

From Bacon we learn something of the difficulties with which the medieval scholar had to contend. Among other things, he complains of the indifferent value of the translations, through whose aid alone knowledge was possible. " Though we have numerous translations of all the sciences . . . there is such an utter falsity in all their writings that none can sufficiently wonder at it." [3] The scarcity of books placed a great obstacle in the way of those who wished to profit by them. " The scientific books of Aristotle, of Avicenna, of Seneca, of Cicero, and other ancients, cannot be had except at great cost; their principal works have not been translated into Latin, and copies of others are not to be found in ordinary libraries or elsewhere." [4] The

---

[1] Cf. Taylor, *op. cit.*, vol. II., p. 527.
[2] *Opus Tertium*, Ch. XXIX., trans. by Taylor.
[3] *Opera Inedita*, ed. Brewer, p. lix.
[4] *Op. cit.*, p. lxii.

scarcity of competent teachers, especially in mathematics, still further intensified the difficulties. " Without mathematics, nothing worth knowing in philosophy can be attained. And, therefore, it is indispensable that good mathematicians be had, who are very scarce. Nor can any obtain their services, especially the best of them, except it be the pope or some great prince." [1] Moreover, there was the scarcity and the expense of obtaining the necessary scientific apparatus: " without mathematical instruments no science can be mastered; and these instruments are not to be found among the Latins, and could not be made for £200 or £300. And besides, better tables are indispensable requisites, for although the certifying of the tables is done by instruments, yet this cannot be accomplished unless there be an immense number of instruments." [2] The question of expense is a matter that Bacon frequently refers to, as he found that inability to meet the expenditure necessary for the work he desired to carry out effectually checked the projects he had in his mind. " I know how to proceed," he writes, " and with what means, and what are the impediments; but I cannot go on for lack of the necessary funds. Through the twenty years in which I laboured specially in the study of wisdom, careless of the crowd's opinion, I spent more than two thousand pounds on occult books and various experiments and languages and instruments and tables and other things." [3]

Details are also available of the curriculum for the bachelors who were to determine at Oxford in 1267. This included :—

Logic. The bachelors " shall swear on the gospels that they have gone through all the books of the old Logic in lectures at least twice, except Boethius, for which one hearing is enough, and the Fourth Book of Boethius' Topics, which they are not bound to hear at all; in the new Logic, the book of Prior Analytics, Topics and Fal-

[1] *Op. cit.*, p. lxxv.
[2] *Op. cit.*, p. lxxv.
[3] *Opera Inedita*, ed. Brewer, pp. 58, 59.

lacies twice; but the book of Posterior Analytics, they shall swear that they have heard at least once."

Grammar. Priscian and Donatus.

Natural Philosophy. " De Anima, De Generatione et Corruptione." [1]

For the fourteenth century we have the writings of Chaucer, which serve to throw some light upon what was taught in the schools. He tells us of :—

> " A litel scole of Cristen folk ther stood
> Doun at the ferther ende, in which ther were
> Children an heep, y comen of Christen blood
> That lerned in that scole yeer by yeer,
> Swich maner doctrine as men used there,
> That is to seyn, to singen and to rede,
> As smale children doon in hir childhede." [2]

Among these children, he describes a " widwes sone, a lytel clergeon, seven yeer of age " who had been taught by a pious mother to kneel down and say an " Ave Marie " whenever he saw " th' image of Cristes moder." The little boy heard his elders singing the " Alma redemptoris," and asked one of them to " expounden this song in his langage, or telle him why this song was in usage." The older boy explains that it was sung in honour of the Mother of Christ, " Hir to salue and eek hir for to preye." However, he could tell his questioner little more.

> " I can no more expounde in this matere ;
> I lerne song, I can but smal grammere,"

i.e. he was learning how to read and sing, but his knowledge of Latin was slight.

These extracts from Chaucer enable us to see that schools were common at this time, and that the curriculum of the schools consisted of Latin reading, of song, and, for those who showed aptitude, a further study of Latin grammar.

Chaucer also describes for us :—

> " A clerk ther was of Oxenford also,
> That unto logik hadde longe y go,"

---

[1] Anstey : *Munimenta Academica*, I., p. 34.
[2] Chaucer : *Canterbury Tales*, ed. Skeat, p. 299.

but the only information we glean of the academic studies of this clerk was, that he had,

> " at his beddes heed,
> Twenty bokes, clad in blak or reed,
> Of Aristotle and his philosophye." [1]

At the close of the fourteenth century, the statutes of New College, Oxford, which were also partly those of Winchester College, give us the curriculum of the time. The university scholars were to study Theology, Canon and Civil Law, Arts, and Philosophy ; the choristers were to be taught to read and sing ; this is subsequently explained to mean " reading, plain song and old Donatus." The " pauperes scholares " of Winchester were expected to be proficient in grammar.[2]

From this time onwards we begin to get fuller particulars of the school curriculum. Hence it is only necessary for us to quote representative examples.

I. IPSWICH.

Some particulars of the curriculum of a grammar school may be gleaned from an extract from an entry in the Ipswich Court Book of 1476-7. It runs:—

" The grammar master shall henceforth have the jurisdiction and governaunce of all scholars within the liberty and precinct of this town, except only petties called " Apeseyes " and song, taking for his salary from each grammar scholar, psalter scholar, and primer scholar, according to the tariff fixed by the Bishop of Norwich, viz. for each grammarian 10d., psalterian 8d., and primerian 6d. a quarter." [3]

This extract brings out four grades of instruction.

1. The petties or infants, consisting of those who learnt the A B C.[4]

2. Those who were studying a primer.[5]

3. Those learning the Psalms.

4. Those studying Donatus and Priscian.

---

[1] *Ibid.*, p. 421.
[2] *Statutes of the Colleges of Oxford*, vol. I. ; *Ed. Ch.*, pp. 349-373.
[3] Brit. Mus. Add., MS. 30158, f. 34.   [4] *I.e.* the " Apeseyes."
[5] Cf. article in *Cyclopaedia of Education.*

II. CHILDREY.

The first full curriculum of a school which we have been able to trace, is that which was drawn up for the use of the school which was founded in 1526 at Childrey, in Berkshire, by Sir William Fettiplace. The priest to be appointed to the school was required to be well instructed in grammar. The children in the school were to be taught, first, the alphabet, and then in Latin, the Lord's Prayer, the "Hail Mary," the Apostles' Creed, all things necessary for serving at Mass, the De Profoundis, collects for the departed, and grace for dinner and supper; and in English, the Fourteen Articles of Faith, the Ten Commandments, the seven deadly sins, the seven sacraments, the seven gifts of the Holy Spirit, the seven works of mercy, the manner of confession, good manners and good conduct. In addition, if any of those who attended the school were capable of profiting by further instruction, the master was required to instruct them in grammar.[1]

III. ETON.

We also possess a full account of the curriculum adopted at the school founded by the will of Edmund Flower, a "citizein and marchaunt tailor of London."[2] Previous to his death, Flower had "for certeine years past at his cost and charge caused a fre Gramer Scole to be maintained and kept at Cukfelde." This school was further endowed by William Spicer, the incumbent of Balcombe in 1528, who required that the schoolmaster should "teach the said school grammar after the form order and usage used and taught in the grammar school at Eton near Windsor from form to form." For this purpose, a copy of the Eton time table was obtained. This original has, unfortunately, been lost, but a copy, which dates from the Stuart period, is still preserved in a book in the possession of the Vicar of Cuckfield.[3] The Eton time table of this period was also sent to Saffron

---

[1] Carlisle : *Grammar Schools*, I., p. 314.
[2] *P. C. C.*, 8 Maynwaryng.
[3] See Carlisle, *op. cit.*, II., pp. 594-598.

Walden School, and, together with the time table of Winchester, was incorporated in the Saffron Walden School statutes.[1]

The statutes show that the Latin grammar in use was that by Stanbridge, so far as the lower forms were concerned, and that by Whittington in the higher forms. John Stanbridge, who was made master of Banbury Hospital School in 1501, wrote several Latin Grammars. The teaching of grammar "after the manner of Banbury" was subsequently prescribed at a number of grammar schools, e.g. Manchester, Cuckfield, and Merchant Taylors.[2] Whittington was the master of the school at Lichfield, in connection with St. John's Hospital in that city; he brought out an improved version of the grammar of Stanbridge.[3]

The Latin authors mentioned in these statutes include Terence, Cicero, Sallust, Caesar, Horace, Ovid, Virgil, thus showing that the influence of the Renaissance was beginning to be felt. Here, however, we touch upon a topic which must be reserved for future consideration. It is possible to read too much into this list of authors, as Colet, in his statute of 1518, when dealing with the choice of authors to be studied at St. Paul's School, mentions Lactantius, Prudentius, Proba, Sedulius, Juvencus, and Baptista Mantuanus, even though he expressly stated that he wished to select only "good auctors suych as have the veray Romayne eloquence joyned with wisdome."

We may, therefore, summarise the school curriculum of the Middle Ages as consisting mainly of grammar, meaning by the term the study of the reading of ecclesiastical Latin, and the acquisition of the power to speak Latin. During the twelfth and thirteenth centuries, Logic was also studied

[1] A copy of this time table is reprinted in Leach; *Educational Charters*, pp. 448-451; see also *Archaelogia*, XXXIV., p. 37, *seq.* Foster Watson gives a full account of the projected statutes for Cardinal College, Ipswich (1528) in *Old Grammar Schools*, pp. 16-18.

[2] For an account of the manuals of Stanbridge, see Foster Watson : *English Grammar Schools*, pp. 385-386.

[3] *Ibid.*, pp. 238-45.

and, for a time, was the supreme study. Gradually the study of Logic returned to a subsidiary position, due, partly, to the fact that new studies were slowly finding their way into the curriculum owing to the humanistic influences which began to manifest themselves in Italy in the fourteenth century; and partly to the fact that the barren nature of the study of Logic was being realised by men of thought.

A new subject began to win a place in the school curriculum towards the close of the fifteenth century—the study of the Scrivener's art, or the art of writing. We have already dealt with this subject in previous chapters.[1] Here it may suffice to set forth the reason which Thomas Rotherham, Archbishop of York, gave for introducing the subject into his Foundation of Rotherham College in 1483 :—[2]

"Tercio que, quia multos luce et ingenii acumine preditos juvenes profert terra illa, neque omnes volunt sacerdotii dignitatem et altitudinem attingere, ut tales ad artes mechanicas et alia mundi Concernia magis habilitentur, ordinavimus tercium socium, in arte scribendi et computandi scientem et peritum."

[1] Among the records of the chantry schools, six are mentioned as teaching writing ; see *E. S. R.*, II., pp. 66, 98, 251, 305, 307, 312.
[2] *Yorkshire Schools*, II., p. 109.

CHAPTER IX.

THE PROGRESS OF EDUCATION.

In reviewing the educational progress which our country has made during the later Middle Ages, our starting point must be the consideration of the ideals which at various times dominated education, and created a supply of, and a demand for, facilities for education.

The ideal behind the schools first established in this country was essentially religious. The early missionaries clearly realised that the Christian religion could not exist side by side with ignorance. It was necessary that provision should be made to enable converts effectively to participate in the divine service offered by the church; it was imperative that Latin should be taught to those who wished properly to understand the teaching of the church and to those who were desirous of being admitted to office in the church. Latin was the native language of the Christian missionaries; the services of the church were conducted in that tongue; and medieval ecclesiastical literature was written in the Latin language. More than this, Latin was the universal language of the civilised world of the time and, it must be remembered, there was no standard language in this country which could act as a substitute. It was in response to this ideal of the Church, the ideal which required that facilities for religious education should be within the reach of all, that the Church set herself to see that in every parish, in every town, in every city, a school should be found.

The progress of the Christian religion entailed a progress

in morality. Progress in morality necessarily involved progress in civilisation. With the growth of civilisation, there developed gradually an interest in the things of the mind as well as the things of the body. Thus it came about that education began to possess a value for its own sake, apart from its service in connection with religious progress.

But the ideal of education, as necessary for moral perfection, never ceased to be the ideal behind the establishment of church schools. From the earliest date three things have been considered necessary for religious education: there must be a training in habits of worship and devotion, the mind must be stored with adequate and systematised knowledge of the doctrine of the Church to serve as a guide to conduct, and there must be held before the mind of the pupil the ideal character of Christ, human and divine.

Hence we note that the curriculum of the schools evolved in response to this ideal. It consisted, as we have seen, of song and grammar: song, because of its value in the training of habits of worship and devotion ; grammar, because it put the scholar in possession of the key to unlock the store of knowledge which the Church possessed.

Gradually another ideal came into existence. People began to realise that these church schools were useful for "bread and butter" purposes. Just as the ideal which we have first outlined and which created the supply of schools was the highest possible, so the motive which exercised an important influence upon the demand for schools was the lowest possible. Yet, it must be confessed that the "bread and butter" motive proved to be a most powerful one in stimulating the demand for schools. Throughout the history of the human race self-interest has always been a powerful stimulant to action. Under normal circumstances and in the great majority of cases, as soon as a man freely realises that a certain course will be of service to him, he proceeds to take the necessary action.

These two ideals were in operation, side by side, during the period from the eleventh century to the close of the

Middle Ages. The authorities of the church, believing in
the value of education as an agency for the elevation of
the human character sought to provide schools ; the principle of self-interest, in many cases, led children to attend
these schools.

Towards the latter part of the period we are now concerned with, a new ideal and a new agency gradually
manifested itself. The new ideal arose out of the percep-
tion of the value of education. Education began to be
conceived of as a preparation for a life in this world as
well as a life in eternity ; now " learning and manners "
begin to be combined just as previously "religion and
letters " were linked together. Thus we read that the
school at Wisbech was founded that children might be
instructed in "godly and vertuos leruinge," [1] and the
school at Tewkesbury " for the bringynge up of the saide
youths in knowlege of vertue and good learninge." [2]

With this realisation of a social ideal for education,
schools began to be provided by civic societies and by
merchants who had gained a fortune for themselves. The
social ideal arose out of the value of religious education,
hence the curriculum was not affected. There was a change
in the agency through which the school was provided,
there was a change in the mode of governing the schools,
there was a change in the relationship of the teacher to
the church, but there was no change in the curriculum.
Inspired originally by a religious ideal, it was now known
to serve a social purpose.

Among the early merchant founders of schools may be
mentioned William Sevenoaks, a grocer of London, who
founded Sevenoaks Grammar School in 1432, Edmund
Flower, citizen and merchant tailor of London, the founder
of Cuckfield Grammar School in 1521, Richard Collyer,
mercer, who founded Horsham School, Sussex, in 1532,
and William Dyer, mercer, who founded a school at
Houghton Regis in 1515.

Bearing these general principles in mind, we find that
the main events connected with the progress of education

---

[1] *E. S. R.*, II., p. 21.   [2] *E. S. R.*, II., p. 85.

during the later Middle Ages may conveniently be considered under three headings.

1. Circumstances which influenced the demand for schools.
2. Lollardism and Education.
3. Educational Legislation.

(1) The circumstances which influenced the demand for schools arose out of the existing social conditions. The Church, as a profession, offered considerable attraction to the able but penniless youth. Many of the outstanding churchmen of the Middle Ages were men who had come from a comparatively lowly origin. Thus William of Wykeham was the son of a yeoman whose ancestors for generations had "ploughed the same lands, knelt at the same altar, and paid due customs and service to the lord of the manor." Henry Chicheley, afterwards Archbishop of Canterbury, famous as the founder of All Soul's College, was also the son of a yeoman. William Waynflete, afterwards Bishop of Winchester and Lord Chancellor of England, was of lowly origin and at one time occupied the comparatively humble position of grammar master at Eton College at a salary of £10 a year.

But apart from the great prizes of the church available to those of outstanding ability, there were also a large number of openings possible to the man who had availed himself of the educational facilities offered by the church schools and had there mastered the elements of grammar. He might proceed from the parochial church schools to the school of a collegiate church, and possibly he might make his way to the university and ultimately obtain ordination to the priesthood.

The financial advantages of the education offered by the church became obvious after the Norman Conquest, and arose out of an undesigned circumstance. Prior to the Conquest, the parishes of this country were under the spiritual care of Saxon rectors who were generally well-born and whose position was well-endowed. The Norman Conquest ultimately resulted in these men being deprived of their cures and being replaced by ill-paid vicars or parochial chaplains. The chief factors which brought about this condition of things were impropriations, papal provisors, pluralities, and the custom, which gradually grew up, of appointing to livings men who had only been admitted to minor orders in the church.

The practice of impropriation was an indirect result of the revival of the monastic principle. The custom of endowing a newly founded monastery with the patronage of existing churches gradually came into being. When a vacancy occurred, the monastery as patrons of the benefice bestowed it upon themselves as a corporation, and drew the stipend attached to it, appointing a " vicar " to perform the requisite spiritual duties, and allowing the vicar only a comparatively insignificant share of the temporalities of the benefice. The position of the incumbent was consequently considerably degraded both in dignity and in emolument.

The custom of papal provisors dates from the thirteenth century when the popes began to assume a power of nominating to vacant benefices. In this way foreigners were appointed to many of the most lucrative of the English benefices. Naturally they never came near their parishes, but contented themselves with the appointment of an ill-paid parochial chaplain to discharge the necessary duties. This custom was put an end to by the Statute of Praemunire (1392).

We must also note that the system of pluralities was carried on in the Middle Ages to an extent which seems to us almost incredible to-day. One man might hold several valuable livings which he never went near, whilst a clerk, who was frequently paid a miserable wage, was expected to do the work. Equally vicious was the custom of appointing to benefices men who had only been admitted to minor clerical orders. " A glance at the lists of incumbents of parishes in any good county history will reveal the fact that rectors of parishes were often only deacons, sub-deacons, or acolytes. It is clear that in many of these cases—probably in the majority of them—the men had taken minor orders only to qualify themselves for holding the temporalities of a benefice and never proceeded to the priesthood at all." [1] Just as in the other cases we have mentioned, these men drew the revenues of the living and then appointed a deputy at a small salary to be responsible for the duty.

Whilst the spiritual effects of this policy were disastrous, the policy itself resulted in education becoming an object of desire to men in the lower social grades, as they saw in education an opportunity of escape from their existing circumstances. It does not follow that these men made either incapable or undesirable priests. One of the most charming pictures drawn by Chaucer is that of the poor parson of the town, but his social position is indicated by the fact that "with him there was a ploughman, was his brother."

The number of possible ecclesiastical appointments does not end with vicars and parochial chaplains. In addition there were the numerous chantries, which existed in connection with so very many churches in the country, and for each of which one or two priests would be required. Then again the gilds to which we have already referred usually maintained one or more chaplains. In these ways employment would probably be found for a large number of priests. "There were at the Reformation, ten gilds in Windham in Norfolk, seven at Hingham, seventeen at Yarmouth. Moreover, a gild like a chantry, had sometimes more than one gild priest. Leland tells us that the gild of St. John's in St. Botolph's Church, Boston, had ten priests 'living in a fayre house at the west end of the parish churchyard.' In St. Mary's Church, Lichfield, was a gild which had five priests." [2]

Besides all these regular appointments, there were a large number of priests who earned fees by taking "temporary engagements" to say masses for the souls of the departed. Thus Archbishop Islip in his "Constitutions" speaks of this class as those who "through covetousness and love of ease, not content with reasonable salaries, demand excessive pay for their labours and receive it." [3] Chaucer

[1] Cutts : *Scenes and Characters in the Middle Ages*, p. 200.
[2] Cutts : *op. cit.*, p. 205.　　　　[3] Johnson : *Canons*, II., p. 421.

introduces one of these characters into his *Canon Yeoman's Tale* :—

> " In London was a priest an annueller,
> That therein dwelled hadde many a year
> Which was so pleasant and so serviceable
> Unto the wife there as he was at table
> That she would suffer him no thing to pay
> For board ne clothing went he never so gay
> And spending silver had he right ynoit."

Employment for qualified men was also available in connection with the establishments of great nobles. The household books which are available usually contain a record relating to a "maister of gramer." In addition to grammar masters, these establishments often afforded opportunities for employment for a number of priests. The " Household Book of the Earl of Northumberland " gives us information which enables us to see that he maintained a dean, ten other priests, and six children, who formed a choir for his private chapel.[1]

It was not only noblemen of high standing who numbered chaplains on their establishment. Knights and gentlemen and even wealthy tradesmen and yeomen also had their domestic chaplains. Sir Thomas More writes : " there was such a rabel (of priests) that every mean man must have a priest to wait upon his wife, which no man almost lacketh now." [2]

We have thus demonstrated that there existed a considerable demand for men who had received a certain amount of education, and that as a result the demand for schools was stimulated. The account we have given in the preceding part of this work shows that a supply of schools was forthcoming to meet this demand. We have confined ourselves here to treating of the demand for men of education in connection with ecclesiastical positions, but it would also have been possible to show that men of education were also needed in connection with commerce and law.

---

[1] *Household Book of Henry Algernon, fifth Earl of Northumberland*, Antiq. Repertory, IV., p. 242.
[2] *Dialogue of Heresies*, III., c. 12.

(2) Turning next to the second of the three headings we have indicated, we note that Lollardism is the general term applied to the political and theological doctrines associated with the name of John Wycliffe. His main ideas are embodied in his *De Civili Domino* and *De Domino Divino*. The chief subject discussed in these works is the nature of the relationship between a ruler and his subjects and between divine and civil lordship. His conception of this relationship is based on a feudal view of society, and he continually borrows illustrations of the relationship of divine to civil lordship from the connection between feudal lord and vassal. It was his application of this doctrine to questions touching temporal property that brought him under the imputation of heresy because he taught that " ecclesiastical persons or corporations had no indefeasible right to temporalities which might be taken away in case of misuse." [1] This theory cut across the doctrine of the supremacy of the spiritual power. The State, according to Wycliffe, possessed the power of determining the function of the Church, and when the Church either extended the sphere of its legitimate operations or misused the revenues entrusted to it for spiritual purposes, then it was the duty of the State to take such action as might be necessary for the reformation of the Church.

Poole points out [2] that the main principle contained in the writings of Wycliffe is the recognition of the significance of the individual whom Wycliffe regarded as directly responsible to God, and to no one else. Wycliffe divorced the Church from any necessary connection with the State and conceived of it simply as a spiritual idea and as consisting of individuals in a certain relation to God. It is to the uniqueness of Wycliffe's idea of individualism that Poole considers the claim of Wycliffe to rank as the " precursor of the Protestant reformation " to be due.

The doctrines associated with Wycliffe seem to have made great progress among the teachers of the time. This is not a matter for surprise. Facilities for education were

[1] Dunning : *Political Ideas*, p. 263.
[2] *Illustrations of Medieval Thought*, p. 305.

abundant and education was free. Either by means of begging, or by exhibitions, or through social interest, a student might be maintained without expense to himself until his course was completed. What happened then? Owing to the system of patronage prevailing in the Church, the clerk found that all the lucrative positions were usually given to men who on account of their social connections could command influence, regardless of their merits or demerits. This is brought out clearly when we consider the presentees to benefices by patrons whom Bishop Grosseteste refused to institute. One presentee was refused by the bishop because he was a " boy still in Ovid ";[1] another on the ground that the young man was practically illiterate;[2] in answer to a request of the papal legate, to institute a son of Earl Ferrers to a living, the bishop asks to be excused ; when pressed, he suggests that the son of Earl Ferrers should simply draw the revenues of the living and appoint a vicar to discharge the spiritual duties.[3]

It is not a matter of wonder that the views of Wycliffe found ready supporters among those of the clergy who were of a low social origin. They considered themselves qualified for ecclesiastical positions which they had little hope of ever filling; hence they drifted to the teaching profession, and in their bitterness of feeling would use the opportunity they possessed to propagate among their scholars the new ideas they had acquired.

It is on an hypothesis of the kind which we have outlined that it is possible to interpret the legislation against Lollard teachers which was enacted in the fifteenth century. In 1400, an Act was passed which provided that:—

" None of such sect and wicked doctrines and opinions shall make any conventicles, or in any wise hold or exercise schools." [4]

Any offender against this Act or anyone who in any way assisted or supported an offender, " shall before the people in an high place be burnt."

---

[1] *Letters of Grosseteste* (R. S.), p. 63.
[2] *Ibid.*, p. 68.   [3] *Ibid.*, p. 151.
[4] 2 Hen. IV., c. 15.   *Stat. of the Realm*, II., 127.

In 1406 a petition was presented to the king by the Prince of Wales which drew attention to the propagation of teaching against the temporal possessions of the clergy by certain teachers in "lieux secretes appellez escoles,"[1] and prayed that no man or woman of any sect or doctrine which was contrary to the catholic faith should hold school. The rigour with which this commission was enforced is illustrated by the commission which was issued to the prior of St. Mary's, Coventry, and to the mayor and bailiffs of that city ordering them to arrest and imprison all offenders found there.

The spread of Lollardism among teachers is further illustrated by the "Constitutions" of Archbishop Arundel issued in 1408. He forbade "masters and all who teach boys or others the arts of grammar and that instruct men in the first sciences" to teach theology except in accordance with the customary teaching of the Church, and also prohibited them from allowing their scholars to select as subjects for disputations any topics relating to the catholic faith or the sacraments of the Church.[2]

As the existing legislation was apparently not sufficient to effect the desired purpose, another Act was passed in 1414. By this Act "all of them which hold any errors or heresies as Lollards" and who sustained it in "sermons, schools, conventicles, congregations, and confederacies" were to be arrested.[3]

We have not found it possible to trace the effects of this legislation.

(3) We pass next to consider the Educational Legislation during the later Middle Ages. In our summary of the economic condition of this country at the opening of this period we referred to the scarcity of labour consequent upon the Black Death.[4] As a result an Act was passed in 1388, which provided that "he or she which used to labour at the Plough and Cart till they be of the age of twelve

[1] *Rot. Parl.*, III., 584.
[2] Johnson : *Laws and Canons*, II., p. 465. Wilkins : *Concilia*, III., p. 317.
[3] 2 Hen. V., c. 7. [4] See p. 129.

years, from henceforth they shall abide at the same labour without being put to any Mystery or Handicraft; and if any Covenant or Bond of Apprentice be from henceforth made to the contrary, the same shall be taken for void." [1] The reason for this Act is embodied in the statute itself: "there is so great scarcity of Labourers and other Servants of Husbandry that the Gentlemen and other People of the realm be greatly impoverished for the cause thereof."

Either on account of the prosperity of the labouring classes due to the increase of wages resulting from the demand for labour in the later fourteenth century, or to avoid the provisions of the Act we have just described, or for the purpose of making progress in social status, the custom of sending children to schools seems to have developed. As a result, the Commons of England petitioned the king in 1391 "de ordeiner et comander, que null neif ou Vileyn mette ses Enfantz de cy en avant a Escoles pur eux avancer par Clergie et ce en maintenance et salvation de l'honour de toutz Frankes du Roialme." [2]

Mr. de Montmorency suggests four reasons for this action on the part of the Commons.

(1) The Commons "were anxious to check the further increase in the number of unbeneficed clergy and of those whom the bishops could claim as subject to ecclesiastical law."

(2) Lollardism would be very attractive to the newly educated and "the Legislature must have realised the revolutionary possibility of the first and nobler Reformation."

(3) "The jurisdiction of Rome increased with the increase of popular education," consequently, this "was a serious consideration for the patriotic baronage of England."

(4) If a man became ordained, his services would be lost to the manor. [3]

These reasons do not appear to be very conclusive. The first implies an opposition between the clergy and laity

---

[1] *Rot. Parl.*, 12, R. II., c. 5.
[2] *Rot. Parl.*, 15, Ric. II., 39; quoted de Montmorency, *State Intervention*, p. 27.   [3] *Op. cit.*, pp. 30-32.

which was non-existent; the second and the third are contradictory. If the development of education fostered Lollardism (which is probable, though it has not yet been demonstrated) it could scarcely be regarded as equally favourable to Rome. Further, the desire of limiting the jurisdiction of the Church could have been gratified more simply by the abolition of the " privilege of clergy."

His fourth reason is a more plausible one but it must be noted that the consent of the lord of the manor was required before children could be sent to schools and before ordination.[1] For this reason, legislation would scarcely be necessary to effect this purpose.

The more probable reason for this petition of the commons is that the diminution of the supply of labour had caused employers to become fearful of future possibilities, and that they were afraid that the result of sending children to school would be that the number of those who would be prepared to act as " hewers of wood and drawers of water " would be seriously diminished.

We have just referred to the custom that villeins were not allowed to send their children to school without the consent of their lords. This custom was abolished by a statute of 1406 which provided that " chascun homme ou femme de quele estate ou condicion qil soit, soit fraunc de mettre son fitz ou file dapprendre lettereure a quelconque escole que leur plest deinz le Roialme." [2] The same statute provided that labourers could not apprentice their children to trades and manufactures in the towns unless they owned land worth £1 a year, probably about £40 a year now.

It is difficult to understand the reasons for this legislation. The Feudal System was already crumbling and its complete collapse was not far off. It cannot therefore be assumed that the Act was passed merely to remove a grievance, because the grievance itself was probably lightly felt. It is just possible that the Act might have been intended to facilitate the process by which it was sought to make good the deficiency of priests occasioned by the Black Death.

[1] See p. 200.   [2] *Statutes of the Realm*, 7, Henry IV., c. 17.

The reference to "daughters," however, makes this suggestion improbable. There is also the possibility that the phrase " dapprendre lettereure " meant an education which would provide for " godly and virtuous living," which, as we have shown in the preceding chapter, was becoming recognised as a part of the educational ideal.

The years 1446-7 are important in the history of education in England. In 1446 the Archbishop of Canterbury and the Bishop of London petitioned the king for permission to erect two new grammar schools in London ; the permission was granted and the Letters Patent duly issued.[1] In 1447, a petition was similarly sent to the Commons by four London Rectors for permission to set up four new grammar schools.[2] As we have already considered these petitions in the chapter dealing with the question of the monopoly of school keeping, [3] it will not be necessary for us to deal further with the topic here.

We have now brought to a close our exposition of the educational administration in England in the Middle Ages. Until comparatively recently it was generally believed that the educational provision available in this country could not be traced back further than to the efforts of the Reformers of the Church in the sixteenth century, and to the influence of the Renaissance. We are now able to realise that the two centuries preceding the Reformation, at least, were a period in which facilities for education in England were widespread and practically open freely to all. The educational effect of the Reformation—even though undesigned—was to remove from the great mass of the people the opportunities for attending school which had previously been available for them. It is also extremely probable that the significance of the Renaissance upon the educational development of this country has been considerably exaggerated; this, however, is a question which still awaits investigation.

[1] *Pat.*, 24, Henry VI., pt. ii., m. 28.
[2] *Rot. Parl.*, V., 137.   [3] Bk. II., ch. VI.

APPENDIX.

WORKS CONSULTED.

A.—Sources.

Aelfric: *Homilies* (with translation by B. Thorpe), 2 vols., Lond., 1844-6.

Alcuin: *Opera Omnia Patrologiae Cursus Complexus*, ed. Migne, vols. C., CI., 1851.

Aldhelm: *Opera*, ed. J. A. Giles, Oxon., 1844.

Alfred the Great: *Preface to Gregory's Pastoral Care*, ed. H. Sweet (Early English Text Society), 50.

Ancient Laws and Institutes of England, ed. B. Thorpe, (Rec. Com.) Lond., 1840.

Anglo-Saxon Chronicle, The, ed. B. Thorpe, 2 vols. (R. S.), Lond., 1861.

Annales Monastici, ed. H. R. Luard, 5 vols. (R. S.), Lond., 1864-6-9.

Asserius de Rebus Gestis Alfredi, ed. W. H. Stevenson, Lond., 1904.

Bacon, Roger: *Opera Inedita*, ed. J. S. Brewer (R. S.), Lond., 1859.

Basil, St.: *Opera*, 3 vols., Paris, 1839.

Becket, Thomas à, Materials for a History of, ed. J. C. Robertson, J. B. Sheppard (R. S.), 7 vols., Lond., 1885.

Bede: *Opera Historica*, ed. C. Plummer, 2 vols., Oxon., 1876.

Beverley Minster, Memorials of, ed. A. F. Leach (Surtees Society), Durham, 1898.

Cardwell, E.: *Synodalia*, 2 vols., Oxon., 1842.
  ,,   ,, : *Documentary Annals of the Church of England*, 2 vols., Oxon., 1844.

Charters and Documents illustrating the History of the Cathedral City of Sarum, 1100-1300, ed. W. D. Macray (R.S.), 1891.

Chaucer, Geoffrey: *Complete Works*, ed. W. W. Skeat, Oxon., 1894-7.

Chronica Jocelini de Brakelonda, ed. J. G. Rakewood (Camden Society Publications, XIII.).

Chronica Monasterii St. Albani, Johannis de Trokelowe, Chronica et Annales, ed. H. T. Riley, 2 vols. (R. S.), Lond., 1866.

Chronica Monasterii Gesta Abbatum Monasterii Sancti Albani, ed. H. T. Riley, 3 vols. (R. S.), 1867-9.

Chronica Monasterii, Ypodigma Neustriae a Thomas Walsingham, ed. H. T. Riley (R. S.), 1876.

Chronica Rogeri de Wendover, ed. H. G. Hewlett, 3 vols., Lond., 1886-9.

Chronicon Abbatiae Rameseiensis, ed. W. D. Macray, 2 vols. (R. S.), Lond., 1882-83.

Chronicon Monasterii de Abingdon, ed. J. S. Stevenson, 2 vols. (R. S.), Lond., 1858.

Chronicon Petroburgense (Camden Society, XLVII.), 1849·

Corpus Juris Canonici, ed. A. L. Richter, 2 vols., 2nd ed., Leipzig, 1879-81.

Coventry Leet Book, ed. M. D. Harris (Early English Text Society), 1907.

Dachery, L.: *Spicilegium, sive collectio veterum scriptorum qui in Galliae Bibliothecis delituerant*, ed. nova. a De la Barre, 3 vols., Paris, 1723.

Documents illustrating Early Education in Worcester, ed. A. F. Leach, Lond., 1913.

Dugdale, Sir W.: *Monasticon Anglicanum*, ed. J. Caley, H. Ellis, B. Bandinel, 6 vols., Lond., 1817.

Dunstan, St., Memorials of, ed. W. Stubbs (R. S.), Lond., 1874.

Early Yorkshire Schools, ed. A. F. Leach (Yorks. Archaeol. Assoc. Record Series, vols. XXVII. and XXXII.), 1899-1903.

Fifty Earliest English Wills (1387-1439), ed. F. J. Furnivall (Early English Text Society), No. 67.

Flores Historarium, ed. H. R. Luard, 3 vols. (R. S.), Lond., 1890.

Freemen of York (Surtees Soc.), XCVIII., 2 vols., 1897.

Giraldus Cambrensis, Opera, ed. J. S. Brewer, J. F. Dimondes, A. F. Warner (R. S.), 8 vols., Lond., 1861-91.

Gross, Charles: *The Gild Merchant*, 2 vols., Oxon., 1890.

Grosseteste, Robert: *Epistolae*, ed. H. R. Luard (R. S.), Lond., 1861.

Haddon and Stubbs: *Councils and Documents relating to Great Britain and Ireland*, 2 vols., Oxon., 1877-8.

Higden, Ranulf, Polychronicon (with the English translation of John Trevisa), ed. C. Babington, J. R. Lumby, 9 vols. (R. S.), Lond., 1865-83.

Hingeston-Randulph, F. C.: *The Episcopal Registers of the Diocese of Exeter*, Lond., 1886.

Historia et Cartularium Monasterii St. Petri Gloucestriae, ed. W. H. Harte, 3 vols. (R. S.), Lond., 1863-67.

Historians and Archbishops of the Church of York, ed. J. Raine, 3 vols. (R. S.), Lond., 1879-94.

Historical Papers and Letters from the Northern Registers, ed. J. Raine (R. S.), Lond., 1873.

Historical Works of Gervase of Canterbury, ed. W. Stubbs, 2 vols. (R. S.), 1879-80.

Household Books of John, Duke of Norfolk, and Thomas, Earl of Surrey, Roxburg Club, 1844.

John of Salisbury : *Omnia Opera*, ed. J. A. Giles, 5 vols., Oxon., 1848.

Johnson, J. : *A Collection of the Laws and Canons of the Church of England*, 2 vols., Oxon., 1850-1.

Lanfranc : *Opera*, ed. J. A. Giles, Oxon., 1844.

Leach, A. F. : *Educational Charters*, Lond., 1911.

Leach, A. F. : *English Schools at the Reformation*, Lond., 1897.

Liber Censualis Vocati Domesday Book, ed. Sir H. Ellis (Rec. Com.), Lond., 1816.

Liber Vitae Ecclesiae Dunelmensis, ed. J. Stevenson (Surtees Society), 1841.

Manners and Meals in the Olden Times, ed. F. J. Furnivall (Early English Text Society), O. S. XXXII.

Memorials of St. Edmunds Abbey, ed. T. Arnold, 3 vols. (R. S.), Lond., 1890-1891.

Migne: *Patrologiae Cursus Complexus*, vols. XXXI., LXVI., CXXXVII., CXXXVIII., CXXXIX.

Monumenta Academica, ed. H. Anstey, 2 vols. (R. S.), Lond., 1868.

Monumenta Franciscana, ed. J. S. Brewer, R. Hewlett (R. S.), 4 vols. 1858-1882.

Neckham, Alexander: *De Natura Rerum*, ed. T. Wright (R. S.), Lond., 1863.

Northumberland Household Book, ed. Bishop Percy, 2nd. edition, Lond., 1827.

Norwich, Visitations of the Diocese of, 1492-1532, ed. A. Jessop (Camden Society, XLIII.).

Paston Letters, ed. J. Gairdner, 6 vols., Lond., 1904.

Pecock, R. : *Repressor of Over-Much Blaming of the Clergy,* ed. C. Babington, 2 vols. (R. S.), 1860.

Pertz, G. H. : *Leges,* 5 vols., Hanover, 1853.

Proceedings and Ordinances of the Privy Council, ed. Sir H. Nicholas, 7 vols. (Rec. Com), 1834-37.

Register of St. Osmund, ed. Rev. W. H. R. Jones, 2 vols. (R. S.), 1883-5.

Registrum Palatinum Dunelmensis, ed. Sir T. D. Hardy, 4 vols. (R. S.), Lond., 1873-78.

Rotuli Hugonis de Welles Episcopi Lincolniensis, ed. W. P. W. Phillimore, F. H. Davies, 3 vols. (Lincoln Record Soc.), 1911.

Sharp, R. R. : *Calendar of Wills proved and enrolled in the Court of Husting,* Lond., 1889-90.

Simpson, W. Sparrow: *Registrum Statutorum et Consuetudinum Ecclesiae Cathedralis St. Pauli,* Lond., 1897.

Smith, J. Toulmin : *English Gilds* (Early English Text Society), Lond., 1870.

Sonner, W.: *Dictionarium Saxonico-Latino-Anglicum,* Oxon., 1659.

Southwell Minster, Visitations and Memorials of, ed. A. F. Leach (Camden Society), N. S., 1891.

Statutes of the Realm, ed. Sir T. E. Tompkins, J. Raithby, J. Caley, and W. Elliot (Rec. Com.), 9 vols., 1819-28.

Stow: *A Survey of London,* ed. C. L. Kingsford, 2 vols., Oxon., 1905.

Valor Ecclesiasticus, ed. J. Caley, Rev. J. Hunter (Rec. Com.), 1817-34.

Waltham Abbey, The Foundations of, ed. W. Stubbs, (R. S.), Lond., 1861.

Wharton, H.: *Anglia Sacra seu Collectio Historiarum de Archiepiscopis et Episcopis Angliae*, 2 vols., Lond., 1861.

Wilkins, D.: *Concilia Magnae Britannicae et Hiberniae*, 4 vols., Lond., 1737.

William of Malmesbury: *De Gestis Pontificum Anglorum*, ed. N. E. S. A. Hamilton (R. S.), Lond., 1870.

William of Malmesbury: *De Gestis Regum Anglorum*, ed. W. Stubbs (R. S.), Lond., 1887-89.

Wulfstan: *Vita St. Aethelwoldi*; Migne: *Patrologiae Cursus Complexus*, CXXXVII.

Yorkshire Chantry Surveys, ed. J. Rainer, 2 vols. (Surtees Society), Lond., 1898.

Calendars of the Charter Rolls.

Calendars of the Close Rolls.

Calendars of the Patent Rolls.

B.—Other Works.

Adams, G. B.: *Civilisation during the Middle Ages*, New York, 1894.

Allain, L'Abbé: *L'instruction primaire en France avant la Révolution*, Paris, 1881.

Ampère, J. J.: *Histoire Littéraire de la France avant la Douzième Siècle*, 3 vols., 1839-40.

Ashley, W. J.: *Introduction to English Economic History*, 2 vols., Lond., 1886.

Azarias, Brother: *Essays Educational*, Chicago, 1896.

Bateson, M.: *Medieval England*, Lond., 1903.

Böhmer: *Kirche und Staat in England und in der Normandie. im XI. und XII. Jahrhundert*, Leipzig, 1899.

Brodrick, G. C.: *History of the University of Oxford*, Lond., 1896.

Burrows, Montague: *Collectanea*, Second Series (*Oxford Hist. Soc. Publications*, vol. XVI.), Third Series, vol. XXXII., Oxon., 1890, 1896.

Capes, W. W.: *The English Church in the Fourteenth and Fifteenth Centuries*, Lond., 1900.

Cavendish, G.: *Life of Cardinal Wolsey*, ed. H. W. Singer, Lond., 1827.

Chevrier, Fischer de: *Histoire de l'instruction populaire en France*, Paris, 1898.

Church, R. W.: *St. Anselm*, Lond., 1884.

Clark, J. Willis: *The Care of Books*, New York, 1901.

Compayré, G.: *Abelard, and the Origin and Early History of the Universities*, New York, 1893.

Conybeare, E.: *Alfred in the Chronicles*, Lond., 1900.

Cooper, C. H.: *Annals of Cambridge*, 4 vols., Camb., 1842-1852.

Cornish, F. W.: *Chivalry*, Lond., 1901.

Coulton, G. C.: *Monastic Schools in the Middle Ages*, Lond., 1913.

Cunningham, W.: *The Growth of English Commerce and Industry*, Camb., 1882.

Cutts, E. L.: *Parish Priests and their People in the Middle Ages*, Lond., 1898.

Cutts, E. L.: *Scenes and Characters in the Middle Ages*, Lond., 1873.

Davidson, Thos.: *Aristotle and the Ancient Educational Ideals*, New York, 1892.

Denifle, H.: *Die Enstehung der Universitatem des Mittelalters bis* 1400, Berlin, 1885.

Dill, S.: *Roman Society in the Last Century of the Western Empire*, 2nd edition, Lond., 1899.

Dittes, Fr.: *Gesichte der Erziehung und der Unterrichtes*, Leipzig, 1890.

Drane, A. T. : *Christian Schools and Scholars*, Lond., 1881.

Draper, J. W. : *Intellectual Development of Europe*, 2 vols., New York, 1876.

Dunning, W. A. : *History of Political Theories*, New York, 1905.

Edgar, J. : *History of Early Scottish Education*, Edinburgh, 1893.

Emerton, E. : *Introduction to the Study of the Middle Ages*, Boston, 1883.

Emerton, E. : *Medieval Europe*, Boston, 1894.

Fletcher, C. R. L. : *Collectanea*, First Series, (*Oxf. Hist. Soc. Pubs.*), vol. V., Oxon., 1885.

Froude, J. A. : *History of England from the Fall of Wolsey to the death of Elizabeth*, 12 vols., 1856-70.

Furnivall, F. J. : *The Babees Book*, Lond., 1868.

Gaskoin, C. J. B. : *Alcuin*, Lond., 1904.

Gasquet, F. A. : *The Black Death*, 2nd edition, Lond., 1908.

Gasquet, F. A. : *The Old English Bible and Other Essays*, Lond., 1897.

Gautier, Leon : *Chivalry*, Lond., 1891.

Green, Mrs. J. R. : *Town Life in the Fifteenth Century*, 2 vols., Lond., 1805.

Hartson, L. D. : *A Study of Voluntary Associations* (Ped. Sem., Vol. XVIII., No. 1), Worcester, Mass., 1911.

Hazlitt, W. C. : *Schools, School Books and Schoolmasters*, Lond., 1887.

Healy, J. : *Ireland's Ancient Schools and Scholars*, Dublin, 1890.

Hibbert, F. A. : *Influence and Development of English Gilds*, Camb., 1891.

Hodgkin, T. : *Italy and her Invaders*, 4 vols., Camb., 1880-5.

Hodgson, G. E.: *Primitive Christian Education*, Edinburgh, 1912.

Holman, H.: *English National Education*, Lond., 1898.

Hunt, W.: *The English Church from its Foundation to the Norman Conquest*, Lond., 1899.

Jessop, A.: *The Coming of the Friars*, Lond., 1901.

Kemble, J. M.: *Saxons in England*, 2 vols., Lond., 1849.

Lacroix, P.: *Le Chevalrie et Les Croisades*, Paris, 1890.

Lacroix, P.: *L'école et la Science jusqu'à la Renaissance*. Paris, 1887.

Lacroix, P.: *Le moyen Age et la Renaissance*, 5 vols., Paris, 1848-51.

Laurie, S. S.: *Rise and Constitution of the Early Universities*, New York, 1886.

Leach, A. F.: *A History of Warwick School*, Lond., 1906.

Leach, A. F.: *History of Winchester College*, Lond., 1899.

Little, A. G.: *The Grey Friars at Oxford* (*Oxf. Hist. Soc. Pubs.*, vol. XX.), Oxon., 1891.

Lyte, Sir H. C. M.: *A History of Eton College*, Lond. 1875.

Lyte, Sir H. C. M.: *History of the University of Oxford*, Lond., 1886.

Maitland, S. R.: *The Dark Ages*, Lond., 1899.

Maître, Léon: *Les écoles épiscopales et monastiques*, 769-1180, Paris, 1866.

Medley, D. L.: *English Constitutional History*, 4th edition, Lond., 1907.

Meredith, H. C.: *Economic History of England*, Lond. (n. d.).

Mignet, F. A. A.: *Mémoire sur la conversion de l'Allemagne par les Moines*, Paris (n. d.).

Monnier, M. F., *Alcuin et Charlemagne*, Paris, 1860.

Montalembert, Count de : *The Monks of the West*, 7 vols., Lond., 1861-79.

Montmorency, J. E. G. de: *State Intervention in English Education from the Earliest Times to 1833*, Camb., 1902.

Mullinger, J. B.: *History of the University of Cambridge*, Camb., 1873.

Mullinger, J. B.: *The Schools of Charles the Great*, Lond., 1877.

Munroe, P.: *Source Book for the History of Education for the Greek and Roman Period*, New York, 1901.

Ozanam, A. F.: *La Civilisation Chretienne chez les Francs*, Paris, 1872.

Parker, H.: *The Seven Liberal Arts; in Eng. Hist. Rev.*, vol. V., pp. 417-461, July 1890.

Poole, R. L.: *Illustrations of Medieval Thought*, Lond., 1844.

Putnam, G. H.: *Books and their Makers during the Later Middle Ages*, 2 vols., Lond., 1896.

Rashdall, H.: *Universities of Europe in the Middle Ages*, 2 vols., Oxon., 1895.

Report of the Schools Enquiry Commission, Lond., 1868.

Rogers, J. E. T.: *History of Agriculture and Prices in England*, 4 vols., Lond., 1866-82.

Roper, W.: *Life of Sir Thos. More*, ed. S. W. Singer, Chiswick, 1882.

Sandys, E. G.: *History of Classical Scholarship*, 3 vols., Camb., 1903.

Seebohm, F.: *The English Village Community*, Lond., 1883.

Smith, J. G.: *Rise of Christian Monasticism*, Lond., 1892.

Taylor, H. O.: *The Medieval Mind*, Lond., 1912.

Theiner, A.: *Histoire des Institutions d'Education Ecclesiastique*, 2 vols., Paris, 1841.

Timbs, J.: *School Days of Eminent Men*, Lond. (n. d.).

Townsend, W. T.: *Great Schoolmen of the Middle Ages*, Lond., 1881.

Traill, H. D.: *Social England*, 6 vols., Lond., 1894.

Vinogradoff, P.: *English Society in the Eleventh Century*, Oxon., 1908.

Watson, Foster: *English Grammar Schools*, Camb., 1908.

   ,,   ,, : *The Old Grammar Schools*, Camb., 1916.

West, A. F.: *Alcuin and the Rise of the Christian Schools*, New York, 1892.

Wilkins, A. S.: *National Education in Greece in the Fourth Century*, B.C., Lond., 1873.

ABBREVIATIONS.

Ed. Ch.   Educational Charters.

E. S. R.   English Schools at the Reformation.

S. M. E.   Schools of Medieval England.

INDEX.

256